iTQ FOR IT USERS
USING OFFICE® 2010

LEVEL 2   STUDENT BOOK

Karen Anderson

Alan Jarvis

Allen Kaye

Richard McGill

Neela Soomary

D1464989

ALWAYS LEARNING

PEARSON

Published by Pearson Education Limited, Edinburgh Gate, Harlow, Essex, CM20 2JE.

www.pearsonschoolsandfecolleges.co.uk

Heinemann is a registered trademark of Pearson Education Limited

Text © Pearson Education Limited 2012
Typeset by Kamae Design, Oxford
Original illustrations © Pearson Education Limited 2012
Illustrated by Kamae Design
Cover design by Andrew Magee Design Limited
Cover photo/illustration © Corbis/David Arky

The rights of Karen Anderson, Alan Jarvis, Allen Kaye, Richard McGill and Neela Soomary to be identified as authors of this work have been asserted by them in accordance with the Copyright, Designs and Patents Act 1988.

First published 2012

16 15 14 13 12
10 9 8 7 6 5 4 3 2 1

British Library Cataloguing in Publication Data
A catalogue record for this book is available from the British Library

ISBN 978 0 435 07523 1

Printed in Spain by Grafos S.A.

Websites
Pearson Education Limited is not responsible for the content of any external Internet sites. It is essential for tutors to preview each website before using it in class so as to ensure that the URL is still accurate, relevant and appropriate. We suggest that tutors bookmark useful websites and consider enabling students to access them through the school/college intranet.

Contents

The following Level 1 optional units are available on the Pearson Education website www.pearsonschoolsandfecolleges.co.uk/ITQLevel2 using the password IT_user_level2.

Credits and acknowledgements

The publisher would like to thank the following for their kind permission to reproduce their photographs:

(Key: b-bottom; c-centre; l-left; r-right; t-top)

Alamy Images: Ingram Publishing 129, 134b, James Boardman 26; **Digital Stock:** 133b; **Digital Vision:** 104l; **Glow Images:** Corbis / Image 100 160-161; **Imagestate Media:** John Foxx Collection 133t; **Pearson Education Ltd:** Malcolm Harris 134t; **Shutterstock.com:** Valerie Potapova 57, vectomart 104r

Cover images: Corbis: David Arky

All other images © Pearson Education

Every effort has been made to trace the copyright holders and we apologise in advance for any unintentional omissions. We would be pleased to insert the appropriate acknowledgement in any subsequent edition of this publication.

The publisher would also like to thank Microsoft® Corporation, Google™ and Skype™. Microsoft® product screenshots reprinted with permission from Microsoft® Corporation.

Introduction

The qualification

The iTQ provides an **up-to-date, 'hands-on' nationally recognised IT user qualification** based on the National Occupational Standards (NOS) for IT Users 2009 that helps people to develop the IT skills they need in their day-to-day life. It is designed to help you improve your IT skills whether, you are using technology at work, in education or in your free time. The iTQ is also designed to help you prepare for employment in jobs within the IT industry.

You may be studying the iTQ alongside other qualifications, as part of a Foundation Learning programme, as a standalone course or as part of an IT User Apprenticeship at school, college or in the workplace. Whatever level you are studying at, the iTQ can:

- provide you with **good employability skills** to help you get a job
- allow you to **progress through the levels**, whatever level you start at
- give you the chance to **put into practice the skills you learn** in your daily life and in the workplace
- equip you with the IT skills you need to help you with a **variety of tasks**, such as book keeping and fundraising for voluntary and charitable work.

iTQ is available at four levels: Entry 3, Level 1, Level 2 and Level 3. At each level the qualification is offered in three sizes: Award, Certificate and Diploma.

You can select units from different levels to make up your qualification. The minimum credit value for each size at Level 2 is as follows:

- Award – 10 credits, 7 of which must be achieved at Level 2
- Certificate – 16 credits, 10 of which must be achieved at Level 2
- Diploma – 38 credits, 21 of which must be achieved at Level 2

Units in the qualification

The table below shows the credit value for each unit at the different levels.

- The units covered in this Level 2 book have been highlighted in purple, together with their credit value.
- The additional Level 1 units available on the website have been highlighted in green, together with their credit value.

	Credit value (E3)	Credit value (L1)	Credit value (L2)	Credit value (L3)
Improving productivity using IT	–	3	4	5
IT communication fundamentals	–	2	2	–
IT software fundamentals	–	3	3	–
IT user fundamentals	2	3	3	–
Audio and video software	2	–	–	–
Audio software	–	2	3	4
Bespoke or specialist software	2	–	–	–
Bespoke software	–	2	3	4
Computer accounting software	–	2	3	5
Data management software	2	2	3	4
Database software	2	3	4	6
Design and imaging software	2	–	–	–
Design software	–	3	4	5
Desktop publishing software	2	3	4	5
Drawing and planning software	–	2	3	4
Imaging software	–	3	4	5
Multimedia software	–	3	4	6
Personal information man. software	1	2	2	–
Presentation software	2	3	4	6
Productivity programmes	1	–	–	–
Project management software	–	3	4	6
Spreadsheet software	2	3	4	6
Video software	–	2	3	4
Website software	–	3	4	5
Word processing software	2	3	4	6

	Credit value (E3)	Credit value (L1)	Credit value (L2)	Credit value (L3)
Computer basics	1	–	–	–
IT security for users	–	1	2	3
Optimise IT system performance	–	2	4	5
Setting up an IT system	–	3	4	5
Computer security and privacy	1	–	–	–
Using collaborative technologies	–	3	4	6
Using mobile IT devices	1	2	2	–
Using email	1	2	3	3
Using the Internet	1	3	4	5
Digital lifestyle	1	–	–	–
The Internet and worldwide web	1	–	–	–

Mandatory unit

For the Certificate and Diploma sizes, you must complete Unit 1 *Improving productivity using IT*. This is a mandatory unit. For this unit, you will be required to demonstrate evidence of planning, evaluating and improving procedures that use IT to make them more efficient. The evidence can be generated from tasks that you carry out in your day-to-day work, through written scenarios/situations or knowledge tests.

How the qualification is assessed

Assessment is by means of a portfolio of evidence – either paper based or, where possible, as a digital portfolio – that demonstrates your competence. At Level 2, your portfolio will be assessed by an External Verifier.

Types of evidence

For each unit you need to gather evidence to include in your portfolio to show that you have successfully achieved the required standard for each of the assessment criteria. This evidence is likely to include:

- observation of your performance by your assessor
- responses to oral or written questioning
- projects that demonstrate your work
- assignments
- personal statements that demonstrate planning and decision-making skills and explain your decision-making process
- Witness testimonies – that can be used to support your personal statements.
  - Witnesses can include your line manager, experienced colleagues in your workplace or customers and clients.
  - The witness needs to be able to testify to your performance.
  - Witness testimonies normally take the form of a written statement about the quality and authenticity of your work and need to be dated and signed by the witness.
- Professional discussion (which may be used for the assessment of the mandatory unit.)
  - You will meet with your assessor (or have a series of meetings with your assessor) and have the opportunity to present a range of evidence for discussion. You will be required to take the lead in the professional discussion.
  - The discussion can be used to explore and explain situations in which you have used IT, i.e. to demonstrate your problem-solving skills, to explore and explain how you undertook tasks, to explore your reasons for choosing different options, (e.g. selecting the best software for a task and to reflect on the final product or outcome).
- Knowledge tests to assess your knowledge and understanding of, for example, an organisational procedure or the knowledge requirements for units.
- Simulation of work tasks and activities within a realistic working environment – the mandatory unit may be assessed in this way.
  - Scenario-based evidence (may be used for the mandatory unit – *Improving productivity using IT*). If you undertake this type of assessment for the mandatory unit, you will be given a written scenario/situation and you will need to write a response explaining how IT can be used in the situation.
- Recognised prior learning – this allows you to count any other relevant units towards your iTQ. Your assessor can give you further guidance on this.

Collecting your evidence

The main ways in which evidence can be collected include:

- from a current job role – you build an assessment portfolio by gathering evidence of ICT skills that you have applied to your day-to-day work in the workplace
- from a learning/training programme – you may be studying at a training centre and produce evidence from a mixture of knowledge tests and scenario-based evidence
- Accreditation of Prior Achievement (APA) – qualifications that you have already achieved and that meet the assessment criteria for the optional units of the iTQ may also be used as evidence – for example, a presentation that you have done as part a geography project.

A combination of the above methods of collecting evidence can be achieved. Other valid evidence can come from social and voluntary activities (e.g. posters/websites of a club or society you belong to), enterprise activities (such as creating a business plan or marketing materials) and job searches (e.g. CVs, application forms and emails to potential employers).

ECDL Extra

The following Level 2 units make up the ECDL Extra qualification:

- Improving productivity using IT
- Presentation software
- Spreadsheet software
- Word processing software.

This book provides complete coverage of the content of these units.

How to use this book

Unit introduction and learning outcomes

These introductions give you a snapshot of what to expect from each unit – and what you should be aiming for by the time you finish it!

The learning outcomes are ways to measure your learning and progress. After completing a unit you should be able to achieve all of the learning outcomes listed. The assessment activity and activities will help you achieve this.

Assessment activity

At the end of each unit you will find an assessment activity. The activity will be broken down into steps and you'll be asked to complete tasks. The tasks will be based on the content you have learned in the unit and will cover the learning outcomes. These may take a variety of forms – but each task will require you to demonstrate the skills and knowledge you have developed over the course of the unit.

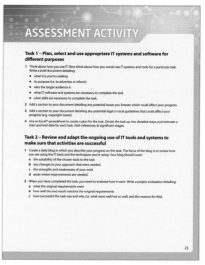

Activities

There are different types of activities for you to do and they will appear at different points throughout each unit. The aim of these activities is to give you a broader grasp of the IT world through the practical application of your skills and knowledge.

Activity: Planning a task

You work in a photo printing shop. Your supervisor has asked you to produce a leaflet advertising a new range of themed products (mugs with personalised photos, and personalised key rings and calendars). Your supervisor would also like you to email the leaflet to the business' customers. How will you go about planning this task?

1 Create a plan for how you are going to tackle the task. You will need to use sub-tasks to help you plan effectively.
2 Create a list of sub-tasks for taking and preparing photographs of the products.
3 What additional things do you think you will need to consider (for example, copyright of photos; layout of the leaflet, etc.)? Create a list of at least five points.

How to... activities

These activities run though the steps involved in carrying out an IT task. You will need to be able to successfully carry out these activities in order to complete the assessment activities in this book and in your IT career.

How to create a plan

1. Identify all of the different things you need to do (sub-tasks) to complete the overall task. You should go into as much detail as you can and make sure you don't forget any important sub-tasks.
2. List all the sub-tasks in the order in which they should be done. You might find that a word-processed table or a spreadsheet is a good way to collect this information.
3. Estimate how long it will take you to complete each sub-task. This can be quite difficult to do, but use your experience of completing similar tasks in the past. If you have never done a task like it before, ask a colleague or a supervisor who has.
4. Working back from the completion date for the whole task, work out when each sub-task must be completed. Add a deadline date beside each sub-task in your plan.

Figure 1.1: A spreadsheet will help you to plan complex tasks

Case studies

These are extended activities which focus on genuine business cases or real-life working scenarios. There might be one case study used throughout a unit; or there could be more than one case study per unit.

You will be provided with a scenario and asked to weigh up the information, assess the facts and then complete a series of tasks based on the information provided.

Case study: Cherry's Chocolates

Your friend Cherry runs a small business making and selling handmade chocolates. She works from home, making and packaging the chocolates in her kitchen and living room. She sells her chocolates locally to a gift shop, florist and friends. Now she wants to expand the business and sell her chocolates through a website. She also wants to be able to communicate regularly with customers and suppliers using email.

Until now, Cherry has only used the Internet occasionally. She has a desktop computer in her living room and uses an Internet dongle which plugs into a USB port. This is a slow and expensive Internet connection. She has a printer which is connected to her PC by a USB cable. She is also thinking about buying a laptop but is unsure how she will connect this to the Internet or to the printer. She needs a fast, reliable Internet connection and has asked you to:

- recommend a suitable connection method that can be used to access the Internet
- help her get online with an Internet connection.

You are aware that Cherry may have some Internet connection problems from time to time, so you are also going to advise her on the help facilities available so that she can sort these out herself.

Check your understanding

At the end of some sections you will find a series of questions. These are designed to focus in on some of the key topics and knowledge areas covered in the section. Make sure you can answer these questions before moving on to the next section.

Check your understanding

1. When creating a project schedule, what are milestones?
2. What sort of factors can affect your ability to complete a task to schedule?
3. How can you check the validity and accuracy of information you find on the Internet?
4. What is the Data Protection Act? Who does it apply to?

Key terms

Technical words or phases you might be unfamiliar with have been placed in bold font (black). The terms and definitions can also be found in the glossary at the back of the book.

IT terms

IT terms and functions, such as **Caps Lock** and **desktop** have been made red and are placed in bold so that you can spot them easily. Some of the terms will be explained using the Key terms boxes. However, not all IT terms will be explained. If you're unsure about a word's meanomg then ask your tutor.

Did you know?

This feature provides you with additional knowledge about a particular topic or sheds some light on an interesting area of information which might not have been touched upon in the content.

Remember

In these feature boxes you'll find helpful reminders and top tips relating to the information covered in a unit.

Improving productivity using IT

This is a mandatory unit so you must complete it to obtain your ITQ qualification.

IT is an amazingly powerful tool for doing all sorts of tasks. This unit is about planning how to use IT to complete a task efficiently and how to evaluate your use of IT so your productivity and skills improve.

To complete this unit you must plan, carry out and review an IT project. Your project can consist of one large task, such as creating a website or newsletter, or several smaller but related tasks, such as creating a set of marketing materials for an event.

Learning outcomes

After completing this unit you should be able to achieve the following learning outcomes.

» **LO1** Plan, select and use appropriate IT systems and software for different purposes

» **LO2** Review and adapt the ongoing use of IT tools and systems to make sure that activities are successful

» **LO3** Develop and test solutions to improve the ongoing use of IT tools and systems

1

1 Plan, select and use appropriate IT systems and software for different purposes

Simple tasks using IT, such as sending an email to a friend, usually need little **planning**. Larger or more complex tasks, such as creating a multi-page newsletter, will require a lot of planning and the task should be broken down into several smaller tasks. Before you start a complex task, plan what you will do and how you will do it. Decide which IT systems and software you are going to use. Time spent planning and selecting the right systems and software will save you time and effort.

1.1 Purpose for using IT

Who or what the information is for

Before starting a task, make sure you know who you are completing the task for. It is important to check that your understanding of the task is the same as the person asking you to complete the task. You do not want to spend time and effort producing something which is not correct. Speak to the person about the task; find out what is required and what the information is to be used for. This will help you to select the IT systems and software to complete the task successfully.

Project dates and what information should be included

You also need to understand what information should be included in the finished product and how it will be presented. For example, should the finished product be a printed document, an onscreen presentation or presented in some other format?

You also need to be clear about when the task needs to be completed. It is advisable to create a **schedule** and establish the start date, the end date and any **project milestones** along the way. This will help keep you on track and give you an end point to work towards.

Where IT will be used

Whether during your time at college or in the workplace, you may be required to contact people using email. You may have to email your tutors or peers, or customers or suppliers. Make sure you know who you are addressing (who the person is and their role) and why you are emailing them (what your email is about). If you are discussing the details of a project, be sure to provide clear details. For example, if you are discussing promotional materials for an advertising campaign, you need to establish who the audience is (e.g. informing people about how to recycle plastic items) and how you want the materials to look (e.g. A3 colour posters with images of young people putting items in a recycling bin).

Key terms

Planning – the process of breaking down a large project or task into several smaller tasks, or sub-tasks, and identifying what you need to do in order to complete each sub-task.

Schedule – a list of tasks and the dates you plan to start and complete them.

Project milestones – are dates when significant events are planned to occur within a project. For example, you might include a milestone in your schedule such as 'Project proposal agreed by customer'.

1.2 Reasons for choosing IT

There are many benefits of using IT.

Time and cost

In most cases, using IT means tasks can be completed quicker than they could be done manually. For all businesses 'time is money', so by being able to do more work in less time businesses can save money. For example, suppose a company needed to write a letter to all of its customers, telling them about a change in prices. Even if the letter was typed using a word-processing program, it would take hours to enter hundreds of customers' names and addresses independently and then print each letter off. Using **Mail merge** would save a considerable amount of time, with the entire task taking less than 30 minutes.

Professional presentation

IT can be used to present information in a more professional manner. For example, two local estate agents advertise their services by putting leaflets through letter boxes in their area. One is a photocopied handwritten letter; the other is a well-formatted, word-processed leaflet with photos of recently sold properties. The word-processed letter might take longer to produce than the handwritten one, but the end product looks more professional and is more likely to lead to new business.

Convenience and effectiveness

Over time, you will have formed your own opinions on the effectiveness and convenience of different application programs. You may find some products or features frustrating to use, or that they don't provide you with the features you need to complete the task at hand. Some applications may be too basic, or some too complicated to use successfully. As your knowledge, skills and experience develops, so will your ability to assess and select the right IT tools and programs. As your familiarity and expertise of IT tools and applications grows, your ability to produce quality, accurate work more quickly and effectively will also develop.

> **Key term**
>
> **Mail merge** – when information stored on a database (e.g. people's names, company names and addresses) is dropped into a letter template. This process means that the same letter can be sent to hundreds of people. The system inserts everyone's name and address, rather than each name and address having to be added manually.

Activity: Use IT efficiently and avoid problems

If possible, work with a partner or in small groups to complete this activity.

1 Discuss what procedures might help you use IT efficiently and help avoid problems.
2 Create and deliver a five-minute presentation based on your findings. You can present to your tutor, friends or colleagues.

1.3 Plan how to carry out tasks

Once you are clear about what is required, you can begin work on planning how to achieve it.

How to create a plan

1. Identify all of the different things you need to do (sub-tasks) to complete the overall task. You should go into as much detail as you can and make sure you don't forget any important sub-tasks.

2. List all the sub-tasks in the order in which they should be done. You might find that a word-processed table or a spreadsheet is a good way to collect this information.

3. Estimate how long it will take you to complete each sub-task. This can be quite difficult to do, but use your experience of completing similar tasks in the past. If you have never done a task like it before, ask a colleague or a supervisor who has.

4. Working back from the completion date for the whole task, work out when each sub-task must be completed. Add a deadline date beside each sub-task in your plan.

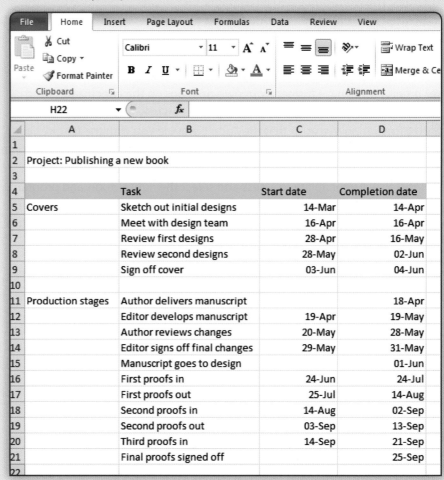

Figure 1.1: A spreadsheet will help you to plan complex tasks

You can use your plan to track your progress as you complete the overall task.

Skills and resources

You need to consider the skills that you have in different software packages, as this might influence your choice of application.

If you are taking photos then you will need a digital camera. You might also need access to specialist software to prepare and edit the photos. If you are planning to carry out complex editing of the photos, then you will need to have the skills and know-how to use the software in order to achieve the desired effects.

Factors that may affect a task

When planning and preparing for a task, there are multiple factors that will affect your ability to complete it successfully and on schedule.

- **The time available**: You need to consider if you have sufficient time to complete the task by the deadline (if there is one).
- **The skills needed**: If you don't already have the skills needed to complete the tasks then you will need to add in time to learn the skills.
- **Resource availability**: Depending on the nature of the task, you might need to access a range of resources, including things like application software and equipment such as digital cameras, scanners, colour printers, etc.
- **Contingency**: Even the best-made plans can go wrong. Equipment failure may affect your ability to complete the task, as can software corruption or lost files. When planning a task it is wise to build in a certain degree of contingency to allow extra time if things go wrong.

What information sources are needed?

You will probably need to provide or share information with colleagues or friends at some point. The information will have an original source point. For example, if your project involves gathering data on rainfall levels, then you might need to provide statistical reports or surveys from sources like The Met Office. Or if you are including images or quotations or video, then you will need to acknowledge where this information came from and make sure you have permission to use it.

Activity: Planning a task

You work in a photo printing shop. Your supervisor has asked you to produce a leaflet advertising a new range of themed products (mugs with personalised photos, and personalised key rings and calendars). Your supervisor would also like you to email the leaflet to the business' customers. How will you go about planning this task?

1 Create a plan for how you are going to tackle the task. You will need to use sub-tasks to help you plan effectively.
2 Create a list of sub-tasks for taking and preparing photographs of the products.
3 What additional things do you think you will need to consider (for example, copyright of photos; layout of the leaflet, etc.)? Create a list of at least five points.

How to find and evaluate information sources

The Internet provides access to a huge amount of information. Search engines like Google™ and Yahoo! will produce hundreds, if not thousands, of results for most searches. This can leave you with a problem of too much data. When using a search engine, try to do the following.

- Be as specific as possible when entering your search text into the search engine. If you search for 'car' you will get literally millions of results. Searching for 'hybrid electric cars' or 'low emission cars' will still produce a lot of results but more of them are likely to be relevant.
- Restrict the date range. The Internet contains a lot of out-of-date information. Google™ has a feature that helps you to narrow down the search results based on how long the information has been available on the Internet. On the left-hand side of the Google™ search results page, there is a heading called 'Any time' and a list of time periods under it (e.g. 'Past hour', 'Past 24 hours', 'Past week', and so on). If you click 'Past week', for example, then you'll only see the pages which have been updated in the last week.

Another issue is that the Internet is not censored or checked by anyone. Therefore, not all the information on the Internet is reliable and trustworthy. How can you be sure the information is accurate? One way is to use reputable websites like the BBC News website; another is to find at least two different independent sources to back up your findings.

What application software and IT systems will be used

You will need to choose what software to use to prepare your project. This might depend on how many different sources of materials you plan to use. If you just need to crop photos and do some minor adjustments, you might be able to use the application that you are creating the project in, such as Microsoft® Word®. If more complex preparation is needed, then a proper photo-editing application like Photoshop® might be needed.

Microsoft® Word® includes a lot of features, which means it can be used to produce a wide range of documents. However, if you are not producing a printed document you might need to use different software, such as Microsoft® PowerPoint® to produce presentation slides, or Dreamweaver to produce web pages.

As well as selecting the application software to use, you may also need to consider the IT systems you will use. You may be able to use the IT system you have in your workplace, but you may also need to use your own computer or laptop, if you have one. There may be differences between the application software you have installed on your own computer and the one installed on your work computer, which may cause problems. You may also have different versions of the software, which can cause compatibility issues.

Requirements for content, structure and layout

As well as planning the tasks, you also need to plan the design or layout of the materials you will produce. Depending on the type of materials you need to produce, you can draw a sketch diagram of the layout. You will need to decide the format of the resulting document. For example, is the leaflet A4 or A5? Single or double sided? Monochrome or colour? In addition, you will need to consider the style and design of the document, including the colour scheme (background and text colours), text fonts and sizes, and the use of text features like bullet points, number lists and tables.

Activity: Creating a plan

You have been asked to create materials for a college end-of-term trip to a theme park. You need to produce posters to be displayed around campus and also **mail merge** a letter to all students/parents providing details of the trip and asking them to complete a permissions slip. You also need to keep track of who is coming on the trip, who has paid and which people have completed permission slips. The trip is in four weeks' time, but the posters need to go up and the letters sent out at least two weeks before the trip.

1 Make a list of all the tasks you need to complete and all the information you need to collect in order to complete this project.
2 Estimate how long you think it will take to complete each task.
3 Create a plan for this project. It should show the order in which you will do each task, and the resources and information you need to complete the task.

1.4 Legal or local guidelines or constraints

There are a number of issues related to laws, local guidelines and constraints that may affect your project.

Data protection, copyright, software licensing

You must be aware of **copyright** when sourcing materials for your project. Unless you have created the material yourself or it is copyright free, you may break copyright laws if you use material without permission. You may also find there are issues with **software licensing**. For example, you might find it useful to have a copy of a software application you use on your school or college computer installed on your computer at home. However, you will normally need to purchase a licence for that software to be allowed to install it on your computer at home, unless your school has agreement to allow you to do this.

You must also comply with the Data Protection Act. This protects the rights of people who have data stored about them on computer systems. You cannot store information about living individuals unless you are registered on the Data Protection Register.

Key terms

Copyright – a law which protects the creator of original works (music, art, photographs, etc.) from people copying and using their work without permission. For example, you cannot use someone else's photograph on a blog without getting their permission.

Software licensing – unless the software you are using is classified as 'freeware' or open source, you will need to purchase a licence to use it. Using unlicensed software breaks copyright law.

Did you know?

If you store personal information about living individuals (e.g. people's names and addresses) then you are legally required to register with the Information Commissioner's Office. You are also legally required to comply with the key principles of the Data Protection Act. These include keeping the data secure, not sharing the data with people who have no reason to have access to it, and making sure it is accurate and up to date.

Key term

Attachments – these are files (e.g. a photograph or a word-processed document) which are linked to emails and sent along with them to the recipient.

Local guidelines

Many businesses and all colleges and schools have guidelines on how you can use their computers and what you can and cannot do on the Internet. This may restrict some things you plan to do. You might find, for example, that sites like Facebook and YouTube are blocked.

Security

There are also guidelines to protect you from a range of security threats. This can include things like the importance of using strong passwords to help prevent people breaking into your online accounts, to taking care with emails you receive which might have **attachments** containing viruses, or that may be trying to trick you into revealing account passwords. (*See Unit 5 Section 5.4, page 56* for more information on password security.)

Organisational house-style or brand guidelines

Many companies also have rules about how their documents are designed. This includes things like how their logo is used and their requirements relating to fonts and colours used. This is called their house style. If you are preparing materials for a company which has a house style, then whatever you produce must conform to this style.

Activity: Internet and computer usage policies

1 Find out what the Internet and computer usage policy is at your school or college. There should be a written document which lists the things you can and cannot do. For each rule listed, discuss why the rule is necessary and what problems might occur if the rule is broken.

2 Find some examples of workplace policies or procedures related to computer and/or Internet usage. Ask your family, friends or tutor to help if you do not have access to a workplace.

Check your understanding

1 When creating a project schedule, what are milestones?

2 What sort of factors can affect your ability to complete a task to schedule?

3 How can you check the validity and accuracy of information you find on the Internet?

4 What is the Data Protection Act? Who does it apply to?

2 Review and adapt the ongoing use of IT tools and systems to make sure that activities are successful

2.1 Evaluating use of IT tools and systems

In order to gain extra benefits from using IT tools, it is useful to review how you have used IT and to consider ways in which you could improve your use.

You might find it useful to collect information on the way you use IT by keeping a diary over a period of several weeks. Note down the applications you use and what you use them for. Use the diary to keep track of any problems you come across and how you dealt with them. These can be technical problems with the computers, or difficulties you have using the software. You can then review the diary and see where you are having the most difficulties.

2.2 Evaluating selection of IT tools and systems

In some cases the most appropriate IT tool (like a word processor or spreadsheet) to tackle a particular task will be obvious. However, in other situations you may need to make a choice.

For example, if you need to produce a poster advertising an event, you may have to choose between using a word-processing or a **desktop publishing (DTP)** application. Another example would be if you needed to create a list of names and addresses. Should you use a spreadsheet or a database?

Factors to consider

The choice will be based on some technical considerations, such as the facilities available in the software, but other considerations such as your skill level in different applications will also play a part. In a work- or school/college-based setting you might not have the choice of which software to use you might be told which product you must work with. You will usually want to choose the application which will get the job done quickest, because it has the facilities needed to do the task efficiently. However, if your skill level in that application is low, you might be wise to choose an application which you feel more confident about using, even if it is not ideal for the task.

Cost and availability of software may be another consideration. For example, although a DTP package might be the best choice to complete a poster, it may not be worth purchasing if you already have word-processing software which can do the job adequately.

Transferability of information into other formats

You may also have to consider how easy it is to transfer data from one application to another. For example, if you need to complete a mail merge, you should select a word processor which is compatible with the application that holds the list of names and addresses or other data for the merge.

> **Key term**
>
> **Desktop publishing** – or DTP, is the use of application software (e.g. Microsoft® Publisher®) to create complex printed documents which combine text, graphics and other features. Examples of documents that might be produced using DTP software include magazines, brochures and newsletters.

Speed of Internet connection

Depending on the task you are completing, you may also need to consider the speed of your Internet connection. If the project you are completing creates large files (like graphic, audio or video files) and you are planning to email these files to other people, you need to ensure your Internet connection is fast enough to download the files in a reasonable time. Remember also that many email systems restrict the size of files you can send. If you need to send really big files you may need to save them onto a CD or DVD and post them.

Activity: Creating a newsletter

A friend asks you to create a newsletter for his five-a-side football team.

1 What software might be needed to create the newsletter?
2 Should you use a word processor or a DTP program?
3 The newsletter needs some photos included in it. What software will you need for this?

2.3 Strengths and weaknesses

As you complete a task or project you should assess its strengths and weaknesses. This can help you focus your attention on those aspects of your work that need improving (the weaknesses). As well as reviewing your own work, you might find it helpful to ask other people to look at it and identify what they think are its strengths and weaknesses.

2.4 Improvements to work

Identifying specific ways in which your work could be improved is a good way to ensure that it is of the highest quality. It may also help you next time you need to complete a similar task. Simply saying that your work could be made better or more accurate, or the quality should be improved, is not sufficient. Below are some areas where you may be able to improve things.

Correct mistakes

You need to proof-read written work very carefully to make sure all the mistakes are corrected. It is often very difficult to spot mistakes in your own work, so asking someone else to proof-read it will help eliminate errors. As well as checking for spelling and grammatical mistakes, you should check carefully for layout and formatting errors. This applies to graphics you may have produced as well as written documents.

Find better ways of doing things

Although the end result you have achieved may be fine, it could be that, having completed the task, you can now see that there is a much more efficient or effective way of doing it next time.

Learn new techniques

There may have been things you would have liked to add to your work but you did not know how to use the required technique. Most applications have many facilities that allow you to do things that would really improve your work. Unless you know how to use these facilities, you won't be able to take advantage of them.

Avoid affecting other people's work

It is likely that on some projects you will need to work in a team. In these situations you will need to ensure that the way you work fits in with everyone else in the team. This might include things such as ensuring you are using the same formatting or layout, or making sure that work is saved in a file format which is compatible with other people's applications.

2.5 Review outcomes

Reviewing your task when it is complete is useful, but it's also important to review work as your task progresses, as you may be able to correct problems and adjust things before it is too late. As well as checking for errors in the document, you should also check that the result is fit for the purpose that it is intended for and is likely to appeal to its target audience.

Produce drafts

Producing draft copies of the document you are creating is one way of doing this. You can ask other people, including those that the task is for, to review the draft and let you know if you are heading along the right lines. This is much better than showing them the final version and finding out you have misunderstood what is required when it is too late.

Check with intended audience

If the material you are producing is aimed at a particular audience, such as a poster inviting young people to come to an after school-club, you should check that it does actually appeal to that audience and that they can understand the material. The easiest way to do this is to ask someone from the target audience group for their opinion on what you have produced.

Review against initial plans

You should also regularly review your progress against the plan you initially created. If you find you are falling behind when compared with your plan you may be able to take action to try and get back on track, perhaps by spending more time on the task.

Evaluate the quality of the information used

You also have to consider if the information you have collected for the task is good enough. Was it the right information? Was it up to date? Did it meet the purpose? For example, you might be completing a science project and use science journals to collect some information. The information may be too complex or high level for your audience, so you need to decide how to make it accessible, relevant and engaging.

Effect of own mistakes on others

Mistakes in your work can have an effect on other people, confuse them and cause them inconvenience. Suppose you were writing a letter to a job applicant, inviting them to an interview, and you typed the wrong date for the interview on the letter. This would cause a serious problem for the applicant, who might come for the interview on the wrong day.

Once you have completed the task, take a critical look at what you have produced and think about what the strengths and weaknesses of your work are. You should consider both the technical aspects of the layout of the document (for example, is your use of different fonts and alignment consistent?) and also the suitability of the document for its purpose and intended audience. As mentioned earlier, it's often difficult to critically review your own work so you might find it helpful to ask other people to comment on it.

Activity: Reviewing IT tools

1 Select one piece of work that you have used IT to complete. Discuss with your tutor or with a friend the IT tools you used to complete this piece of work. Explain why you chose those particular tools and whether you think they were appropriate for the task and for the purpose of the work.

2 Was there anything else you had to consider? For example, would you have preferred to use a different program which was not available in your school, college or office?

Check your understanding

1 List some of the ways that you may be able to improve a piece of work.

2 What are the different ways you can review your work?

3 Develop and test solutions to improve the ongoing use of IT tools and systems

Having reviewed the way you use IT tools, hopefully you will have identified ways in which you can further improve your productivity and efficiency.

3.1 Review the benefits and drawbacks of IT tools and systems

How can you review the ways in which IT tools have helped you complete a task? To do this you need to review the benefits and drawbacks of using different application software and computer systems (including things like printers, digital cameras, scanners) and the impact they had on your productivity and efficiency in completing a task. Did they really make things easier? Were you able to complete tasks more quickly than you could have done using manual methods?

The best way to do this is to keep a detailed record of the work across all stages of a project. Log all the problems you have, both with software and hardware, and also note down when things went well and the tasks you were able to complete easily and quickly.

3.2 Ways to improve productivity and efficiency

There are a number of ways in which you may be able to develop your use of IT in such a way that you can improve your productivity (the amount of work you can do in a given time) and your efficiency (how much time you spend doing actual work as opposed to doing things like resolving technical problems).

Save time

You may be able to save time by customising the software you are using to make repetitive tasks easier and quicker to complete. Creating short cuts and using macros may help you do this. It may also help if you investigate more efficient ways of doing tasks. For example, you may find that there are features in a software package which you were not aware of, which help you do the task more quickly.

Save money

Being able to do a task in less time may save your employer money as, overall, they may need to employ less people to get the same amount of work done (or enable the same number of people to do more work).

Reducing the cost of a solution is important to all employers, so being able to find ways to reduce costs is an important skill for employees. There are many ways that the cost of a solution can be reduced, perhaps by being able to produce it more quickly, or by reducing the amount of hardware or software required to produce the solution.

Streamline work processes

Streamlining work processes involves making repetitive tasks easier and less frustrating. This is a benefit not only because it saves time but also because it reduces stress and frustration. Streamlining processes can include making things (like programs or files) easier to find. There is nothing more frustrating than, having created an important document one day, not being able to find it the next.

Increase output

In a modern workplace you are expected to produce quite a lot of work (i.e. output), and this can be quite stressful. Improving your knowledge of how to use software functions, so you can produce work more quickly, is important so you can stay on top of your workload.

As well as being expected to produce a lot of work, you need to ensure the work you produce is of high quality. As with increasing your output, knowing how to use the facilities in the software you are using is important to help you improve the quality of your work. For example, in a graphics editing program you need to know how to use features like guidelines, snap to objects, grouping, etc. to enable you to produce accurate graphics.

3.3 Develop solutions

You also need to be able to develop solutions which will help you achieve savings in time, or the improvements in quality you are hoping for.

Set up short cuts

Setting up short cuts to make accessing applications and files easier is one way that you can streamline your use of IT tools. A short cut is simply an icon you can place anywhere, but usually on your desktop, which provides a link to a file, folder or application. You usually place short cuts on your desktop as this is the easiest place to find them.

Remember that a short cut is not the actual file, folder or application itself, it's just a link to the actual item. If you need to copy a file or folder onto a **USB memory stick** to take it somewhere and use it on a different computer, copying the short cut won't work – you must copy the original file or folder. Also, if you create a short cut to a file or folder on a USB memory stick, the file or folder won't be available if you remove the USB stick.

Key term

USB memory stick – a device used to store files which plugs into the USB port on a computer.

How to create a short cut on your desktop

1. Select the file or folder you want to create a short cut for.
2. Right click on the file or folder and a menu will appear.
3. Click **Send to**. Then click **Desktop (create shortcut)**.

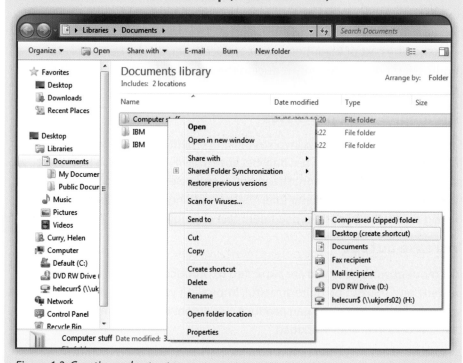

Figure 1.2: Creating a short cut

continued

4. The file or folder will now appear as an **icon** on your **Desktop** so that you can open the item just by **double clicking** on it.

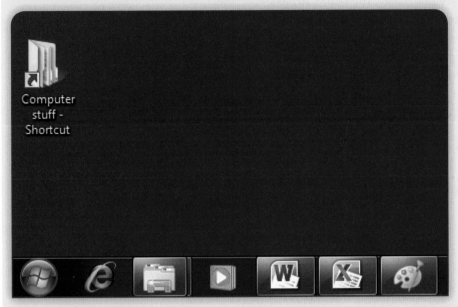

Figure 1.3: Short cut on the desktop

5. If you want to create a short cut somewhere other than on the **Desktop**, you can choose **Create shortcut** when you **right click** on the item. This will create a short cut in your current location. You will then need to **copy** and **paste** the short cut to where you want it.

Activity: Organising folder and files

Are your folders and files organised as well as they could be?

1   Look at your **Documents folder** or **USB memory stick**. Could it be better organised to make things easier to find? For example, is your ITQ work divided into folders for each unit?

2   Make sure that all your folders and files have meaningful names.

3   Do you have folders or applications you use regularly? Create short cuts on your desktop to these folders and applications.

4   Once you have reorganised everything, create a **backup** of your documents.

Customise the interface

Many application programs allow you to customise the user interface to suit your preferences and the type of work you most commonly do. For example, you may be able to select which **toolbars** are shown and what options are available.

All the applications in the Microsoft® Office® 2010 suite have a feature called the **Quick Access toolbar**. This sits at the top left of the application window and gives access to commonly used functions. By default it just has icons for **Save**, **Undo** and **Redo**. (See Figure 1.4.)

Figure 1.4: Quick Access toolbar in Word®

How to add icons

You can add to the **icons** shown in the **Quick Access toolbar** by clicking the **down pointing arrow** to the right of the bar. This will then display a menu of other icons you can add to the Quick Access toolbar.

Figure 1.5: Adding icons to the Quick Access toolbar

How to add a command

1. If the command you want to add to the toolbar isn't shown, you can click on the **More commands** option at the bottom of the menu. This will open the **Word options** dialog box.

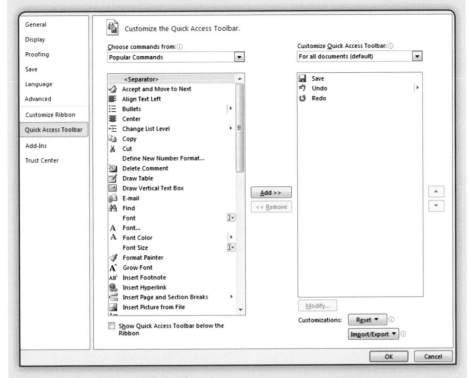

Figure 1.6: Word Options dialog box

2. On the right-hand side you will see the current **command icons**. On the left-hand side you will see a list of all the available **commands**. You can add or remove command icons by using the **Add** and **Remove** buttons.

Activity: Customise the Quick Access toolbar

1 What commands do you use most often in Word® or Excel®?
2 Add these commands to your Quick Access toolbar.

Record macros

Some application programs allow you to record **macros**, which automate procedures and make it quicker to carry out repetitive tasks. Macros can also be used to simplify complex tasks.

For example, let's say you want to record a macro to add a **header** to an Excel® worksheet. Instead of having to set up a header each time you use a new worksheet, the macro will automatically do it for you. The 'How to record a macro' step-by-step guide below shows you how to do this.

How to record a macro

1. Switch on the **macro recorder**.
2. Open Excel® and select either a new worksheet or one that does not already have a header set up.
3. Click the **View** tab on the ribbon. Then click the **Macros** button. This will display the Record Macro dialog box. (See Figure 1.7.)

Figure 1.7: The Record Macro dialog box

4. There are a number of things you must enter in the Record Macro dialog box.

Macro name	Each macro must have a name. Excel® will insert a default name (Macro1) if this is the first macro you have recorded. You should change the name to something more meaningful, like MakeHeader.
Short cut key	You can assign a **shortcut key** to the macro. This will enable you to run it by pressing the **CTRL key** along with another key of your choice. In this example the 'H' key has been chosen (for 'Header').
Store macro in	The default setting in this **drop-down box** is the current workbook. This means that the macro will only be available in this workbook. If you want to be able to use this macro in any workbook, the drop-down box should be set to **Personal Macro Workbook**.
Description	You can add information here to describe the macro.

continued

5. Once you have made the required entries in the dialog box, click **OK**. Be careful – as once you do this the **macro recorder** is on and everything you do will be recorded in the macro.

You can now start creating the header macro.

6. Go to the **Insert** tab. Click **Header and Footer** in the **Text** section. This will change your view of the spreadsheet to **Page Layout** view.

7. Position your **cursor** in the header box (see Figure 1.8). Add a header, including your name and the page number.

8. To add an automatic page number, click the **Page Number** button in the **Header and Footer Elements** section of the **Design** tab.

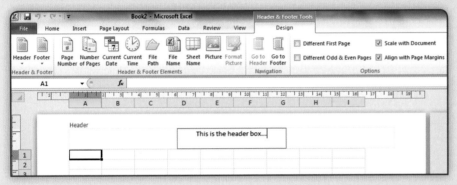

Figure 1.8: Adding a header

9. Click in one of the **spreadsheet cells** to close the **Design** tab.

10. To return the spreadsheet to **Normal view** rather than **Page Layout view**, click the **View** tab in the ribbon. Then click the **Normal** button on the left of the tab. This will return the spreadsheet to the view you had when you started to record the macro.

11. The final step is to stop the **macro recorder**. Click the **Stop recording** option in the **Macros** section of the **View** tab.

How to test your macro

You can't test your macro on the current worksheet, since it now has a header. You need to move to a new worksheet.

1. Select a new worksheet using the **worksheet tabs** at the bottom of the worksheet.

2. Then press the **Ctrl+H shortcut key** combination that you set for the new macro. You won't see very much on the screen (it will flash a few times as the macro changes in and out of **Page Layout** view).

3. Go to the **View** menu and choose **Page Layout**. You will see that this sheet now has a header, set by the macro.

Did you know?

You can't have a space in a macro name. Instead, you can use capitalisation to show where a space would normally be inserted. It is important to give macros meaningful names. For example, instead of calling a macro 'Make header' you would need to call it 'MakeHeader'.

3.4 Testing solutions

Testing a simple solution like a short cut requires checking that it links to the correct folder or application. With more complex solutions like a macro, you will need to think of the different ways in which the macro could be used and test all of these to make sure it works correctly in every situation.

You can ensure your testing is done properly by creating a test plan. This is a document which lists all the things you are going to test and what you expect to happen as the result of each test. A test plan is usually formatted as a table (see Table 1.1).

Test description	Expected outcome of the test	Actual outcome of the test	Action required
Click short cut to Invoices folder	Invoices folder opens		
Click short cut to Customers folder	Customers folder opens		
Click shortcut to Excel®	Excel® opens		

Table 1.1: Example of a test plan

If the actual outcome of the test does not match the expected outcome then the test has failed. An entry must be made in the **Action required** column explaining how this error will be resolved.

Activity: Recording and testing a macro

You work for an IT support department. Your manager has decided that everyone in your team needs to use Excel® to record customer issues and calls. You have been asked to use a different workbook for each call/issue. For consistency, each workbook will need to record the same information – so you will need the same headings (e.g. name, department, date and time, phone extension, problem description).

1   Record a macro which will create a new workbook and copy the titles and headings to the new sheet. Test the macro to ensure it works correctly.

Check your understanding

1   Give an example of how IT could save time and money.
2   Explain what a short cut is and how it can be used.
3   Why is it not a good idea to create a short cut to a folder or document held on a USB memory stick?
4   Where can you find the Quick Access toolbar? What is it used for?

ASSESSMENT ACTIVITY

Task 1 – Plan, select and use appropriate IT systems and software for different purposes

1   Think about how you use IT. Now think about how you would use IT systems and tools for a particular task. Write a brief document detailing:

- what it is you're creating
- its purpose (i.e. to advertise or inform)
- who the target audience is
- what IT software and systems are necessary to complete the task
- what skills are necessary to complete the task.

2   Add a section to your document detailing any potential issues you foresee which could affect your progress.

3   Add a section to your document detailing any potential legal or local guidelines that could affect your progress (e.g. copyright issues).

4   Use an Excel® spreadsheet to create a plan for the task. Divide the task up into detailed steps and estimate a start and end date for each task. Add milestones at significant stages.

Task 2 – Review and adapt the ongoing use of IT tools and systems to make sure that activities are successful

1   Create a daily blog in which you describe your progress on the task. The focus of the blog is to review how you are using the IT tools and the techniques you're using. Your blog should cover:

a   the suitability of the chosen tools to the task
b   any changes to your approach that were needed
c   the strengths and weaknesses of your work
d   areas where improvements are needed.

2   When you have completed the task, you need to evaluate how it went. Write a project evaluation detailing:

a   what the original requirements were
b   how well the end result matches the original requirements
c   how successful the task was and why (i.e. what went well/not so well, and the reasons for this).

Task 3 – Develop and test solutions to improve the ongoing use of IT tools and systems

Based on your experience of completing Task 1 and Task 2, you now need to develop and test solutions which will improve your future use of IT.

1 Add to your blog a review of the benefits and drawbacks of the IT tools you used, considering productivity and efficiency.

2 Describe ways that you could improve the productivity and efficiency of the tools you have used.

3 Develop solutions which demonstrate how productivity and efficiency can be improved (e.g. short cuts, interface customisations and macros).

4 Test the solutions you create using a test plan to ensure they work correctly.

Using the Internet

You may already find that the Internet is an exciting and essential part of your life and feel able to surf it well to find information, keep in touch with friends and to play online games with others.

This unit will build upon these skills and enhance them so you will get even better at surfing the net.

You will start by understanding how the computer you use is able to connect to the Internet and how different hardware devices can be used to plug your computer into the worldwide web.

A lot of people use their browser without any thought of how it can be set up and configured to help keep them safe when visiting websites. You will gain an understanding of safety issues when using the Internet and find out the actions you can take to set up your browser to minimise these risks.

The unit will show you how to use professional techniques to improve your web searching skills. You will also practise downloading and communicating information online, such as completing web-based forms.

Finally, you will add to your understanding of how to keep safe and to practise good security when working online.

Learning outcomes

After completing this unit you should be able to achieve the following learning outcomes.

» **LO1** Connect to the Internet

» **LO2** Use browser software to navigate web pages

» **LO3** Use browser tools to search for information from the Internet

» **LO4** Use browser software to communicate information online

» **LO5** Understand the need for safety and security practices when working online

1 Connect to the Internet

1.1 Types of connection methods

There are many methods to allow your computer to connect to the Internet. Some of these methods are used by large organisations. Other methods are used in small businesses or the home.

LAN

Most organisations use a **Local Area Network (LAN)** to connect their computers together. The LAN enables them to communicate, connect to the Internet and share information and resources such as printers. Many homes also have a LAN to connect computers to each other and to other devices such as a printer or to the Internet.

A basic LAN may be a **Wifi router** through which a personal computer or a laptop can connect to the Internet. A printer may also be plugged into the **router**. Some LANs are very large and connect many computers together.

VPN

Some large organisations have offices in different locations with their own individual LANs. The LANs can be connected together in a **Virtual Private Network (VPN)**. The VPN enables fast and secure connections between the LANs. To set up a VPN the routers need to be configured to connect to each other and to stop unauthorised connections to the VPN. The VPN can also be configured to **encrypt** the data between the LANs to keep it private and secure.

Modem

A **modem** is a device that gets data ready for transmission, or sending. The modem sends the data through a connection to another modem that receives the data into the destination system.

Router

The **router** is used to find the best route a **packet** can take when sent from one system to another. There are usually many choices of route. The router finds the easiest route for each packet sent in a data transmission.

Often the router and modem are combined into the same device, but they can be separate components, or parts.

The router modem often has **network ports** and **Wifi**. The network ports can be used to plug in network cables connecting the Internet to other parts of the network, or to connect a printer to the network.

Key terms

Router – a device that sends and receives data between systems through the Internet.

Encrypt – data is changed into a code so it can only be read by authorised users. The encrypted data will need to be decrypted by the receiving system so it can be understood.

Modem – a device for transmitting and receiving data. The word modem is made from MODulator and DEModulator. These were used in old dial-up modems to turn data into sound that could be sent through an ordinary voice telephone system (modulate) and also to receive the sound made by another modem to translate back into data (demodulate).

Packet – when data is transmitted, it is broken down into thousands of small pieces of data, called packets. Each packet is sent independently to the receiving system. When the packets arrive they are put back together so that the data appears complete once again.

Did you know?

A combined router and modem are often called by different names: router-modem, router/modem, router modem or modem router. Some people simply call it a router, while others call it a modem.

Wireless

Wireless Wifi networks are widely used by both organisations and individuals. Laptops have Wifi built in as standard to enable them to connect to a network or the Internet through a **wireless access point (WAP)**.

Some routers have a **USB** connection where a single computer can attach to the router.

Dial-up

Before broadband, people used a dial-up connection through their home telephone line to connect to the Internet. This was the usual method for private households in the 1990s. Businesses used a different system to connect to the Internet. They paid for an **ISDN** telephone line through which they could connect to the Internet.

A dial-up connection uses an ordinary telephone line. The modem rings the telephone number of the **Internet service provider (ISP)**. Dial-up connections are used by people who:

- use the Internet occasionally and do not want the regular cost of a broadband contract
- live in an area where the telephone system does not have broadband and they do not have access to a connection through a cable provider
- are away from home and choose to connect a laptop to a telephone socket to dial up the Internet.

Dial-up usually offers speeds up to 56 **kilo bits per second (kbps)**, which is around a hundred times slower than many broadband connections.

Some dial-up ISPs offer a faster service than 56 kbps. These are known as high-speed dial-up or **DSL** speeds over regular telephone lines. This is achieved by compressing the data before transmitting it. The method increases the speed to around 1 **mega bits per second (mpbs)**. Graphics or images sent in this way look blurred because of the amount of compression used.

Broadband

Broadband is used by most people to access the Internet. There are two main ways of delivering broadband to the home or a small business: cable and DSL.

Cable

Cable uses a fibre-optic connection, which uses flashing light signals for transmissions. It is currently able to carry up to 40 mbps. It is often bundled with other services such as television.

Your friend Cherry runs a small business making and selling handmade chocolates. She works from home, making and packaging the chocolates in her kitchen and living room. She sells her chocolates locally to a gift shop, florist and friends. Now she wants to expand the business and sell her chocolates through a website. She also wants to be able to communicate regularly with customers and suppliers using email.

Until now, Cherry has only used the Internet occasionally. She has a desktop computer in her living room and uses an Internet dongle which plugs into a USB port. This is a slow and expensive Internet connection. She has a printer which is connected to her PC by a USB cable. She is also thinking about buying a laptop but is unsure how she will connect this to the Internet or to the printer. She needs a fast, reliable Internet connection and has asked you to:

● recommend a suitable connection method that can be used to access the Internet

● help her get online with an Internet connection.

You are aware that Cherry may have some Internet connection problems from time to time, so you are also going to advise her on the help facilities available so that she can sort these out herself.

Did you know?

Giga bits per second (gbps) is a measure of data transfer speed, approximately a thousand million bits every second. Many networks use the Gigabit Ethernet standard which runs at 1 gbps.

Key terms

Protocol – a set of rules used by computers to control how they communicate. There are many protocols, including the wireless application protocol.

WAP – an acronym that has several possible meanings, including wireless application protocol and wireless access point.

Hyper Text Markup Language (HTML) – HTML is behind every web page, used by browsers to understand how to display the page. HTML is plain text with commands on how to lay out the page and where the images are stored on the web server hosting the page.

DSL

A **digital subscriber line (DSL)** is a broadband-enabled telephone line. It uses a filter to divide the voice call and modem router signals.

DSL uses an ordinary phone line that has been configured in the exchange to carry a range of frequencies that are used for both voice and Internet. This type of connection uses electrical transmissions and is currently able to carry up to 20 mbps.

Mobile phone with WAP or 3G technology

Mobile phones are able to surf the Internet using:

1. wireless application **protocol** (WAP)

2. 3rd Generation (3G) technology.

WAP dates from 1997 and is now old technology. It brought emails and the Internet to mobile phones. WAP includes WAP push, a technology that alerts users to new emails, rather than them having to open their email software to look for emails.

WAP worked with **WML (Wireless Markup Language)** to show web pages. WML is a selection of some of the **HTML (Hyper Text Markup Language)** chosen to work on a handheld device with a small screen. eBay Mobile is an example of WML pages.

Modern mobile phone users expect to be able to see any web page, which they can with 3G phones that can easily display HTML.

WAP has been largely replaced in the UK with 3G, which arrived in Europe in 2003. 3G promises up to 7.2 mbps, but for most users the actual data transfer rate is 1–2 mbps.

Intranet server

Many organisations operate an **intranet** inside their IT network. An intranet looks like the Internet, but all the pages in an intranet are produced by the organisation and are used by their employees. The usual connection to an intranet is through network cabling or Wifi, although there might be some computers connected through USB switches to the network and intranet. Some very old systems used serial cables to connect to a modem and parallel cables to connect printers.

1.2 Benefits and drawbacks of connection methods

There are usually benefits and drawbacks to any connection method.

Speed

Speed is a major benefit for any connection method. Usually, the greater the speed, the better the connection. Downloads are brought to your computer quicker, pages appear almost instantly and web browsing is an enjoyable experience.

On the other hand, a slow connection can limit what you can do. If every web page takes a long time to load, you are less likely to explore and visit new pages.

Stability

Stability is important. You want a connection that keeps working. Some people prefer to have a reliable connection and a slightly slower speed.

Instability can be a major drawback. If the connection is regularly dropping out, you may need to reconnect with the web pages you are visiting. This can become frustrating.

Services offered by ISP

Some ISPs offer extra services. These may be web-based, such as free **website hosting**, or the connection may be bundled with on-demand television or telephone. For example, the Internet provider Plusnet has a range of bundles available which can Include internet, phone line and up to 500MB of website hosting.

If a user wants these services, then not having them provided as part of their Internet bundle is a drawback. They will either need to go without, or pay extra to get the services from elsewhere.

Accessibility

Accessibility is not likely to be an issue in the workplace or at home where there is a connection to the Internet. Outside the workplace or home, accessibility becomes more important, particularly if you need to pick up or send emails.

A 3G connection method will allow access from anywhere with a suitable 3G signal. This, of course, depends upon the coverage provided by the ISP, just like a mobile phone.

Figure 5.1: Broadband filter to separate voice and data signals

Key terms

Website hosting – the website host provides storage and Internet connections for a website.

27

Email access becomes a lot easier from different locations if the ISP provides a web interface for emails. This allows you to log onto the ISP website to receive and send emails.

Activity: Connecting Cherry's Chocolates

Write a report recommending a suitable connection method for Cherry's Chocolates. Make sure your report covers the points below, and remember to include the benefits and drawbacks of the method you have chosen.

Cherry lives a couple of doors along the road from you and you have the same telephone STD code and postcode.

1 What are the technologies available to connect to the Internet for your postcode or telephone STD code?

2 What is the cheapest broadband Internet package you can find for your postcode? This needs to be calculated over the year to allow for any introductory offers.

3 What is the fastest connection available to your postcode and how much would it cost for the first year?

4 How can Cherry's USB printer be connected to the router so that she can print to this device from her laptop? What is the cost of this? Is there a new printer that could connect directly to the router for a similar cost?

1.3 Getting online with an Internet connection

For your assessment you need to be able to demonstrate you can get online with an Internet connection. To do this, you could use any of the methods below.

Wired router using cable or DSL

To get online with a wired router using cable or DSL, you need to connect your computer to the router using a network cable. The router will be set up to connect to the ISP with whatever settings are needed to do this.

Router ISP connection settings are different for each ISP. Some ISPs, such as Sky, pre-configure the free router they provide so it simply plugs into the broadband socket and works. Other ISPs will provide instructions which could be sent to the new user or can be found on their website.

Sky uses a system called **MAC encapsulated routing (MER)** which only allows a router with a recognised **MAC address** to connect to their system. Many ISPs use a system called **point-to-point protocol over ethernet (PPPoE)** which requires a username and password to connect to the ISP.

Key term

MAC address – every network communication device, such as a network card or a router, has a Media Access Control (MAC) address in the electronic circuits which is unique to that device. No two devices have the same MAC address. This is used in security systems to help authenticate connected devices.

Wireless router using laptop

To get online with a wireless Wifi router, you need to connect to it using the password that has already been set to restrict unauthorised access. The Wifi router should be configured so that the **SSID** is enabled thus helping you to locate the network. This means you will see the name of the network easily when searching for the Wifi connection. SSID can be turned off after the connection is made, to improve security.

Dial-up WAP and 3G technology

To get online with dial-up, you need a modem with a wired connection to a telephone point. The modem needs to be configured with the telephone number of the ISP and the password to gain access to their system.

To get online with a mobile phone using WAP or 3G technology, you need to start up the appropriate app to connect and browse.

To get online using a netbook with 3G technology, you need to start up the browser to connect and surf the Internet. The 3G settings will already be in place to enable access to the Internet.

1.4 Using help facilities to solve connection problems

The router and Internet have help facilities to solve Internet connection problems. Many routers have setup screens at the 192.168.0.1 address that can be typed into the address bar of your browser. The default **IP addresses** for home networks start with 192.168.0; the device number is the fourth digit.

The setup screens usually need an administrator ID and password before you can gain access. The setup screens each have a help section to explain the parts of the screen, the effects of changing any of the settings and the meanings of any options and acronyms.

To access Internet help you need the Internet to be working. This means that you need to use a different computer or device from the one that has the problem. The best Internet help is likely to be on the ISP's website, which will clearly explain the exact settings needed for your router to connect to its system.

> **Key terms**
>
> **SSID** – service set identifier. Every Wifi system has a SSID, which is the name of the network. The SSID is the name you see when searching for a connection in the available networks.
> **IP address** – most devices on a network have an IP address which needs to be different for each of them. An IP address consists of four numbers separated by full stops. Each of these numbers needs to be in the 0–255 range.

Check your understanding

1 What is a packet?
2 How is a VPN different to a LAN?
3 What type of Internet connection do you have at home? Find someone with a different connection type. How do they compare?
4 What is 192.168.0.1?

2 Use browser software to navigate web pages

2.1 Browser tools

Every browser offers a number of tools that are designed to help with your web browsing. They include:

- **Enter** to accept the current page
- **Back** to retrace steps to previous pages visited
- **Forward** to retrace from a previous step towards the pages where **Back** was used
- **Refresh** to reload a web page from the Internet
- **Stop** to stop a page loading
- **History** to see pages recently visited
- **Bookmark** to remember a page
- **New tab** to open a fresh web page in the browser.

Many web pages act like a form to gather information before moving onto the next web page.

Enter

The **Enter** key can often be used to accept the current page content and move onto the next page.

Back

The **Back** button on most web browsers is used to return to the last page visited. You might use a **search engine** such as Google™, then click on one of the links the search engine offers you. If the page you see after using the link is not what you were hoping for, then clicking on the **Back** button will return you to the search engine list.

Some browsers use **Alt+ ←** or the **Backspace** key as a keyboard alternative to the **Back** button.

Forward

Forward is similar to **Back** as it is used to revisit web pages. Whereas **Back** returns to previous pages, the **Forward** button can be used to return along the pages already seen using **Back**, eventually returning to the web page where **Back** was first used.

Some browsers use **Alt+ →** or **Shift+Backspace**, a keyboard alternative to the **Forward** button.

Key term

Search engine – a website where you can enter something you want to find on the Internet. The search engine shows you a list of websites that contain the information you want.

Refresh

Refresh is a powerful tool that is often used by experienced Web surfers. This tool reloads the web page directly from the Internet. This can be useful when looking at online listings such as eBay™ or Gumtree where the information on the page regularly changes. Clicking on **Refresh** will update the page to show the latest information.

Some browsers use the **F5** key as a keyboard alternative to the **Refresh** button.

Stop

Stop is used to prevent a web page from completely loading into the browser. This can be useful if there is a problem with the contents of the web page or connection to the website. The browser may freeze if the page takes a very long time to load. **Stop** will prevent the browser from freezing so it is usable again.

Some browsers use the **Esc** key as a keyboard alternative to the **Stop** button.

History

History keeps track of all the websites you have visited.

> ### How to look at your website history in Microsoft® Internet Explorer®
> 1. Open the **View** menu and select **Explorer Bars**.
> 2. Select **History** and the **History** window will appear on the left side of the browser.

You will see a list of the websites visited using the browser. These may be grouped by dates, such as last week.

Using **History** you can revisit a recent site you have seen but not saved as a bookmark.

Some browsers use **Ctrl+Shift+H** as a keyboard alternative to show the browser history.

Bookmark

Bookmarks are also known as **Favorites**. They are an essential feature of web browsing for many users. Adding a website page as a favourite or bookmark creates a menu option to return to the website easily at any time in the future.

Bookmarks can also be seen as a window in the browser, alongside History.

Bookmarks are different to History as you add them to your favourites, whereas History is simply a list of every site visited. The websites in History are also automatically removed after a few weeks. A bookmark stays until you choose to delete it.

Some browsers use **Ctrl+Shift+I** as a keyboard alternative to show bookmarks.

Did you know?

Refresh is also used by IT professionals when producing websites. After a new page is uploaded to the web server, the browser will still show the older page until **Refresh** is used to reload the page.

New tab

Starting a new tab allows you to open a new window in your browser so that you can see another website. You can start the new tab either by clicking on the **New Tab** button in your browser, or by holding the **Ctrl** key as you click on a link to the website that is wanted in the new tab. Use the **<Close>X** button at the top right corner of a tab to close it.

Some browsers use **Ctrl+T** as a keyboard alternative to starting a new tab and **Ctrl+F4** to close a browser tab.

Toolbar

Modern browsers offer a choice of **toolbars** to help you improve your browsing skills. Each toolbar has its own selection of buttons and can be turned on or off from the **View** menu.

Search bar

You can add a **search bar** to your browser. This will make it easier to use a search engine such as Google™. The search bar contains a box where you can type in what you want to search the Internet for.

Address bar

The **Address Bar** is where you can type in the address of a web page to visit it directly, rather than using a search engine to find the website.

Home

The **Home** button returns you to your homepage in the browser. The homepage is the page you see when the browser is first started. Many users set their homepage to the website they like to visit first.

Some browsers use **Alt+Home** as a keyboard alternative to bringing up the homepage.

Go to

The **Go to** option in the **View** menu gives you a quick way of returning to searches you have typed into your browser.

Follow link

You can **follow a link** by clicking on it in the browser. Links can usually be recognised on a web page as they are underlined and in a different colour. If you hold down the **Ctrl** key when you click on a link, the page will open up in a new tab in the browser.

URL and save web address

Every website has a **uniform resource locator (URL)** that can be used in the address bar to bring the site up in the browser. URL is the name of the website, for example **http://www.pearson.com**.

2.2 Browser settings

You can set or change your browser settings to make Internet surfing easier and safer.

Homepage

Many organisations want their employees to visit the same first page when they open their browser. For example, the homepage could show the organisation's intranet, with news and forthcoming events.

How to set the homepage for the Internet Explorer® browser

1. Open the **Tools** menu and select **Internet Options**.

2. In the **Internet Options** dialog box that appears, open the **General** tab.

3. In the **Home page** box, press the **Use current** button to set the web page that is showing, or type in the website address of the homepage that you want to appear.

4. Click the **Use current** button and then click **OK** to save your choice.

Autofill

Autofill makes using forms on web pages much faster, as it remembers similar typing from a previous form to save you re-entering the text. For example, if you buy something on the Internet, you will be asked to fill in a form with your name, delivery address and payment details. The next time you buy something from the same website, the information you entered will be entered for you each time you click into a text box on the form.

Setting up **Autofill** will be offered to you the first time you start to use a similar field on a web form that you have used before.

> **Did you know?**
>
> Some organisations believe that Autofill is a security risk, as previously typed sensitive or confidential information can be brought back.

How to change the Autofill setting in Internet Explorer®

1. Open the **Tools** menu and select **Internet Options**.

2. In the **Internet Options** dialog box that appears, open the **Content** tab.

3. In **AutoComplete**, click the **Settings** button.

4. In the **AutoComplete Settings** dialog box that appears, check the boxes where you want **Autofill** to work (see Figure 5.2).

5. Click **OK** to save your choice.

Figure 5.2: AutoComplete settings

Cookies

Cookies are small amounts of text and numbers that are stored in your browser by a website to keep information about you. For example, when you visit a website such as eBay™, cookies enable the website to 'remember' you so that you can check your saved searches, messages and current bidding information. Without cookies you would need to log onto eBay™ every time you looked at a page from the site.

Cookies are often not wanted as they can secretly track your use of websites. You can stop this by using the **Tools Options** dialog box **Privacy** tab, where cookies can be blocked for all sites except those web pages selected to allow cookies.

How to block cookies

1. Open the **Tools** menu and select **Internet Options**.
2. In the **Internet Options** dialog box that appears, click on the **Privacy** tab.
3. Under **Settings** you will see a scrollbar which provides six different privacy settings:

   - Block All cookies
   - High
   - Medium High
   - Medium
   - Low
   - Accept All cookies.

4. Select the setting you require and click **OK**.

Security

You can set the level of security on your browser to help you surf the Internet safely and to protect your computer from security risks.

How to set security options in Internet Explorer®

1. Open the **Tools** menu and select **Internet Options**.
2. In the **Internet Options** dialog box that appears, click on the **Security** tab.
3. Select the zone where you want to change the security settings and click **OK** to save your choice.

There are four zones:

- **Internet** – this allows you to control the types of code, downloads, pop-ups and objects that are allowed to run on visited websites.
- **Local intranet** – this allows you to control security in a similar way to the Internet, but for sites within an organisation's intranet.
- **Trusted sites** – this allows you to identify safe sites.
- **Restricted sites** – this allows you to block unsafe sites.

Pop-ups

Pop-ups are often caused by advertisements. You can block pop-ups from appearing on all websites and then allow pop-ups on any individual websites you use that needs them.

How to block pop-ups on websites

1. Open the **Tools** menu and select **Internet Options**.
2. In the **Internet Options** dialog box that appears, click on the **Privacy** tab.
3. Check the **Turn on Pop-up Blocker** box.
4. Use the **Settings** button to add any websites where you want pop-ups.
5. Click **OK** to save your choice.

Appearance

You can change the appearance of web pages using the **Tools** menu. Select **Internet Options** and in the dialog box that appears open the **General** tab. Here you will find buttons for:

- colours of default text and background
- fonts used when displaying web pages
- choosing which language to use on web pages and the address bar
- accessibility.

Personalisation

You can **personalise** your browser by downloading add-ons to provide extra toolbars or links to videos, music, news, search engines, social, travel or shopping websites.

Accessibility

The **Tools, Options dialog box General tab** has an **Accessibility** button which allows you to set the browser to ignore colours, font styles and font sizes that are specified on web pages and to use the colours you specify.

Privacy

The **Privacy** settings in the **Tools, Options dialog box Privacy tab** controls cookies, pop-ups and **InPrivate browsing**.

Software updates

Software updates can bring your browser up to date with the latest version of the software. This helps to improve security and includes the latest features.

Key term

InPrivate browsing – can be turned on using the Tools menu. The browser will now not remember any sites you visit in History or anywhere else.

Did you know?

Software patches are regularly released to fix problems found as software is used. Windows® will install these when the system is closed down and restarted.

Temporary file storage

Your browser uses temporary file storage to keep copies of websites you visit on your hard disk. These are used to make the web pages load faster when you return to them.

Deleting temporary file storage will free up some space on your hard drive, remove traces of websites you have visited and slow your browser down a little if these websites are revisited.

How to delete temporary file storage

1. Open the **Tools** menu and select **Internet Options**.
2. In the **Internet Options** dialog box that appears, click on the **General** tab.
3. In the **Browsing history** section, check the **Delete browsing history on exit** box and click **OK** to save your choice.

You can also change the location of temporary file storage to a location of your choice. Follow steps 1 and 2 above, then work through points 1–3 in the box below.

How to change the location of temporary file storage

1. In the **Browsing history** section, click the **Settings** button.
2. In the **Temporary Internet Files and History Settings** dialog box that appears, click **Move folder** in the **Current location** section.
3. In the **Browse for Folder**, click on the location where you want to move the temporary Internet files and click **OK** to save your choice.

Search engine

The default search engine depends on your browser. It is likely to be a search box near the top of the browser window.

Some search engines such as Google™ allow you to download a search bar for your browser. This then becomes the default search engine.

Zoom

The **View** menu allows you to zoom in or out of the web pages to make them larger or smaller. Zoom in to 150% and everything on the web page is a lot larger – you will need to use the scroll bars to the right and below the browser to move the page and see the edges. Zoom out to 75% and everything on the web page is smaller, or to 100% to return to where you started.

2.2 Browser performance

The browser performance can affect how quickly your computer seems to work. A faster computer gives a better experience when surfing the web.

Delete cache and temporary files

To speed up your browser, delete the **cache** and temporary files (follow steps 1–3 in 'How to delete temporary file storage'). Next time you open the browser, it will not need to load History data and your computer will appear to work faster. The drawback of deleting the cache is that some web pages will load more slowly.

Work offline and save websites

If you have a slow connection or find a website that is very slow, you can use the **File** menu to save the website pages, then work offline.

How to bring up saved web pages when working offline

1. Go to the **File** menu and choose the **Open** menu command.
2. Browse for the saved website page.
3. Press OK to open the page.

> **Key term**
>
> **Cache** – memory in a web browser. This is when pages are kept on your computer so they do not need to be downloaded again from the Internet. This can make revisiting a web page a lot quicker.

Case study: Greenfields Sports Club

You are a member of Greenfields Sports Club, which is based in a building on the edge of playing fields. The Club building consists of changing rooms, a storehouse and a social area with a bar and children's area.

The Club's Committee has decided to set up some PCs in the children's area which will have a DSL Internet connection through the Club's broadband-enabled telephone line. The Committee wants the PCs to be set up to keep web browsing restricted to safe sites and to reduce risks to the systems.

1 The Committee has asked you to research the following browsers:

- Google Chrome™
- Firefox®
- Microsoft® Internet Explorer®
- Opera®
- Safari™.

2 Write a report showing your findings. Your report should include:

- a review of each browser
- the benefits and drawbacks of each browser
- a guide to how to reduce risks from web browsing.

Check your understanding

1 Why are **Stop** and **Refresh** useful when browsing the Web?
2 Identify similarities and differences between **History** and **Bookmarks**.
3 Why can a cookie be helpful when web browsing?

3 Use browser tools to search for information from the Internet

Case study: Cherry's Chocolates moves premises

Cherry's Chocolates is growing fast. Cherry has so many orders that she needs to take on three new members of staff: one to help in the kitchen, and two to deal with sales and orders. Her tiny kitchen is too small to allow her business to expand and she needs space for an office.

She has decided to move to a small shop. It needs to have space to sell her chocolates at the front, and room at the back for a kitchen and an office.

Cherry is wondering how she is going to find the time to carry out an Internet search for her new premises.

3.1 Search techniques

The worldwide web is a vast source of information. You need to use search techniques to find the information you want from this huge collection of web pages.

Search keywords

To find information on the Internet you need to use a search engine (see below for more information on search engines). Search engines look for websites containing the keywords you type into your search. A search engine can do this because it regularly looks at every website on the world wide web to build up the search engine database it uses to find the websites you are looking for.

Carefully chosen keywords are words that you would expect to be in a website you want to visit, but that are not in websites you do not want to find. If you are looking to buy something, then including UK in your keywords will increase the number of sites you find that sell the product or service in the United Kingdom.

Quotation marks

Quotation marks are very powerful in searches because they force the search engine to look for the exact phrase inside the marks, rather than every combination of the words. For example, searching "internet search techniques" with the quotation marks will return web pages with this phrase. The same search without the quotation marks will return any web pages with these words both scattered and together.

Search within results

You may want to search 'within the results' that the search engine finds for you. Google™ does this automatically as you type keywords into the search box. Each new word you type refines the results that Google™ shows to include everything you entered.

Relational operators

Relational operators are used to find results that are less than, more than or not equal to. These are difficult operations to carry out in most search engines.

For example, Google™ allows some relational operations in the **Advanced search** screen in the **Date, usage rights, region, and more section** where you can specify a date or a numeric range between two figures.

The not equal to relation can be used in a search by using the minus sign; for example, –Toshiba will bring out a result without any references to Toshiba.

'Find' or search tool

To find a word or phrase on a page of results from a search, or on a web page you are visiting, you can use the **Find** or search tool.

How to find a word or phrase using Find

1. Open the **Find** dialog box either by clicking on the **Find** icon within the **Home** tab, or using the **Ctrl+F** shortcut key combination.

2. Type a word or phrase into the search box.

3. Click on **Next** or **Previous** to jump to the required word. If you click away from the **Find** box, you will see all the found search word(s) highlighted.

If the **Find** box is not visible, you can use the **Edit** menu to select **Find on this page** or use the **Ctrl+F** keyboard shortcut.

Turn questions into keywords for an online query

The keywords you use in a search are important because these are what the search engine will use to find websites for you. So you need to turn the question you are asking into the keywords needed for an online query. For example, if you want to find a manual for a BMW R100RS motor cycle, you only need the keywords, BMW R100RS manual. This is what you would type into the search engine.

Choice of search engine

There are many good search engines. A lot of people use the Google™ website as their search engine. The best option for a search engine is the one you find easiest to use. For example, Microsoft® Internet Explorer® has Bing™ as standard in the toolbar as a search engine.

Multiple search criteria

A search uses multiple search criteria when more than one word is typed into the search engine. Multiple search criteria can be even more powerful using logical operators and wild cards.

Did you know?

There are metasearch engines such as Dogpile and Metacrawler that use the results from other search engines to find information for you from the Internet.

Logical operators

Google™ and other search engines allow **Logical (or Boolean) operators** in your searches. The main logical operators are AND, OR and NOT (-).

- AND is the default in a search and does not even need to be typed into the search. This is because the search engine will look for matches for every word you type.
- OR can be used to give the search engine a choice of words to look for. A search may have the years 2011 2012 which will look for web pages with both these years. The OR operator could be used to specify that either of these years is wanted, so 2011 OR 2012 in the search will look for pages with one of these years as well as both of them.
- NOT is when you want to remove something from your search results. Google™ uses the minus sign (–) before the word you do not want in your search results. A search for Stratocaster –squier will not return matches for Squier Stratocaster.

Wild cards

Google™ and other search engines allow the * wild card, which acts as a placeholder in your search text. For example, to search for lyrics to a song that you have partly forgotten, you would type in the lyrics you remember and then use * to represent the missing words.

3.2 Information requirements

You must be able to recognise how well information you find meets your requirements. In particular, you need to assess information for the following:

- Reliability – do you trust the information?
- Currency – is the information up to date?
- Relevance – is the information what is needed?
- Accuracy – do you think the information is correct?
- Bias – is the information fair, or is it misleading?
- Level of detail – do you have enough information for your purpose?
- Sufficiency – how complete do you think the information is?

Recognise intention and authority of provider and bias

Reliability is important as you need to recognise how much you can depend upon the information. Knowing the intention and authority of the provider can help you to recognise possible bias in the information.

A manufacturer or advertiser is legally bound to be truthful, but this still offers a lot of opportunity to present information which can be misleading or biased.

Currency of the information

Information needs to be current and up to date. Look for a date on the website. It is often at the bottom of the page, or it may be in the title.

Relevance

Sometimes the information you find may not be suitable for the purpose you need it for, or only some of the information you find may be relevant.

Data that is no longer up to date may also have lost its relevance.

Accuracy

Accurate information is an important part of your search results. Look out for figures which are rounded off to the nearest thousand or million, as these are not as accurate as the original data.

Beware of misleading graphs or charts that distort data by careful use of scaling to emphasise differences (see Figure 5.3).

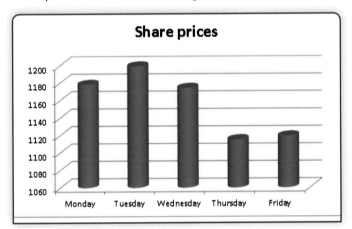 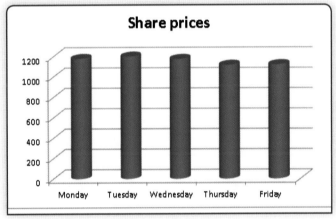

Figure 5.3: Charts can be misleading by showing only part of the chart

Level of detail and sufficiency

There needs to be a sufficient level of detail in the information you discover from searching the web. Often, you will need to find several websites to gather enough information for your needs.

Synthesise information from a variety of different sources

The Internet is a massive resource that you can use to bring information together from many places to find enough detail to meet your needs. Using different sources adds more to your findings, with each bringing a new slant to your research topic.

3.3 Managing and using references

As you search the Internet you will come across useful websites and pages. If you do not make a record of these, you could easily forget them. There are ways to store references to websites so that you can quickly return to them if needed. These include using:

- **History**
- **Favorites**
- **Bookmarks.**

The number of references can become large after a while, so you should also be able to manage these by deleting references that are no longer wanted.

History

The **History** is created automatically by your browser and can be useful to revisit sites you loaded during the last month. As these entries will be deleted after a few weeks by the browser, History is not a good place to keep, or depend upon, links to visited sites.

How to increase the time that visited websites are remembered in the History

1. Open the **Tools** menu and select **Internet Options**.
2. In the **Internet Options** dialog box that appears, open the **General** tab.
3. In the **Browsing history** section, click the **Settings** button.
4. In the **Temporary Internet Files and History Settings** dialog box that appears, use the up/down arrows in the **History** section to change the number of **Days to keep pages in history**.
5. Click **OK**, and **OK** to save your choice.

You can manage the History by:

- individually deleting entries that are not wanted. This sort of action is more suitable to use with the favourites, as they are kept as long as you want them (see below).
- deleting browser history every time you exit the browser. To do this, follow the step-by-step instructions for 'How to delete temporary file storage' (*see page 36*).

Favourites and bookmarks

Favourites are known as bookmarks in some browsers.

You can use favourites to remember websites that you expect to revisit in the future. Internet Explorer® has a **Favorites** menu where the currently viewed website can be added to the menu and where the already saved favourites are shown.

How to return to a website that has been saved in Favorites

There are three ways you can do this:

1. Open the **Favorites** menu – this lists all the websites that have been added to the favourites (Figure 5.4). Click a favourite or use **Alt+A** on the keyboard to open it followed by the first letter of the website.

Figure 5.4: The Favorites toolbar can be used to show or hide the Favorites explorer bar

continued

2. Show the **Favorites** toolbar. This is a button that can be shown in your browser which will show or hide the **Favorites Explorer Bar** when clicked (see Figure 5.5). You can turn this button on or off – in the **View** menu, select **Toolbars**, then check or uncheck the **Favorites Bar**.

Figure 5.5: The Favorites explorer bar can be used to revisit websites

3. Show the **Favorites Explorer Bar**. This is a window that can be shown in your browser to list all the websites that have been added to the favourites. These can be selected using the keyboard or clicked with the mouse (see Figure 5.6). To open or close the window: in the **View** menu, select **Explorer Bars**, then Favorites.

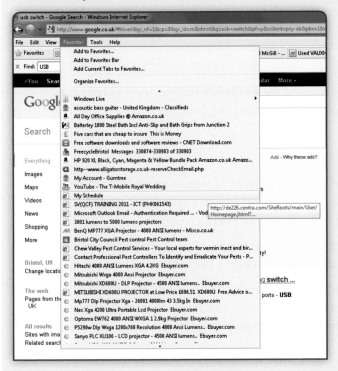

Figure 5.6: The Favorites menu can be used to revisit websites

If you have a lot of favourites you may want to organise them so that you store similar websites in a folder. You can add folders to your favourites to help organise different types of websites.

How to organise your favourites in folders

1. Open the **Favorites** menu and select **Organize Favorites**.

2. In the **Organise Favorites** dialog box that appears, click **New Folder** (see Figure 5.7). A **New Folder** appears at the bottom of the list of favourites.

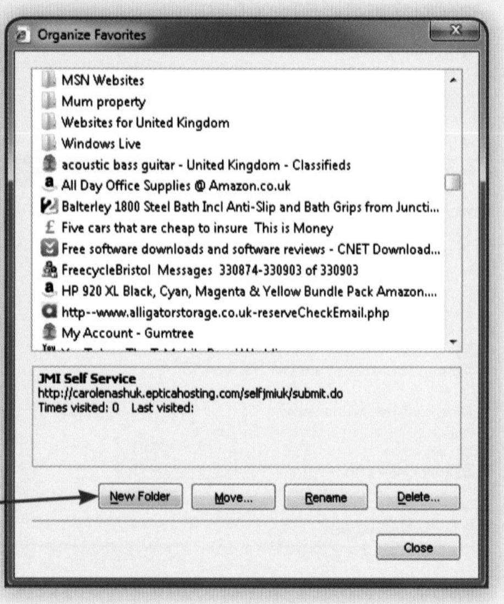

Use this button to create a new folder in your favourites

Figure 5.7: Adding a new folder to the Favorites menu

3. You can now type the name of the new folder.

4. You can move an existing favourite into the folder by selecting the favourite, then using the **Move** button and then clicking on the folder.

5. You can rename any favourite by selecting it, then using the **Rename** button.

Links

The **Links** toolbar is now called the **Favorites** toolbar, used to hold links to websites. *See the section on Favourites and bookmarks, page 42,* for more information.

Log useful sites

As you search the Internet you may want to make a list, or log, of any useful sites you find. To do this, create a Microsoft® Word® document, copy the website URL from the **Address bar** and paste it into the document.

You can then add comments to these links and return to any of the websites by holding the **Ctrl** key down as you click on a link with the mouse.

Remember to save your document and give it a suitable file name. The document could be sent to another user which would then give them a quick and easy way of visiting the websites you have found.

RSS and data feeds

Data feeds are found in the **Favorites Explorer Bar** window with favourites and History.

Your browser can identify a web page with feeds you can subscribe to by making a sound and changing the colour of the feed detector button. You can then click on a link in the page to subscribe to the feed, which will add the feed to the **Explorer Bar**.

Data feeds use RSS (Really Simple Syndication) technology to receive changing information from the feed site. This means that you can get up-to-date information as it happens, such as when new job vacancies are added to a website.

Saved search results

You can easily save the results of a search by adding it to your favourites in the same way you would add a website.

3.4 Downloading and organising information

There are many types of information you might want to download, including:

- web pages and websites
- images, text and numbers
- sound, games, video, television and music.

Web pages and websites

A **web page** from a **website** can be saved to your computer so you can open it again if there is no Internet connection.

In Internet Explorer® use the **File Save** or **Save As** menu options to save the web page or website into **My Documents** . To open the web page or website offline, use the **File**, **Open** menu, then browse to where it was saved.

If there is no Internet connection the web page will look as it did when saved, but none of the links on the page will work. If there is an Internet connection the links will work.

Saving a web page is different to making a bookmark, as you have downloaded a copy of the web page to your hard disk so do not need the Internet to see it again. A bookmark is a link to enable your browser to quickly revisit the bookmarked site.

Images, text and numbers

An image can be downloaded by right clicking on it, then choosing **Save Picture As** from the pop-up menu. You can then specify the folder where you want to save the image.

To download text or numbers, highlight the text or numbers on the web page, then copy and paste them into a suitable document or spreadsheet.

> **Key term**
>
> **Data feed** – a data feed is when a website sends fresh or changed information to your browser.

> **Did you know?**
>
> The Favorites Explorer Bar window is shared with history and feeds, any of which can be selected using the tabs at the top of the window.

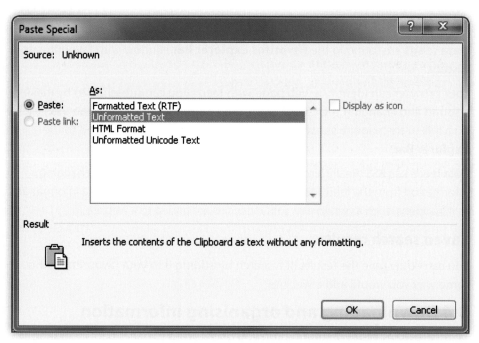

Figure 5.8: Use the Paste Special menu to paste text or numbers without any formatting

Sound, games, video, television and music

Downloading video, television, games, sound or music is quite similar, as they all involve downloading the media file from the website to your computer.

Once you have found the media file you want to download, there will either be a button you can press or you will need to right click on it and select the **Download Target As** menu option, or sometimes it might be **Save Target As**, (see Figure 5.9). You will now need to select the folder where the file will be saved.

Figure 5.9: Use Save Target As menu option to choose the folder where you will store your media file

Activity: Researching premises for Cherry's Chocolates

As we saw in the case study on *page 38*, Cherry is so busy that she does not have the time to do the research for her new business premises.

Once again, she has asked you to help her. She wants you to research a suitable property. She is looking for a small shop with space to sell her chocolates at the front, and room at the back for a kitchen and an office. The shop should not be further than 20 miles away from her home (a couple of doors down from where you live). She is getting a loan from the bank, so she has told you not to worry about the price of the shop.

1 Use Cherry's browser to search for suitable properties using the search techniques you have learnt in this section. Add each successful search to a folder named 'Property searches' in the browser favourites.

2 Write some notes for Cherry on how you applied these techniques to your searches..

Check your understanding

1 Describe how a keyword can be identified for a web search.

2 Which of these logical operators (AND OR) is default in most browsers? How could you use the other relational operator in this question?

3 What is currency in a search result?

4 How many types of downloadable information can you list?

4 Use browser software to communicate information online

4.1 Ways to share information

There are lots of ways to communicate information on the Internet, for example by adding to the content of a website, including blogs, review sites and forums.

Saved information

The worldwide web is a great resource for finding information which you will often want to communicate to others.

Saved information such as **podcasts**, text and images is often called 'static', as it does not change. These are held as documents or files on a website and may be downloaded. For example, the BBC's website has many radio shows available as podcasts with free RSS subscriptions, so you can automatically receive the latest version of your favourite show to hear when and where you want.

Key term

Podcast – a recording which can be downloaded and then heard on a media player.

You and your friends have a favourite online game that you like to play together. Usually you play as a team, with a lot of success.

As a celebration of your success, you have decided to set up a blog to attract possible new team members.

Set up a blog to include:

- links and screenshots to the online gaming website
- details about the team
- some gaming tips.

Key term

Blog – An online journal where people post diary entries.

Did you know?

A growing number of businesses have realised the importance of blogs to promote their products and services, and to publicise the latest news. The fashion chain River Island has an official blog called Style Insider which aims to keep customers 'in the know with all things River'.

Real-time information

Real-time information is not saved as it is transmitted live. Millions of people use instant messaging to keep in touch with typed conversations or video links.

Many websites allow you to create new content by typing into the site. This could be a **blog** where you post up images and text because you have something you want to communicate with others. For example, young people travelling during a gap year often keep a blog which can be regularly updated with news and photos, then instantly viewed from anywhere in the world by friends and family.

Many blogs use real-time information, where visitors can enter comments that can be seen by others visiting the blog as soon as they are typed.

File transfer protocol (FTP) and hypertext transmission protocol (http)

There are two main methods used to bring saved information to your computer.

- **File transfer protocol (FTP)** is used when there is a file to download such as a manual or music track. FTP is the technology behind uploading to the web by web-creation software such as Adobe® Dreamweaver®.
- **Hypertext transmission protocol (http)** is used by your browser all the time to bring the web page down from the Internet to your computer, so the browser can lay the page out and display it on your screen.

Voice over Internet protocol

Voice over Internet protocol (VoIP) is a technology where a telephone or headset is plugged into a computer so you can make a voice call. This is very similar to using a telephone except that the call goes through your Internet connection rather than the telephone system, so there is no charge for the call.

4.2 Sharing information sources

You need to be able to share some of the information you find using the browser. You can do this in different ways including sending links, web pages and photographs.

Send links

Sending a link is as easy as highlighting the web page address in the address bar of your browser, copying this and pasting the link into an email or document.

Pasted links usually appear underlined and in a different colour in the document. The link can then be used with the mouse with a double click or **Ctrl+click**, depending on the app document where the link is held.

Send web page

You can send a web page by saving it from the browser using the **File** menu, then attaching the saved web page to an email as you would any other document. (For more information on email attachments, *see Unit 6 Using email, page 71.*)

There are lots of good websites where you can upload your photographs for friends and family to see, using tools such as Google Picasa™.

Some email programs such as Microsoft® Outlook® have a calendar where you can make and show appointments with other Outlook users on the same network or add a plug-in to Outlook® to share with others in your address book.

RSS feeds can bring live information into your browser. You can share this with others by adding a feed to your own website, so when people visit your site they see the live feed information.

Reference lists

A reference list or bibliography should be used at the end of every piece of work you create which uses Internet research. Identify the websites you used by copying the URL. *See Log useful sites, page 44.*

4.3 Submitting information to the Internet

There are many ways to submit information to the Internet, including:

- adding your own experiences to be shared with others
- entering your details to buy something online.

Fill in and submit web forms

You need to fill in and submit web forms whenever a website needs to know something about you. Web forms are essential for online shopping, both for payment and delivery details.

Many support sites and forums want to know who you are before they allow you to search for information or download pages.

When using online forms for anything to do with money, check that the web address starts with **https** and always make sure you are entering the genuine site.

Did you know?

Never click on a link in an unexpected email to enter a money-related website. This may bring up a spoof website that looks like the real thing but is actually a copy designed to get your bank details.

Ratings, reviews and recommendations

Some websites invite you to comment on products you have bought or used by leaving feedback, writing a review or giving a rating. Your rating or review is then used by other people who are interested in purchasing similar goods to help them decide if the product would be good for them.

Reviews are welcomed on websites that sell goods and also by independent review sites, such as Reevoo. They gather lots of consumer feedback to provide comments on what people found good and bad about products, with an overall score out of ten. Users may use good ratings and reviews as a recommendation that the product or service is worth buying.

Wikis

Wikis are websites where you can add your comments to the information already there. The most famous wiki is Wikipedia.

Activity: Adding to Wikipedia

Add a page of your own to Wikipedia, describing a club you are a member of, or something you find interesting near where you live.

Visit the 'Starting an article' web page on Wikipedia for more information on how to do this.

Discussion forums

Discussion forums are a great way of finding out about products and how to solve problems. They cover a wide range of topics, such as makes of car, computers, washing machines, software apps, and so on. A forum exists for just about everything!

The strength of a forum is that someone posts up a question which can then be seen by everyone who visits that part of the forum. Answers and comments can then be posted, so many opinions and help soon appear. You can often see these simply by visiting, but you usually need to register as a member of the forum if you want to respond to questions, post up a new topic, or search for answers.

Some forums need payment for registration but most are free to join.

Interactive sites

Interactive sites exist for many reasons, often to work out a calculation or conversion for you.

Calculations include currency conversions, where you can type an amount of money in UK pounds to see it converted into euros, US dollars, or any other currency you wish.

You will find it easy to locate sites that are able to convert between sizes, such as inches to centimetres or litres to gallons.

There are even websites you can use to convert English words and phrases into another language.

Netiquette

Netiquette is a set of loose, informal rules that guide you on how to express yourself online. These are useful because they help to communicate feelings that you could easily understand in a face-to-face meeting using facial expressions, body language and tone of voice.

One of the basic netiquette rules is that capital letters are the same as shouting at someone and should only be used to emphasise a point. Otherwise, lower case is used for most online typing.

Netiquette has a lot of acronyms such as IMHO (in my humble opinion), making messages quicker to type and shorter.

There are also a lot of emoticons you can use to show facial expressions when typing, such as :D to represent a big grin and laughing. Some apps convert these to smiley pictures as you type, such as Microsoft® Word® changing :-) into ☺.

> **Did you know?**
>
> Good netiquette includes knowing when not to use emoticons. Although they are great for communicating with friends and family, they should not be used in the workplace.

Activity: Netiquette guide

Produce a guide to netiquette.

1 Use the internet to carry out some research on netiquette.
2 Identify some netiquette examples used across different sectors and different sizes of organisations.
3 Produce your own netiquette guide. Aim to include at least ten rules.

Check your understanding

1 Identify four ways you can post material to websites.
2 What is the difference between FTP and http?
3 What is an interactive site?

---

5 Understand the need for safety and security practices when working online

5.1 Threats to system performance

Every time you go online there are threats to your system from many directions. If allowed onto your computer they may affect the performance of the system.

Unwanted email (spam)

Spam is unwanted email that everyone gets sent all the time. An effective email system will filter out a lot of this spam, so you may not be aware it is happening.

Even the best email system will let some spam through, so it is important to know how to recognise and deal with it. If you do not know the sender or the subject of an email, looks wrong, then it is probably spam.

The simplest way to deal with spam email is to delete it without opening or viewing the email. Never open a spam attachment as this will almost certainly be code that will install malicious software (malware) on your system.

An email in **HTML format** can have malware inside that runs when you open the email. Viewing emails in text format is much safer. The only risks are clicking on links in the email, or opening attachments.

Malicious programs

Malware is any malicious program or software that can run on your computer. Here are some examples:

- **Viruses** are programs that are designed to attach to files on your computer system and infect other files with slightly different types of the virus. A virus keeps changing to make it harder to spot. A virus will corrupt data and can slow down the system.
- **Worms** slow down the system by using up **bandwidth** and may also interfere with data. Worms use computer networks to spread copies of the original worm.
- **Trojans** are named after the **Trojan horse** from Greek mythology. These are programs that are downloaded to do something useful for the computer user. At the same time they also break system security by secretly allowing a hacker access to the computer data, to see what is on the screen, user key presses and to remotely control the system.
- **Spyware** programs install without the user knowing they are there. They send personal information such as websites visited and key presses to hackers outside the system. Spyware is also likely to slow down the system.
- **Adware** creates unwanted pop-ups that appear on your screen to advertise products or services.
- **Rogue diallers** are a security risk only for users with a dial-up Internet connection. Software automatically re-routes the Internet connection to a premium rate phone line. This may lead to very high phone call charges for the user.

Key terms

HTML format – when an email or a web page uses HTML (Hyper Text Markup Language) to improve the appearance.

Bandwidth – Network bandwidth capacity is how much data can travel through a connection at any time.

Trojan horse – trojans are named after the Trojan horse from Greek mythology. This is because, as in the myth, trojans appear to be doing something useful but are secretly letting 'enemies' into your system (see 'Did you know?' box below).

Did you know?

In Greek mythology the Trojans were planning to attack the city of Troy. They gave the people of Troy a gift of a horse. Some soldiers hid inside the horse which was taken into the city. Later, the soldiers got out and opened the city gates, letting in other soldiers who attacked and captured Troy.

Hackers

Hackers are people who gain unauthorised access to a computer system. Some hackers do this for the challenge, but most do it to make money. Once inside a system the hacker can download private information such as details of the user's bank account or credit card. They can then use this information to take money out of the bank account, or sell the details to someone else who can use the information.

Hoaxes

There have been many Internet hoaxes which have spread false information for various reasons, often as humour. A famous hoax on YouTube showed how to recharge an iPod using an onion. This did not work, but the video convinced a lot of people to try it!

5.2 Safety and security precautions

You should always work responsibly and take appropriate safety and security precautions when working online. This will keep your computer running well and will protect any private information on the computer.

Firewall settings and Internet security settings

Firewall security settings are the first line of defence and should be enabled on your router. A firewall stops bad Internet traffic entering your computer system.

Internet security settings can add to this security in various ways, such as blocking bad websites.

Report inappropriate behaviour

You have a right to use the Internet without interference, so report any inappropriate behaviour you find or experience. Tell a teacher or parent/guardian about anything that you feel is wrong, offensive or suspicious, so that they are aware of the problem and able to take the necessary actions. In the workplace, inappropriate behaviour can be reported to a manager, the human resources (HR) department or a union representative.

Report security threats or breaches

In your workplace or at college, where you regularly use IT systems, you should report any security threats or breaches you are aware of to the network administrator. He or she will know the systems already in place and how they need to be adjusted to deal with the threat.

Security threats or breaches can put your own work at risk as well as threatening the smooth running of the system. A security breach could result in a system running so slowly that it is impossible to work with it.

> **Did you know?**
>
> Email hoaxes can be malicious, such as emails sent in October 2010 to the car maker Renault claiming that some employees were being paid for passing on electric car technology to Chinese spies. Three executives were suspended from their jobs and the French intelligence service investigated the claim before finding out that it was a hoax.

Content filtering

The network you use for study or at work will have proxy servers which will be set up to improve firewall security by controlling the websites available to users of the system.

Proxy servers provide content filtering. They look for certain words on the websites you want to visit and will block any website containing these. They can give powerful control of user surfing in other ways, for example they can block users clicking on adverts shown in Google™ or other search engine results.

Automatically blocked websites can be unblocked by the network administrator by adding them to the list of websites the proxy will allow.

Avoid inappropriate disclosure of information

You must never give personal or confidential information to any person or website unless you know that the request is genuine.

Your cashpoint card has a **PIN number** that you must never disclose. An email appearing to come from your bank requesting you to confirm your PIN or to click on a link to the bank website would be an inappropriate disclosure of information, as banks never ask for such data.

Carry out security checks

Every organisation should carry out regular security checks to confirm that staff are using the IT systems responsibly and that computer system security settings are working.

Proxy servers

Proxy servers are used in many networks to control user access to the Internet. These servers give the network administrators good control over blocking potentially unsafe sites, as well as unblocking sites that are needed by users.

A site could be automatically blocked by the proxy server because it contains words the proxy looks for, but these words may be used in a different context on the site a user needs, so the user could request to have it released.

5.3 Threats to information security

The threats to information security when working online are very similar to those towards system performance (*see the section on Malicious programs, page 52*).

Malicious programs and hackers

Many malicious programs have been written to destroy data or send it out from your system to a hacker, so they have enough information to steal from your bank account or gain access to private information.

Key term

PIN number – a secret four-digit password, shared between a user and a system, which enables the user to gain access to the system. PIN stands for personal identification number.

Phishing

Phishing is a clever technique used to get your log-on information to a bank account or similar. This scam works by sending you an email which looks very realistic, as though it was sent from your bank (or similar). The email will tell you of a problem with the account or your card and that you need to visit the bank's website to sort out the problem.

The phishing email will have a link you can click on to bring up the bank's website, but clicking on this will take you to a spoof website that looks real. When you log on, the spoof website captures your ID and password information which can be used by the criminals running the scam to steal your money.

Financial deception

Financial deception on the Internet ranges from emails asking for your help in releasing funds to very sophisticated phishing scams leading you to a spoof website looking just like the real thing. Trust your judgement with all of these because if it looks wrong, it is wrong! Financial deception may also lead to identity theft.

Identity theft

Internet criminals use many different methods to obtain private information about you. This information can be used to withdraw money from your bank account. An even more damaging way to use private information is through identity theft.

Identity theft is when a criminal gets enough information to pretend to be you. Criminal can use your identity to set up credit cards and accounts with online retailers. This means that they can steal a lot more from you than the money you actually have in your bank account by running up debts of thousands of pounds.

Even worse than this is the damage to your credit rating, which can make it difficult or impossible to borrow or obtain finance for years afterwards.

5.4 Accessing personal information online

Managing your personal information securely is always important. There are many people trying to obtain your personal information because they want to steal from you.

Username and password/PIN selection management

Your username and password or PIN are a powerful combination that can give access to your money to anyone who knows them.

You must always manage your personal access to online sources securely by keeping your passwords safe. You should not share your username and password with anyone else or let them see you log on.

Your browser can remember passwords, which is very useful, but if your computer is stolen this will also allow the thief to log on to all the sites with

Did you know?

Some phishing emails and spoof websites can look real. If you think the email might be genuine, you should never click on the link in the email to bring up the website but instead visit it using your usual bookmark.

Figure 5.10: A typical log-in screen

Figure 5.11: An avatar is a character who represents you in a virtual environment

saved passwords. These will also be available to anyone who can use your computer if you leave it unattended.

If you have saved passwords in your browser, you should also have a power-on password for your computer to stop anyone else from using it.

Password strength

Selecting your password is important. There are programs that hackers use which automatically try again and again to gain access to accounts by using a dictionary of possible passwords.

Including a mixture of upper and lower case letters as well as a number creates a stronger password which is a lot harder to crack.

The strongest passwords use a random collection of upper and lower case letters and numbers. These are difficult to remember so you sould probably write the password down. However, this is another security risk.

Online identity/profile

You might have several online identities for different purposes such as online games, shopping, your bank account, and so on. Each of these will have a profile giving some information about you.

Real name

Think carefully about the information you include for online identities. Your real name should only be used where it is needed for shopping or banking.

Pseudonym

When playing online games create a fictitious name (a pseudonym), which your friends easily recognise but will be of no use to a criminal trying to obtain information about you.

Avatar

Avatars are good for virtual worlds, but think carefully about the information you include when setting yours up. You need to keep yourself safe from identity theft.

What personal information to include

The personal information you enter into a website depends on the purpose, e.g. if you are buying something from an online retailer such as Amazon you will need to include your name, address and payment details. Always divulge the minimum personal information you can.

Always consider who can see personal information and what they could do with it if they had bad intentions.

Withhold personal information

You must withhold any personal information that is not directly needed by a website. Otherwise, you will find yourself bombarded by unwanted advertising or, in a worst-case scenario robbed!

5.5 Threats to user safety

There are many threats to your user safety when surfing the web.

Abusive behaviour (cyber bullying)

Abusive behaviour or cyber bullying can take many forms, such as posting bad pictures or words on Facebook. Cyber bullying is anything that a person does to make you feel bad or very uncomfortable.

Inappropriate behaviour and abuse of young people

Inappropriate behaviour is when someone attempts to build up an online relationship with a person where they are not what they appear to be. An older person may pretend to be younger than they are to encourage a young person to communicate with them and build up a friendship.

Grooming of young people can take place over a period of weeks or months. Once a friendship has been established online, the older person may suggest meeting. It is important to be careful when online and be sure not to share personal details with people you do not know.

False identities

False identities are fine for online games but are very dangerous if used as the basis for an online friendship or relationship. The danger here is grooming, where the other person appears to be someone you would like to meet, whereas you would normally avoid any contact with such a person.

5.6 Minimising security risks

You can minimise risks from the Internet by behaving responsibly on the sites you visit and using the software and hardware tools there to reduce risk.

Virus-checking software

Virus checking software is essential on modern computer systems to reduce opportunities for **malware** to enter your computer and to detect any that do breach your security.

Anti-spam software

A virus checker may work with your email system to provide anti-spam protection. Rogue emails are automatically identified when they arrive and are sent to a spam folder instead of the inbox.

Specialist anti-spam software can be installed to reduce this threat.

Key term

Malware – any malicious program or software that can run on your computer. Examples include viruses, worms, trojans and adware.

Firewall

Enabling a **firewall** is a good start to protecting your system but you can also change the configuration to improve the security offered.

The default configuration will allow all outgoing services and block all incoming services. You may add rules to these to block unwanted outgoings or to enable incoming services such as video conferencing.

Internet settings

You can use the browser Internet settings to minimise risk whilst surfing the web. *See section 5.2 Safety and security precautionson pages 53–54* for more information.

Block sites

Blocking sites is accomplished by many organisations using a proxy server (*see Content filtering on page 54*) to prevent staff from visiting websites with inappropriate content or malware.

You can block a site using your browser, either to prevent a revisit or to stop other users of the computer from seeing it.

How to block the current website

1. Open the **Tools** menu and select **Internet options**.
2. In the **Security** tab, click **Restricted sites**.
3. Click **Sites**. You can now **Add** the site.

Parental controls

Parental controls can be included in a virus checker or in your operating system. Virus-checker parental controls can track how children use the Internet and the websites they visit. Microsoft® Windows® parental controls are based on creating an account that children can use for logging on to the computer. The children's account can then be controlled so that they are not able to visit undesirable websites.

Activity: Working safely online at Cherry's Chocolates

Cherry's Chocolates now has its own website and receives lots of emails from customers and suppliers. Cherry and her employees also use the Internet to search for new products, supplies and ideas. She is very concerned about the security of her computers and how to work safely when online.

Cherry has asked you to advise her on how to make her computers secure, and how she and her staff can work safely when online.

Write a report which covers the following areas:

- How to use browser settings to reduce Internet risk.
- How to install an anti-virus program and make sure the virus database is up to date.

5.7 Laws, guidelines and procedures

You should be aware of the laws, guidelines and procedures relating to the Internet, and follow them. This will take away any risk of prosecution and reduce risks to yourself and the organisation you work for, if applicable.

Your employer or organisation will have guidelines and procedures for safe and secure Internet use. These will cover:

- Internet security
- health and safety.

Internet security

In the workplace, employees are expected to sign a code of conduct listing what they can and cannot do when using IT systems and the Internet.

The code of conduct makes the expectations that the organisation has of staff very clear, everyone has to read it and sign their agreement.

Systems and data security is important because organisations must comply with the Data Protection Act. If confidential information becomes known or is misused, an organisation may be prosecuted and fined.

Code of conduct

Things to remember:

- Do not tamper with IT equipment.
- Do not store computer games, music or films on work computers or network space.
- You are responsible for misuse of your log on details, even by someone else.
- If you think someone else knows your password, you should change it immediately.
- IT facilities are only for business-related activities, not personal use.
- Do not enter sites or send emails containing abusive, sexist, pornographic or unlawful material.
- Do not install or download software that has not been provided by the organisation.
- Do not try to bypass the network content-filtering software.
- Do not use the Internet to bring the name of the organisation into disrepute.
- When using information from the Internet, make sure you do not break copyright law.
- Comply with the Data Protection Act – do not store information about living people without authorisation from the organisation Data Protection Officer.
- Do not put any unlawful information onto any system.

Systems need to be protected using physical and logical security. Physical systems such as locked doors and swipe-card access prevent unauthorised people from getting into the system. Logical security, such as passwords, prevents unauthorised people from being able to log in to the system and access data.

Health and safety

Other organisational guidelines and procedures relate to health and safety.

Health and safety is important not only because a healthy workforce is more productive, but also because there is a legal requirement on employers to make the workplace safe.

Health and safety is the responsibility of everyone inside an organisation.

Equal opportunities and disability

Employers are expected to promote equal opportunities in the workplace and provide suitable premises and equipment for employees with a disability.

Laws relating to copyright, software download, and licensing and digital rights

It is important that you understand the relevant laws affecting Internet users. You must not break the law while using the Internet.

See *Unit 1 Improving productivity using IT, Section 1.4 (page 7)* for more information on copyright.

Penalties for breaking the law include:

- up to six months in prison or up to a £5,000 fine for hacking into a computer system
- up to five years in prison and an unlimited fine for more serious hacking with intent to commit further offences or destruction of software or data
- up to five years in prison and an unlimited fine for hacking which deletes data or infects the system, or adds passwords to data files.

Activity: Legislation affecting Internet users

Research the following Acts:

- Defamation Act 1996
- Obscene Publications Act 1964 and Protection of Children Act 1999
- Telecommunications Act 1996 and Interception of Communications Act 1985
- Equality Act 2010
- Computer Misuse Act 1990.

Check your understanding

1 Identify six types of malware.
2 Which laws must be complied with when using IT systems?
3 How does phishing work?

ASSESSMENT ACTIVITY

Task 1 – Connect to the Internet, and use browser software to navigate web pages

You work part time in a local computer shop. The owner has asked you to produce a range of resources that can be seen by or given to customers to help them understand the Internet and what they can do with it.

1 Produce a sales brochure for the shop counter showing methods that can be used to access the Internet, with the hardware these need and a typical ISP package for each.

2 Add a section to your brochure with a table illustrating the benefits and drawbacks of the different connection methods.

3 Record a short video that can be used by the shop to show customers how to set up and use a computer with an Internet connection to get online.

4 Add a FAQ (frequently asked questions) section to your brochure using screenshots from online help systems to answer your questions.

5 Produce a section in your brochure on using Back, Forward, Refresh, Stop and tabs in a browser.

6 Include pages in the brochure on how to set the homepage in a browser and how to add a web page to the favourites.

7 Add to the brochure how to update the browser, turn autofill on, and protect against cookies and pop-ups.

8 Include in your brochure how to delete the temporary files and history.

Task 2 – Use browser tools to search for information from the Internet, and use browser software to communicate information online

You are now going to carry out some market research for the shop owner about other places in the area where computer equipment can be purchased.

1 Use search engines to find all the computer shops within a hundred miles of where you live that do not sell Apple kit. Add these sites to the favourites.

2 Print out the web pages and annotate them, showing how well you think they meet the requirements of the owner.

3 Create a folder in Favorites for your saved websites. Move the websites you found to this folder.

4 Download three manuals for IT components such as motherboards and store them in a new folder you have created.

5 Find a forum that interests you to create a new thread and to post a reply to an existing thread.

6 Set up a blog to promote the computer shop's products.

7 Create an email that you can send to your assessor with links to your forum posts and blog.

8 Create a new email account using Google Gmail™.

Task 3 – Understand the need for safety and security practices when working online

Create a PowerPoint® rolling display on how to surf the web safely.

1 Identify and explain the ways that malware can slow down a computer system, with three named examples of malware and how they attack the system.

2 Record a short video showing how you can be safe while using the Internet.

3 Identify some potential ways that confidential information could be seen when you are working online.

4 Explain the precautions you take to keep your log-in IDs and passwords to online systems secure.

Task 4 – Understand the need for safety and security practices when working online

Create some paper-based resources on how to surf the web safely.

1 Create a code of practice document that the computer shop can offer to business clients for their staff to follow.

2 Create a simple guide, with guidelines and the procedures for safe and secure Internet surfing.

3 Add to your guide a list of the current legislation that affects people who download from the Internet.

Using email

Email is an essential communication tool in business and is also widely used for personal communication. Being able to use email is an essential skill which goes beyond simply being able to send and receive email.

This unit will help you to compose, format and send email messages and attachments to individuals and groups. You will find out how to reply to emails appropriately and how to set up an automatic response when you are not able to reply to emails. You will understand how to use and organise an address book, how to archive email messages and how to deal with email problems. You will also learn how to stay safe when using email.

Learning outcomes

After completing this unit you should be able to achieve the following learning outcomes.

- » **LO1** Use email software tools and techniques to compose and send messages

- » **LO2** Manage incoming email effectively

1 Use email software tools and techniques to compose and send messages

There are two main ways to access an email account.

- Use a **webmail** system such as Microsoft® Hotmail® or Google Gmail™. You use an Internet browser to access and manage your emails, which are stored remotely on the computer servers of the email provider.
- Use an email client program. This runs on your computer and downloads all your emails to a **local system** (i.e. your own computer). The best known example of an email client program is Microsoft® Outlook®. Most businesses use this type of system rather than the webmail-based system. You can also use Outlook® to access webmail accounts.

As well as composing the text for an email, you need to know how to attach files and how to maintain an address book. It is also important that you understand how to stay safe and respect others' privacy when using email.

Key terms

Webmail – you access your email using an Internet browser. All of your emails are stored on the email service provider (e.g. Gmail™, Hotmail®) servers.

Local system – you use an email client program like Microsoft® Outlook® running on your computer. Your emails are stored locally on your computer.

Case study: BigDig Tools

BigDig Tools is a small manufacturing company that makes gardening tools. Its customers include a DIY chain of shops and gardening centres around the UK. It also sells to individual customers through an online store via its website.

You have recently joined the company's administration team. One aspect of your job involves dealing with the many email enquiries that the company receives each day.

1.1 Compose and format email

Once you have opened the Microsoft® Outlook® program, you will see the Outlook® main screen (see Figure 6.1). The Outlook® screen displays a list of folders on the left. There is a folder called **Inbox** where all your incoming emails are stored and a folder called **Sent Items** where copies of all the email you have sent are stored. A folder's content will be displayed in a pane next to the folder list. If you select an email within a particular folder, you will see the contents of that email displayed in the **Preview** pane.

How to create a new email

1. Click the **New E-mail** icon on the **Home** tab of the **ribbon** (as shown in Figure 6.1).

'New E-mail' icon   'Home' tab on the ribbon

Figure 6.1: Microsoft® Outlook® main screen

2. In the **New message** window that opens, enter the email address of the person you are sending the message to in the **To...** box.

3. Enter a subject in the **Subject** box.

4. Then type your message in the box below (see Figure 6.2).

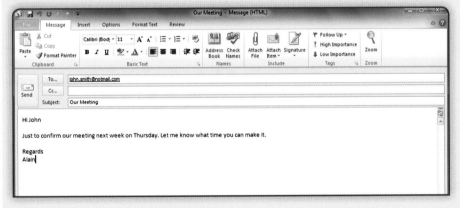

Figure 6.2: The New message window

Did you know?

The terms **Cc** and **Bcc** originated when typewriters were in use. They stand for carbon copy and blind carbon copy. Typists would use three sheets of paper when typing a letter: the letter paper, a sheet of carbon paper and a sheet of copy paper. The carbon paper would 'copy' the typing onto the copy paper. The top copy would list the people who had received the carbon copy (cc).

There are other ways you can send an email.

- The **Cc…** box is used to add the email address of someone who will receive a copy of the email. It is not directly addressed to them. The person who receives the email will see the email addresses or names of people who appear in the **Cc…** box.
- The **Bcc…** box is used to add the email address of someone who will receive a copy of the email. The person receiving the email will not see the email addresses or names of people who appear in the **Bcc…** box.
- You can enter multiple email addresses in both the **To…** and **Cc…** and **Bcc…** boxes. Use a semicolon to separate each address.

Once you have typed your message, look at it again. Will the person receiving your message find it clear and easy to understand? Before sending your email you need to make sure the message looks professional. Remember, when you send an email on behalf of the company you work for, you are representing the company. If your email looks unprofessional, the person receiving it may think your company is unprofessional.

Format text

You can make an email message look professional by changing the format of the text. You can select:

- font
- size
- colour.

The **ribbon** at the top of the **New message** window in the **Message** tab has a section with icons to allow you to choose the font, underline the text, make it bold or italic, or change the colour. See Figure 6.3 for an example of this.

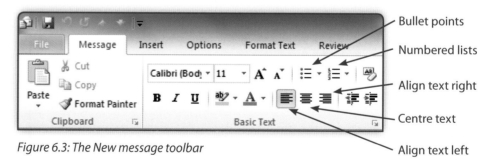

Figure 6.3: The New message toolbar

Format paragraphs

Alignment

You can also change the alignment of the text so that it is:

- aligned to the left
- aligned to the right
- centred
- justified on both sides.

Most of the time your email text will be left aligned. Occasionally you might use centre aligned text, perhaps for a title or subheading if you are sending a longer text email like a newsletter or product update.

The ribbon at the top of the **New message** window has a section with icons to allow you to align the text (see Figure 6.3).

Bullets and numbered lists

Your email may contain a list of items, such as a list of products that your company wishes to buy from a supplier, or a set of instructions. You need to make these lists stand out from the rest of the text by either using bullet points or a numbered list.

The ribbon at the top of the **New message** window has a section with icons to allow you to change the text to a bulleted list or to a numbered list (see Figure 6.3).

You can also start a bulleted list or a numbered list as you type the message. Click the **Bullets** or **Numbering** icon to start the list and each time you press **Enter** the cursor will insert a new bullet or the next number. Remember to turn off the bullets or numbering when you have completed the list.

Spell check

Before you send an email, you should check spelling, punctuation and grammar. A poorly written email with bad grammar looks unprofessional.

Microsoft® Office® uses a program called **Spell Checker** to check spelling and grammar. The Spell Checker program will automatically identify words which are not in its dictionary by underlining them with a wavy red line.

How to use Spell Checker

1. **Right click** on any word which is underlined and a list of possible correct spellings will pop up.
2. Click on the correct one and the word will be changed to the correct spelling. Make sure you choose the correct spelling from the list.

Format

There are a number of different formats you can choose. These are selected by clicking in the **Format Text** tab in the ribbon and choosing the format you want from the **Format** section, choosing the format you want. There are three main format options:

- **HTML** (the default). Select this format if you want to add text formatting features such as bold, italics, different font sizes and colours, etc.
- **Plain Text.** Select this format if you want to send your email with no additional formatting.
- **Rich Text.** This option allows a wider range of formatting options than HTML but is only compatible with Outlook®. Don't use this option unless you are sure the recipient uses Outlook® to view their emails.

In most circumstances, HTML is the most suitable option.

Draft

If you want to save your email without sending it, you can save it as a draft version. You can then return to edit it further before sending it. Simply go to the **File** tab in the ribbon and click **Save**. You can then close the **Message** window. The email is saved in the **Drafts** folder and you can return to it anytime to continue to edit it and eventually send it.

Signature

A signature is text you can add at the end of every email.

How to create an automatic signature

1. Open a new email message. On the **Message** tab, in the **Include** group, click **Signature**, and then click **Signatures**.

2. On the **Email Signature** tab, click the **New** button.

3. Type a name for the signature, such as 'MySig', and then click **OK**.

4. In the **Edit signature** box, type the text that you want to include in the signature. (See Figure 6.4.)

5. To format the text, select the text, and then use the style and formatting buttons to select the options that you want.

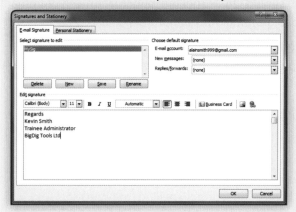

Figure 6.4: Creating a signature

Page set up

If you want to print off an email you may want to adjust the page settings.

How to adjust page settings

1. Open the email you want to print.

2. Click the **File** tab, then click **Print**.

3. On the print window click the **Print options** button. This will open the **Print dialog** box.

4. Click the **Page Setup** button and the **Page Setup** dialog box will open. This dialog box has tabs to allow you to set the paper size, margins and orientation, and add a header and footer.

Backgrounds

You can change the backgrounds, colour schemes and fonts of your emails. Outlook® calls these themes and you can apply the same theme to all the new emails you create.

How to create themes

1. In the Outlook® main window, click the **File** tab in the ribbon. Then click **Options**.

2. The Outlook® **Options** dialog box will open. Choose **Mail** in the menu panel on the left.

3. Then click the **Stationery and Fonts** button, middle right of the window. This will open the **Signatures and Stationery** dialog box. Click **Theme** at the top of the dialog box.

4. You will see the **Theme or Stationery** dialog box (see Figure 6.5).

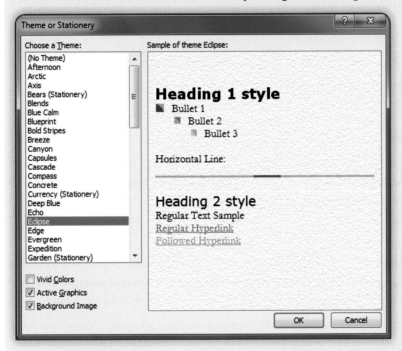

Figure 6.5: Creating a theme

5. Select the theme you like – a preview is shown on the right of the box. Then click **OK** to exit the dialog boxes.

6. All new emails you create from now on will have the theme, including the background you chose.

Sound

You can ask Outlook® to play a sound when a new email arrives. You can turn the option on or off by selecting **Options** (under the **File** tab). Choose **Mail**, then under the **Message arrival** section, use the check box labelled **Play a sound** to turn the option on or off.

Movie

Attaching a movie or video to an email is possible, but it is likely you will run into problems with file sizes. Movies or video attachments tend to be large files and the longer the movie is the larger the file it will occupy. Many email accounts have a maximum size limit, so your email might not deliver if the file size is too large. (*See Section 1.2, page 71*) for more information on file sizes.) In order to avoid attaching large files, it is better to insert a **hyperlink** (see the section below) to where the movie or video can be viewed or downloaded.

You can also attach or insert a simple animation, such as an animated smiley face.

How to insert a picture

1. Open your email program. Then open a new email message.
2. Click **Insert** from the toolbar. Then click on the **Picture** icon and select the file you would like to insert.

Hyperlink

A hyperlink is text (or even an image) within an email or a document which, when clicked on, takes you to a specific website or web page. Hyperlinks are easily identifiable as they are usually underlined and in a different colour to the rest of the text.

You could use a hyperlink to direct an email's recipients to your company website or other relevant online material. The simplest way to do this is to **copy** the web page address from your web browser address bar and **paste** it into the text of your email. Outlook® will automatically recognise it as a hyperlink.

If your hyperlink is not automatically recognised, you can create one yourself.

How to create a hyperlink manually

1. **Paste** your web address in your email. Then highlight the web address.
2. Click the **Insert** tab on the toolbar.
3. Select **Hyperlink** from the drop-down menu.
4. **Paste** the web address into the **Address box**.
5. Click **OK**.
6. The web address in your email should now be a hyperlink.

Working online and offline

One of the advantages of using Outlook® rather than a web-based email client is that you can access old emails and create new emails even if you don't have access to the Internet. This is called **working offline**. It can be useful, for example, if you are working away from the office with a laptop and you need to look up emails you have received or create some new emails when you are somewhere where there is no Internet connection. Any email you create while working offline is automatically sent when you are connected to the Internet again.

Key term

Working offline – when your computer is not connected to the Internet.

Activity: Replying to BigDig Tools email enquiries

You need to reply to some email enquiries about BigDig Tools. Your manager has asked you to create an email theme so that your email replies look more professional.

1 Create an email theme (background) and a signature.

2 Using the text below, create an email.

> Dear Mrs Evans
>
> Re: BigDig – WundaWeeda
>
> Thank you for your enquiry about our new 'WundaWeeda', the revolution in garden weeding. This tool is suitable for both left- and right-handed people. However, left-handed people may find it easier to use if they order the left-handed adapter kit, order number WW1725.
>
> We have recently uploaded a video on YouTube of the WundaWeeda being used. The video also shows the left-handed adapter kit in use. You can view the video here (insert hyperlink).
>
> If I can be of any further assistance please do not hesitate to contact me.
>
> (Your signature)

3 Add suitable formatting to the email. Make the subtitle centred, bold and 16 point. Every mention of the WundaWeeda should be in bold and italics.

1.2 Determining message size

Every message you send has a size in kilobytes (KB) or megabytes (MB). Emails that contain just text are very small (4KB or 5KB). Emails that have attachments may be much larger. The size of an email is important because there are limitations on how large an email you can send.

Managing attachments

As well as sending text in an email you can also **attach** a file. For example, you might attach a copy of your CV when applying for a job by email, or you might attach a photo to an email you are sending to a friend.

Key term

Attach – an attachment is a file which is included in an email, such as a word-processed document or a spreadsheet. You 'attach' this file to an email if you want to send it on to someone else.

How to attach a file to an email

1. Click the **Attach File** icon in the **Message** tab on the ribbon.

2. In the **Insert File** dialog box that opens (see Figure 6.6), choose the file you want to attach to the email.

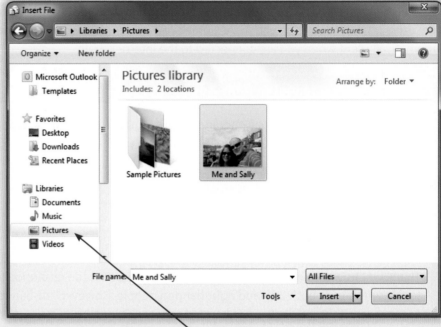

Figure 6.6: Insert File dialog box

You can select the type of file you'd like to attach (e.g. a picture, a video, a document or a music file)

3. Click the **Insert** button. The attached file will be shown in the **Attached** box under the **Subject** box in the email window (see Figure 6.7).

You will see your attached file here

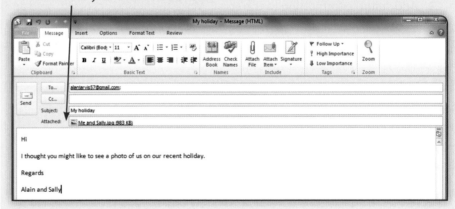

Figure 6.7: An attached file

4. You can add another file simply by clicking the **Attach File** button again.

Mailbox restrictions

When sending an email with several attachments, such as digital photos, the overall size of the email can get very large. Different email providers have different limits on the maximum message size. For example, in Google Gmail™ the largest number of attachments you can send in a single email is 25 MB. This means that if you try to send more than about five or six **high resolution** digital photos your email will be rejected. If you need to send a lot of large files the simplest thing to do is to send multiple emails, each with just a few attachments.

To check the size of an email with attachments before you send it, save the email as a draft. Open the **Drafts** folder and look at the **Size** column on the right of the screen. This will show you the overall size of the email message plus attachments. You can also check the sizes of the individual attachments in the email itself. The **Attached** box shows each attachment with its size. The email shown in Figure 6.8 has three photos attached to it, each of which is 2 MB in size, making a total of 6 MB.

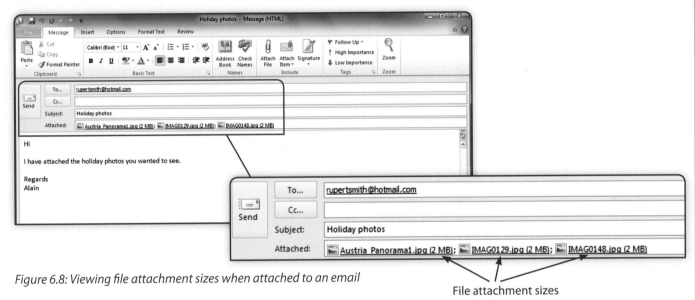

Figure 6.8: Viewing file attachment sizes when attached to an email

File attachment sizes

1.3 Sending emails to individuals and groups

Reply and Reply All

Emails can be used to send a message to a single person or to a group of people. You can either respond to just the sender (**Reply** button) or to everybody included on the email (**Reply All** button).

You can also use the **To...**, **Cc...**, **Bcc...** and **Subject** boxes to compose and send emails (*see page 66*).

How to reply to an email

1. In the email you have received, click the **Reply** icon.

2. In the new window that appears, the email address of the person you are replying to is already completed and the subject is set to the same as the incoming email, with **Re:** in front of it.

3. Type your message at the top of the email. The text of the email you are replying to is shown below your message.

4. Once you have sent a reply, the original email will have a purple arrow icon next to it in the **Inbox** list, indicating that you have replied (see Figure 6.9). The date and time of your reply is also shown in the **Preview** pane.

The 'Replied to' icon

Figure 6.9: The 'Replied to' icon

5. The **Reply All** button sends your reply to everyone the original email was sent to.

Forward

You may receive an email that you want to pass on to someone else. To send on the email with any attachments, click the **Forward** icon.

Distribution lists

There are situations when you will need to send an email to several people. In these instances it is useful to create groups of email addresses (sometimes called a distribution list) so that you can just enter the group name rather than everyone's individual email addresses. For example, if you work with a group of people and need to regularly email everybody in the group, then creating a distribution list/group which contains all their email addresses will make this task easier and save you time.

How to create a group

1. Click the **Address Book** icon in the **Home** tab of the Outlook® main window (see Figure 6.10).

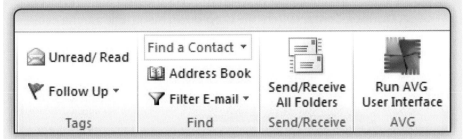

Figure 6.10: The Address Book icon

2. In the **Address Book**: **Contacts** window that opens, select the **File** menu and click **New Entry**.

3. In the **New Entry** window that appears (see Figure 6.11), select **New Contact Group** and click **OK**.

Figure 6.11: The New Entry window

4. In the **New Contact Group** that appears, enter a name for the new group in the **Name** box.

5. Click the **Add Members** icon in the toolbar, and from the drop-down menu select **New Email Contact**.

Figure 6.12: The New Contact Group window

continued

6. In the **Add New Member** dialog box that appears (see Figure 6.13), type the name you want to see displayed and the email address of the person you want to add to the group, and click **OK**. (To add a person to the group who is already in your contacts: when you click the **Add Members** icon, select **Outlook Contacts** from the drop-down menu. Choose the name you want to add from your list of contacts, and click **OK**.)

Figure 6.13: Add New Member dialog box

7. The contact you have added will be listed in the **Contact Group** window. Continue using the **Add Members** icon to add all the people who you want in the group.

Figure 6.14: Completed Contact Group

8. Click the **Save & Close** icon to finish creating your Contact Group.

How to use your contact group

1. Create a new email. In the **New message** window that opens, click the **To…** button.
2. In the **Contacts** dialog box that appears (see Figure 6.15), click on your newly created contact group and then click the **To** button to add the group to the recipients of the email.

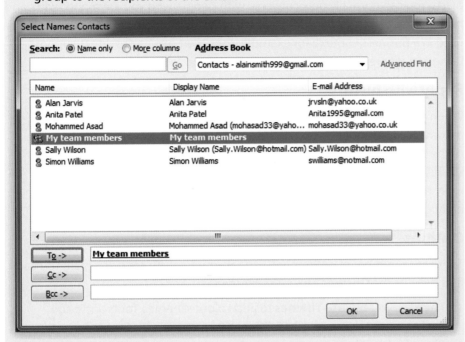

Figure 6.15: Contacts dialog box

3. Click **OK** and the name of the contact group appears in the email (see Figure 6.16).
4. Only the name of the group is shown, not the individual members (although you can display all the contacts in the group by clicking the + icon).

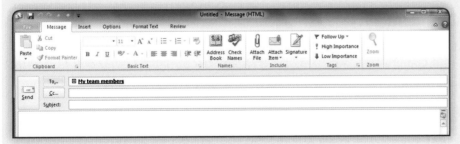

Figure 6.16: Contact group in the email

Instant messaging

Instant messages can be exchanged through applications like Windows® Live® Messenger and Yahoo! Messenger. Messaging facilities are also built into some social networking sites like Facebook. Instant messaging is rather different to sending emails. When you use an instant messaging application, short text messages are sent and received almost instantly, allowing a conversation to take place. You can normally only converse with people who you are friends with, and both parties must be online at the same time. Instant messaging is sometimes used in a business context; for example, some companies provide IT support using instant messaging between customers and technicians.

Reply with history

When you reply to an email, Outlook® and most other email programs automatically include the text of the email you are replying to at the bottom of the new email. If you have swapped a series of emails with a person, then the history of the whole email conversation is included with each email you reply to. You can delete the email history from the bottom of the new email by highlighting the relevant text and pressing the **Delete** key.

Options

There are a number of options you can select when you send an email. You can find these in the **Options** tab in the **Message** ribbon.

- **Themes**: you can use **Themes** to add colour schemes, fonts and page backgrounds to your emails. *See page 69* for more information.
- **Show Fields**: allows you to see the **Bcc...** field.
- **Permission**: allows you to restrict the email so it cannot be forwarded on by the recipient.
- **Tracking**: you can see whether the recipient(s) have read your email.
- **More options**: allows you to control which folder **Sent Items** are saved to, **Delay Delivery** until a certain date or time, and **Direct Replies To** an email to another address.

Confidentiality

It is important that you respect confidentiality and do not send company confidential information in external emails. See *section 1.4 on page 81* for more information.

Response request

Before you send an email to someone, you can request an **automatic return email** to tell you if the email has been delivered and/or if the recipient has read it. To turn these options on, select the **Options** tab in the **New message** window and click the check boxes labelled **Request a Delivery Receipt** and/or **Request a Read Receipt**.

Vote

When you send an email, you can request that people who receive the email vote on something (which they can accept or reject). For example, you might send an email to all your office colleagues asking them if they are free for a meeting tomorrow at 3.00 pm. The voting feature is added to an email from the **Options** tab, by clicking the **Use Voting Buttons** icon and selecting the type of buttons you want (Yes, No, Approve, Reject). The buttons don't show in the email editing window, so you need to add text to the email to explain what questions the recipients are voting on.

Figure 6.17: Voting buttons

1.4 Staying safe

Email is a great way to communicate and is an essential business tool, but it has its dangers. Email can be used to:

- spread computer viruses
- bully and intimidate people
- con people out of money through email scams.

Table 6.1 shows ways to stay safe when using email.

1	Be very careful with emails from people you do not know. Never download attachments or follow links on these emails unless you are sure who they are from and what the attachment or link is. Never disclose personal information such as contact details to strangers.
2	Be careful of strange emails from people you know. Some viruses attack people's email accounts and send emails to all their contacts. If one of your contacts is infected by a virus like this you may get an email from them asking you to follow a link to a web page. Check with the person who sent the email first before following links or downloading anything.
3	Beware of emails offering money in return for a service. There are many scams which involve you providing bank details or paying some money in order to claim 'a large prize'.
4	Beware of emails that appear to come from your bank asking you to follow a link and enter your online banking passwords and security information. Banks *never* send emails like this. This type of scam is known as **phishing** and is used by criminals to obtain your bank log-in details and steal money from you.
5	If you receive an abusive or inappropriate email, do not reply to it. You can block emails from certain senders, as explained on the next page.

Table 6.1: Guidelines to keep you safe when using email

Key term

Phishing – a technique used to obtain individuals' personal details. Phishing emails are designed to look like official emails (e.g. from your bank) and will ask you to click a link and provide personal information (e.g. your name, address and online banking log-in passwords). If you enter your details on the fake page, then your details will become available to the people behind the phishing email, who could use them to steal money from your account.

How to block a sender

1. In your **Inbox** right click on the email from the person you want to block.

2. In the pop-up box that appears, select **Junk** and choose **Block Sender** (see Figure 6.18). A message appears telling you that this sender has been added to your Blocked Senders List and the email has been moved to your **Junk E-mail** folder.

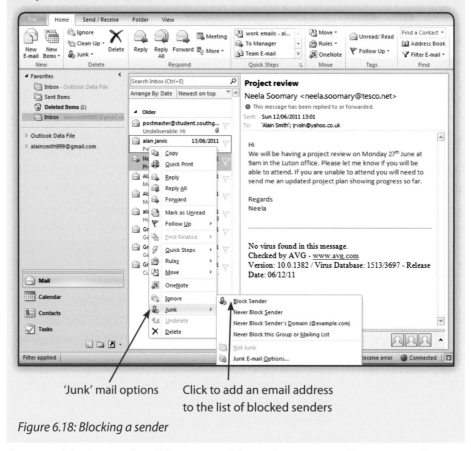

'Junk' mail options   Click to add an email address to the list of blocked senders

Figure 6.18: Blocking a sender

Once you block a sender, all future email from this person will automatically go in your **Junk E-mail** folder.

Avoid inappropriate disclosure of personal information

Always take care when dealing with emails. Do not send your personal information to people you do not know. In a work context, individual customer details such as names and addresses are covered by the Data Protection Act. You should not send these details to anyone who does not have a work-related reason to see them.

Avoid misuse of images

Be careful when sending images to people via email. Your friends might be interested to see an amusing picture of you but once you have sent the picture to other people, you have lost control of what happens to it. You don't know who else might recieve the image and what other people might do with it (e.g. the could post it on various websites). This is the way a lot of online bullying starts. Remember that while you might think a photo is amusing or funny, other people might find it offensive. It is particularly important when using work email not to send any images which might be considered offensive. If in doubt, don't send it.

Use appropriate language, respect confidentiality

The language you use in personal emails to friends will be different to the language used in work-related emails. Although email tends to be informal, you should still ensure that work-related emails are written clearly and coherently, with correct spelling and grammar. Avoid using text message abbreviations such as 'u' for you or 'ty' for thank you. Also remember that some information you deal with at work may be confidential. This particularly applies to people's personal details. Only send emails with people's personal details in them to other people in your company who have a work-related reason for having this information.

Use copy lists with discrimination

In a work context you should use distribution lists with care. Many companies have distribution lists for everyone in the organisation, or at least everyone in the division or department you work in. Only send emails using these distribution lists if the content is genuinely relevant to everyone on the list. Sending out personal adverts for things you have for sale, jokes, or amusing photos is NOT a good idea and you could be reprimanded.

1.5 Using an address book

Microsoft® Outlook® includes an address book which allows you to keep detailed contact information about people, including their phone numbers, company name and postal address. You can also create groups (or distribution lists) so that you can easily send an email to a whole group of people without having to enter their individual email addresses. *See page 74* for more information on distribution lists.

Add contact entries

There are a number of ways of adding an individual email address to your Outlook® contacts.

How to add an individual email address to your contacts

1. In your **Inbox** select an email.

2. Right click the email address shown in the **Preview** pane, and select **Add to Outlook Contacts** (see Figure 6.19).

Figure 6.19: Sdding a contact

Select 'Add to Outlook Contacts'

3. In the **Contact** window that opens, you can add further information about the contact (see Figure 6.20). Once you have done this, click the **Save & Close** icon.

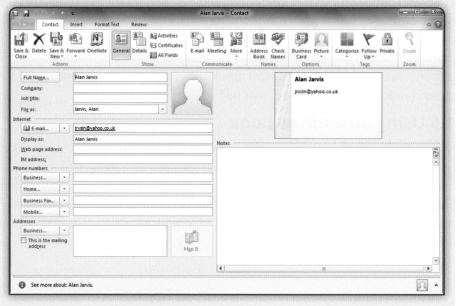

Figure 6.20: Contact window

You can also view your contact list and add additional contacts using the address book.

How to view your contact list and add an individual email address

1. Click the **Address Book** icon on the ribbon of the main Outlook® window to open the address book. A list of your existing contacts appears (see Figure 6.21).

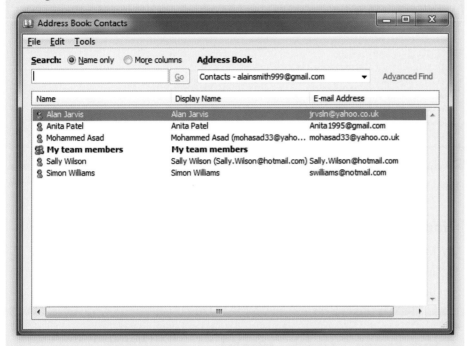

Figure 6.21: Your address list

2. Select the **File** menu, and click **New Entry**.

3. In the pop-up box that appears, select **New Contact** and click **OK**. In the **Contact** window that appears, complete the details of your contact.

4. Click the **Save & Close** icon to save the contact details.

Edit contact entries

To search for a particular person, enter their name in the **Find a Contact** box in the main Outlook® window (see Figure 6.22 overleaf). Click **Enter** and if a match is found the **Contact** window for that contact will appear.

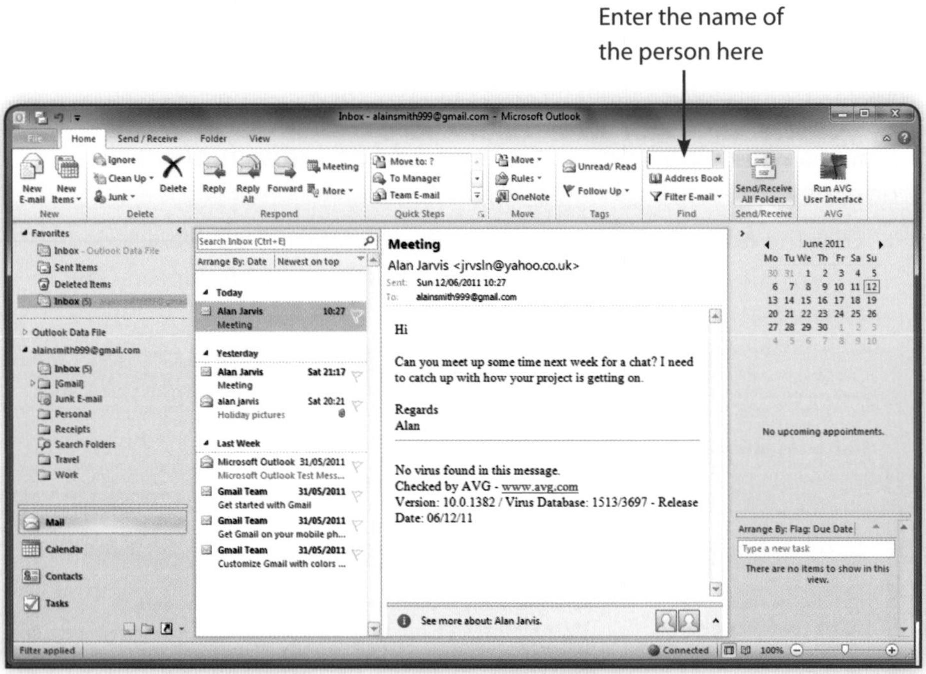

Enter the name of
the person here

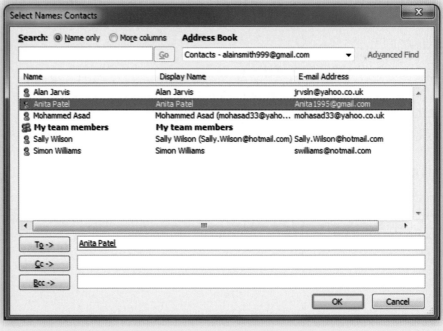

Figure 6.22: The Find a Contact box

How to use a contact when creating a new email

1. Click the **New E-mail** button.
2. In the message window that appears, click the **To...** button and your address list will appear.

Figure 6.23: The Contacts list

3. Click the name of the contact you want to send the email to. Then click the **To->** or **Cc->** buttons to add the contact's email address to the **To...** or **Cc...** list on the email.

How to edit the details of an existing contact

1. Click the **Address Book** icon on the ribbon of the main Outlook® window to open the address book.
2. Double click the entry you want to edit in the **Address Book**.
3. In the **Contact** window that opens, make changes or additions to the contact details.
4. Click the **Save & Close** icon to save the edited details.

Delete contact entries

How to delete a contact entry

1. Click the **Address Book** icon on the ribbon of the main Outlook® window to open the address book.
2. Double-click the entry you want to delete in the **Address Book**.
3. In the **Contact** window that opens, click the **Delete** icon in the Contact tab of the ribbon. The entry is deleted.

Display selected fields

You can select which contact detail fields you display when you view an individual contact. Open the contact window, then use the **Options** tab in the **Show** section of the **Contact** tab to select which fields you want to see.

Activity: Creating a contact group

In your job as a trainee administrator at BigDig Tools, you need to keep a lot of contacts in your Outlook® address book.

1. Using the Address Book, add the contact details of a number of your colleagues (at least 10).
2. Make a contact group called Garden Centres and add some of your contacts to this group.
3. Practise editing and deleting contact entries.

Check your understanding

1. What is the difference between the **To…**, **Cc…** and **Bcc…** fields when you create a new email?
2. You get a strange email from a friend you know well. It includes a link to a free offer for music downloads. What should you do?
3. What is the difference between **Reply**, **Reply All** and **Forward**?
4. What is a hyperlink? What might you use one for in an email?

2 Manage incoming email effectively

In the workplace you are likely to receive a lot of emails. Some of these emails will be important business communications which you will need to keep track of and reply to. Others will be advertising emails that you may wish to ignore. With so much modern business depending on email communication, being able to manage and deal with emails is an important skill.

2.1 Guidelines and procedures

Email can be a source of virus and other types of attack, so there are procedures and guidelines you should follow to help you stay safe.

Set by employer or organisation

Most organisations, including schools and colleges, have guidelines and procedures on the use of email and the Internet. These might be called the Internet and email usage policy, or guidelines, or similar. They list the sort of things you should and should not do when sending emails, such as what is considered inappropriate use of email.

Copyright

You should take care not to send any attachments that you do not have **copyright** to, such as photo or videos you find on the Internet.

Security

It is essential to keep the password to your email account secret – make sure it cannot be easily guessed. Change your password every few months, or if you think anyone might have guessed it.

If other people discover your password, they can send and receive emails as if they were you. This could cause you many problems. People could also change your password and lock you out of your own account.

Netiquette

Be aware of the rules of **netiquette**. These are general rules for electronic communication such as email.

- ✗ Don't abuse or insult people.
- ✗ Don't send 'spam' – i.e. advertising emails.
- ✗ Never say things that you would not want repeated – an email can be forwarded to other people who will read what you say.
- ✗ Don't type whole words or sentences in captial letter – this is considered to be shouting.
- ✗ Don't use **emoticons** or **text language** in work emails.
- ✗ Don't include unnecessary attachments if the content of the attachment could be written in the body of the email itself.

For more information on netiquette, *see Unit 5 Using the Internet, page 51.*

Password protection

Every email account is protected by a password. When you set up an account in Outlook®, you need to create a password. This password will protect you from other people hijacking your email account and using it for other purposes, such as sending spam or distributing email viruses. To protect yourself effectively you must choose a strong password for your account. Using a password which has a small number of lower case letters or is easy to guess (such as 'password' or 'welcome') won't protect you at all. You must use a 'strong' password. A strong password is at least eight characters long and has a combination of at least two:

- upper and lower case characters
- numbers
- symbols.

Examples of strong passwords include 'MyDogisGr8!' and 'Liverpool4theCup'.

2.2 Email responses

Incoming mail is placed in your **Inbox** folder. If it is unread it will be shown in bold (see Figure 6.24). The number next to the Inbox is the number of unread emails you have. If you click on the email you will see a preview of it in the **Preview** pane. **Double click** on it to display the email in a new window (see Figure 6.25).

The number of unread emails you have

'New email' icon

The unread email when opened and displayed in your Preview pane

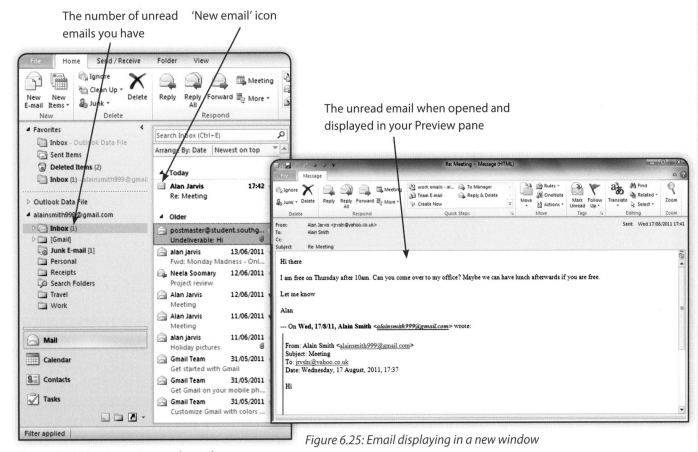

Figure 6.25: Email displaying in a new window

Figure 6.24: How to spot unread emails

Decide on priorities

As well as replying to emails, you may want to mark them as important or needing following up. You might also find it helpful to put all the emails about a particular subject or project in a separate folder.

You can mark emails in any folder as important or needing following up by **flagging** them with a coloured flag. The greyed-out flag icon can be seen to the right of each email in the folder list on the main Outlook® window. Clicking the flag will turn it red (see Figure 6.26). You can use this as a reminder that the email is important.

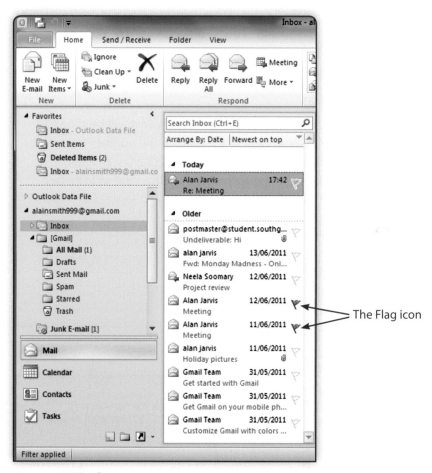

Figure 6.26: The flag icons

Gather information needed to respond

Before you respond to an email you might need to gather some information. For example, in your job at BigDig Tools you might get questions from customers about the suitability of a certain tool for a particular job. You would need to speak to someone in the company to find out if the tool would be suitable and perhaps get hold of an electronic copy of a brochure. Once you have gathered all this information, you are ready to respond to the customer.

Decide when and who to copy in

When replying to an email you can just reply to the sender, or, if the email is to several people you can reply to all of them. Which one you do depends on whether your reply is relevant to just the sender or to everyone. *See the section on* **Reply** *and* **Reply All** *on pages 73–74.*

What to do about attachments

If the email is from a trusted source and contains an attachment, then you can save the attachment in a suitable place on your **hard drive**, such as your **My Documents** folder. You can save an attachment by right clicking on it and choosing **Save As**.

2.3 Automate responses to email

Outlook® can automatically respond to or deal with emails on your behalf. This can make dealing with a large number of incoming emails easier. See the section on *Out of office* on page 90.

Rules

Rules are sets of instructions which you can set up that tell Outlook® how to deal with emails in particular situations. Rules are used for a number of different purposes. For example, you can set up a rule to automatically send all emails from a particular email address/sender to a folder, or you can highlight all emails from an email address/sender in a particular colour. You can also set up a rule for sending 'Out of office' messages. (*See pages 90–93* for more information.)

Changing settings to deal with junk mail

Outlook® will place any email it thinks is junk mail (spam) in the **Spam** folder. You can also **right click** on any email that is spam and select the **Junk** option. This will open up a submenu where you can choose some other options. You can choose to **Block Sender**. This means that this email and any subsequent emails from this sender will automatically be put in the **Spam** folder. Sometimes, Outlook® may put emails in the Spam folder that are not junk mail, so it is worth checking this folder every once in a while. The menu also has **Junk E-mail Options**. Choosing this option will display the **Junk E-mail Options** dialog box (see Figure 6.27).

> **Key term**
>
> **Hard drive** – refers to the disc drive located inside your desktop or laptop computer. This disc is used to store the computer's operating system, application programs like Microsoft® Office® 2010, and all your folders.

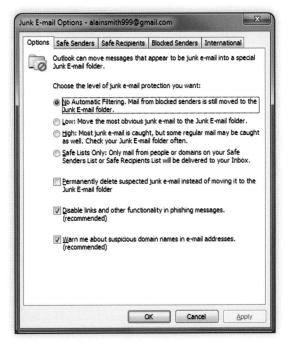

Figure 6.27: the Junk E-mail Options dialog box

The Junk E-mail options dialog box has a number of tabs.

- **Options** allows you to set the level of protection that the junk mail filter provides.
- **Safe Senders** lists any emails that you have said never to block. You can add more emails to the list to prevent them ever being treated as spam.
- **Safe Recipients** lists recipients who will never be treated as spam.
- **Blocked Senders** lists the senders who are blocked. Any emails from these senders will automatically go in the **Spam** folder.
- **International** allows you to block emails from certain **domains** or emails that are written in certain languages.

Out of office

If you go on holiday or are away for some other reason, you are still likely to receive emails. The people sending them will expect a reply. It is polite to tell people that you will be out of the office until a certain date and will reply when you get back. You can do this using an 'out of office' email message.

You can set up Outlook® to reply automatically to all emails, telling the sender that you are away and cannot reply until you return.

How to create a rule to set up an automatic response

1. In the **Home** tab click on the **Rules** icon.

2. In the drop-down menu that appears, select **Manage Rules & Alerts**. This will display the **Rules and Alerts** dialog box.

3. In the **Rules and Alerts** dialog box, click the **New Rule** icon.

4. In the **Rules Wizard** dialog box that appears (see Figure 6.28), in the section **Start from a blank rule** click **Apply rule on messages I receive** and click **Next** .

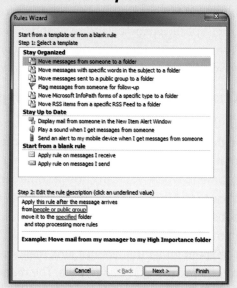

Figure 6.28: The Rules Wizard dialog box

5. In the dialog box that appears, you do not need to make any selection. Click **Next**.

6. A warning box appears, asking if you want to apply this rule to every message you receive. Click **Yes**.

continued

7. In the next step, select **Reply using a specific template**.

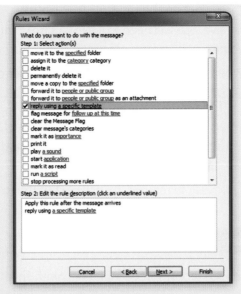

Figure 6.29: The Rules Wizard

8. Click the words **a specific template**. A dialog box appears where you can choose the required template.

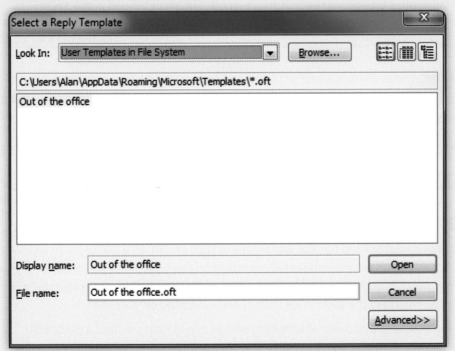

Figure 6.30: Select a Reply template

9. Select **User Templates in File System** and the template you saved earlier should appear in the middle of the box.

10. Click the template to select it and then click **Open**. This will return you to the previous dialog box. Click **Next**.

11. The next step allows you to choose exceptions to this rule. There is no reason to have exceptions, so click **Next**.

12. Click **Finish** and the new rule will be turned on.

Once you have set up the rule it will automatically reply to every email you receive. You will need to leave Outlook® running for the rule to be applied, so you must leave your office computer on while you are on holiday.

When you return from holiday, remember to turn off the rule.

How to turn off rules

1. Click on the **Rules** icon in the **Home** tab of the main Outlook® window.
2. Then choose **Manage Rules & Alerts**, which will display the **Rules and Alerts** dialog box.
3. Click to remove the tick next to the rule you previously created.

Activity: Spam prevention

The BigDig Tools email inbox has recently been inundated with spam emails. You are spending a lot of time identifying the spam emails and then deleting them. You decide to take action to sort this out.

1 Check your spam email settings.
2 Add important contacts to your safe senders list to ensure their emails are never blocked.
3 Add senders of spam email to your blocked list so that these emails automatically go in the **Spam** folder.

Activity: Out of the office

You are going away on holiday for a week.

Set up an 'out of office' automatic reply. The message should explain when you are away and when you will be back.

2.4 Organise and store email

It is essential to keep track of and organise your emails, as some of them will contain important information. Depending on the type of job you are doing, you may need to organise your emails by creating folders for different projects or customers. (See the section on *Folders and subfolders* on page 93.)

There are also a number of features you can use to help you find a particular email. For example, the emails listed in the main Outlook® window are usually displayed in date order, with the most recently received at the top. If you are looking for an email from a particular person but cannot remember when you received it, you can change the way the emails are listed so that they appear in the alphabetical order of who they are from.

How to find an email from a particular person

1. In the main Outlook® window, click on the header at the top of the list of emails.

2. In the drop-down menu that appears, select **From** and the emails will be arranged in alphabetical order of sender.

3. Scroll down the list and find the email from the person you are looking for.

Figure 6.31: Arranging emails in a different order

To return the list to date order, simply click on the list header and select **Date** from the menu.

There is also a search box above the list header. Type any word or phrase into the box and the list below will change to display only those emails which contain that word or phrase.

Folders and subfolders

If you receive a lot of emails, using folders and subfolders can be a helpful way to organise your emails. For example, you might want to create different folders in your **Inbox** for your work emails and your personal ones.

How to create a folder in your Inbox

1. **Right click** your mouse within your **Inbox** and choose **New Folder**. This will display the **Create New Folder** dialog box.

2. Type the name of the new folder you want to create in the **Name** box. Check you have the **Inbox** selected in the list of folders and then click **OK**.

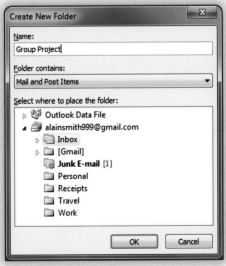

Figure 6.32: The Create New Folder dialog box

continued

93

3. The folder you create will now be shown under the **Inbox** in the list of folders. You can create as many folders as you want. You can also create folders in your **Sent Items** and in other folders too, as well as subfolders within the folders you create.

4. To move emails from your **Inbox** to a folder you have created, simply drag them with the mouse into the folder you want to put them in on the left of the main Outlook® window.

How to create subfolders in your Inbox

1. Right click on the folder you would like to add subfolders to.

2. In the drop-down menu that appears, select **New Folder**.

3. In the **Create New Folder** dialog box that appears, type in a name for the new folder, and click **OK**.

4. You can now drag and drop emails from the list in the centre left of the Outlook® window into your new subfolder in the folder list on the left.

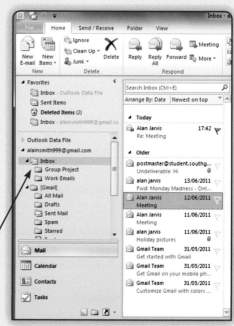

Your new folder will now appear within underneath the folder, and will be indented a little

Figure 6.33: New subfolder

Delete unwanted messages

Over time, the number of emails in your Inbox can get very large. Large numbers of emails in your Inbox will slow down the Outlook® software and make it slow to open.

You should get into the habit of deleting emails that are not important. You can do this by clicking on the email and pressing the **Delete** key, or clicking the **Delete** icon in the **Home** tab.

Backup

You can make a backup of any or all of your Outlook® email folders.

How to create a backup of your email folders

1. Click on the **File** tab of the ribbon, then click **Open**.
2. Select **Export**. This will open the **Import and Export Wizard**.
3. Select **Export to a file**.
4. Click **Next**. In the next step of the Wizard, select the file type as **Outlook data file (.pst)**.
5. Choose which folder you want to export. Then choose where you want the exported file to be saved and click **Finish**.

Move after sending

When you send an email a copy of it goes in your **Sent Items** folder. You can create subfolders in your Sent Items folder and move sent emails to appropriate subfolders to help organise your emails.

Organisation and storage of rules

Rules can be used to automatically direct emails from certain senders to a particular folder. Rules are covered in *section 2.4* (*see page 89*). You can check which (if any) rules are in force by selecting the **Home** tab in the main Outlook® window, clicking the arrow below the **Rules** icon and choosing **Manage Rules and Alerts**. This will open the **Rules & Alerts** dialog box where you can see any rules that apply.

Archive folders

You can build up a lot of emails in your Inbox. You may be able to delete some of these if they are no longer wanted (see the section *Delete unwanted messages* on page 94). Other emails may contain important information that you no longer use from day to day but might need to refer to in the future. To avoid your Inbox becoming a storage area for older emails, it is a good idea to **archive** them.

Outlook® has an **AutoArchive** function which will do much of the work involved in archiving your emails for you, but you need to turn it on. (The default setting for all folders is that Outlook® does not auto archive them.)

Key term

Archive – a storage area which is not immediately accessible but can be accessed if needed. If your house has a loft or a garage, you can use it like an archive. You put things in a loft or garage which you do not want to throw away but need to use occasionally. You can always get them out of the loft or garage when you need them.

How to turn on the AutoArchive setting for the Inbox

1. Select the folder you want to change the **AutoArchive** setting for in the folder list on the left of the Outlook® main window (in this case, the **Inbox**).

2. Select the **Folder** tab in the ribbon of the main Outlook® window, and click the **AutoArchive Settings** icon.

Figure 6.34: The AutoArchive Settings icon

3. The **Inbox Properties** dialog box appears with the **AutoArchive** tab open.

Figure 6.35: The Inbox Properties dialog box

4. To archive this folder, click either **Archive items in this folder using the default settings** or **Archive this folder using these settings**. If you choose the default settings, you can see what they are (and change them if you wish) by clicking the **Default Settings** button to see the **AutoArchive** dialog box.

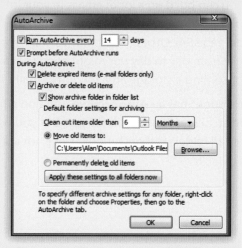

Figure 6.36: The AutoArchive dialog box

You need to select how often **AutoArchive** will run. Every 14 days is the default. You can adjust how AutoArchive works and how old items have to be before they are archived (six months' old is the default).

Emails that are archived will be removed from the Inbox folder and placed in a folder called **Archive**.

Attachments and file compression

If you have one large file to attach to an email that you cannot split up, you can compress it to make it smaller. Figure 6.37 shows a large file which needs to be compressed before it is attached. The size of the file is shown on the right: 9,428 KB is about 9 MB.

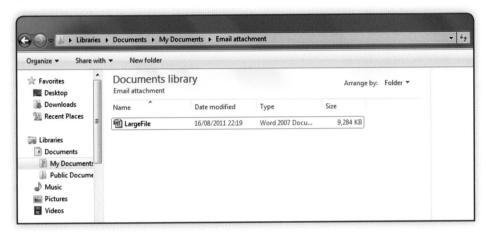

Figure 6.37: Example of a large file which needs to be compressed

How to compress a file

1. Right click on the file and select **Send to** from the drop-down menu.

2. Select **Compressed (zipped) folder** and the file will then be compressed (made smaller) into a separate folder.

3. If the folder contains lots of JPEG images or MP3 audio files it will not get much smaller, as they are already compressed. Figure 6.38 shows the result of compressing a file.

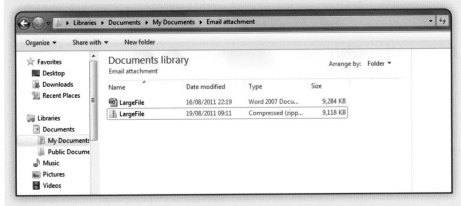

Figure 6.38: Example of a compressed file

To open a compressed folder, **double click** on it. To extract the files from a compressed folder, **right click** on it and choose **Extract All**. Then select the folder location you would like to store the files in.

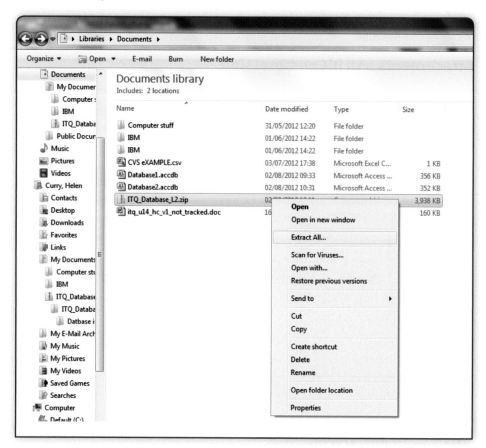

Figure 6.39: How to extract files from a compressed folder

Activity: Organising your Inbox

1   Create different subfolders in your Inbox for emails from garden centres, individual customers and personal emails.
2   Make a backup of your Inbox and set up **AutoArchive** to regularly archive your emails.

2.5 Email problems

The most common problem with sending emails is that the email address is incorrect. When you send an email the address must be exactly right; otherwise it will not get to the right person. In these cases you should get an email response saying your email could not be delivered. When asking people for their email address, make sure that you write it down correctly and check it with the person.

Message size or number of attachments

One problem you may come across, which has been mentioned earlier, is sending large files as attachments (*see page 71*). You will usually get an email response telling you that your email could not be sent because it is too large.

When possible, split the files and send them in several emails. If you cannot do this, compress the files.

Viruses

Many advertising and promotional emails have images included within the email itself (rather than as an attachment). As it is possible to include viruses within images, many email programs hide these images.

If you are sure the email is from a safe source, then you can click on the image and choose **Download Pictures**. The images will then be displayed.

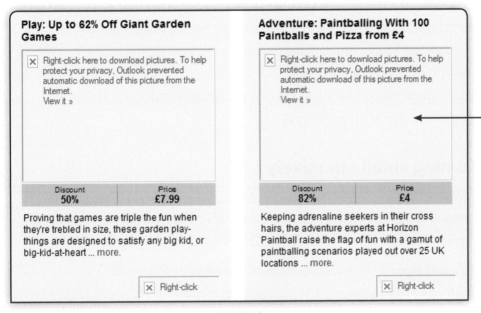

The space where the image should appear is blank. Instead, you will see a message explaining that you need to right-click the image to download it

Figure 6.40: Example of an email with embedded images

Mailbox full

If your mailbox becomes full you will need to use the **Archive** function (*see pages 95–97*) to reduce the number of old emails in your **Inbox** and **Sent Items**. Remember that emails you delete simply go in your **Deleted Items** folder. You need to right click the **Deleted Items** folder and choose **Empty Folder** to permanently delete them.

> ### Check your understanding
>
> 1 What features does Outlook® have to deal with junk (or spam) email?
> 2 What makes a strong password? Give some examples of strong passwords.
> 3 If you type an email in capital letters, what might the recipient think you are doing?
> 4 How can you flag an incoming email as important?

ASSESSMENT ACTIVITY

You volunteer at a local youth club. The club has decided to invest in a new computer so that it can use email to improve communication with the local community and other youth clubs in the area.

Task 1 – Use email software tools and techniques to compose and send messages

The club's social secretary is not very familiar with email. The club's chairperson has asked you to produce a blog and to use your entries to discuss different aspects of using email.

1 Produce a blog for each of the topics below. Illustrate your blog with screenshots or images where possible.

- The different software tools you can use to write and format emails – include images of each.
- How to attached files to emails and how to estimate the overall size of the email.
- How to send emails to individuals and groups of people.
- How to maintain lists of contacts in the address book and create distribution lists.
- The do/don't rules on how to stay safe when using email.

Task 2 – Manage incoming email effectively

The club creates its own web page and has a contact email address. It is soon inundated with emails from people in the local community wanting information, and enquiries from other clubs wanting to know if they can organise joint events. The social secretary asks for your help to manage incoming email effectively.

1 Create a web page which lists guidelines and procedures for dealing with incoming email.

2 Make a video which shows examples of how to respond to emails appropriately and in different ways.

3 Add content to your video which explains how to use rules to automate responses to emails and how to organise incoming emails into folders.

4 Create a step-by-step guide to how to archive email, using screenshots to illustrate each step.

5 Create a FAQ document which explains how to deal with common problems with email.

Database software

Databases are at the heart of many organisations' information systems. They are used to keep vast amounts of data and to deliver just the right amount of information to anyone in the organisation who has the right to see or change it.

The type of data kept in a database can range from employee details such as pay rate, bank details and address, through product details such as suppliers, quantity held in the warehouse and cost, to customer details such as name, orders placed, address and so on.

Many organisations would not be able to exist without their databases.

Some of the most highly paid IT professionals are database specialists, able to create complex databases and to solve difficult problems around storing data and bringing out exactly what information is wanted from this huge resource.

In this unit you will learn some database skills needed to create and edit a non-relational database which contains just one table.

Organisations use relational databases which have several tables. Although relational databases are not covered in this unit, the skills you will develop from creating tables, queries, forms and reports will help you when you come to work on more complex databases.

Learning outcomes

After completing this unit you should be able to achieve the following learning outcomes.

» **LO1** Create and modify non-relational database tables

» **LO2** Enter, edit and organise structured information in a database

» **LO3** Use database software tools to run queries and produce reports

1 Create and modify non-relational database tables

A database can be either relational or non-relational. A **relational database** has more than one table, whereas a **non-relational database** only has one table. A table looks like a spreadsheet and is used to store information (data) in a database.

In this unit you will be looking at non-relational databases. You will gain experience in using tables that you can then build upon when you start to work on relational databases.

Case study: Library database

A small local charity provides support for anyone acting as a carer for a member of their family. The charity has a number of volunteers who spend time with a carer when required.

The charity has just received a donation of 50 books and plans to set up a library to loan books to carers.

You have offered to help the charity set up a simple database it can use to keep track of the books.

1.1 Components of a database design

Before you create your database you will need to make a design for it. This will save time when you write the database. The design will help your database run efficiently. It can also be used to show anyone using the database how it works.

What types of information are stored

Your design must understand the types of information, or data, to be stored in the database. This will help you decide on which fields to include in your table. The design will particularly affect the data type defined and the error checking process.

Some error checking is carried out automatically by the database, such as only valid dates can be entered into a field with the data type defined as date.

Other error checking is defined when the database is created, e.g. a new UK registration number can use an **input mask** to ensure that only two letters, two numbers then three letters can be entered.

Types of information that can be kept in a database include:

- **Text** – for small amounts of writing, e.g. an address
- **Memo** – for longer writing, e.g. notes
- **Number** – e.g. 23
- **Date/time** – e.g. a date of birth

Key term

Input mask – a set of rules which governs the type and length of information a user is allowed to enter in a particular field.

- **Currency** – e.g. £2.40
- **AutoNumber** – used to make a new number, e.g. a key field to make each **record** different
- **Yes/No** – used where there are only two possibilities
- **OLE Object** – used to link to something outside Access®, e.g. a Microsoft® Word® document
- **Hyperlink** – used to link to a web page
- **Attachment** – used in a similar way to OLE, but needing less storage space
- **Calculated** – e.g. cost calculated by multiplying quantity by unit price.

Key term

Record – a record is all the fields in a row in a table where information is kept about one person or item.

Field types

The database table should include fields which are suitable for the types of data stored there and appropriately named.

Field types	
Data type	The data type, e.g. text or number, must be chosen to allow the correct type of data to be kept in the field. Refer to *What types of information are stored* section, page 102, for more information on this.
Field name	The field name should be carefully chosen so that reading the field name gives a good indication of what is kept there.
Field size	The field size property gives control over how many characters can be typed into a field with a text data type.
Format	The format property can be used for most data types, with each of these having different format options to match the data type of the field. The format property of some field types, e.g. Date/ time, can be set using a combo box.
Validation	Validation rules can be set so a field rejects typing that is obviously wrong (invalid). See *Validation rules* in the *Methods for maintaining integrity of existing data in a single table non-relational database* section (page 106) for more information.
Primary key	The primary key is an important field which makes sure each record is different (unique) and automatically sorts the table into the right order. See the *Data integrity* section (page 112) for more information.

Table 8.1: Field types

Use of data entry forms

A data entry form can be used to put information into a database. It also makes the database easier to use.

When designing a database you will also need to design a data entry form. This will show the fields and any other controls, such as buttons, to run queries, reports or to navigate to other parts of the database.

Use of routine queries

There can be one or more routine queries used to show the table in a different way, e.g. a routine query in a stock database could show items that need re-ordering because they are below the minimum stock level.

How data is structured in a single table non-relational database

In a single table database data is structured into **fields**. Each field has a name and a data type, such as 'number'. Names of fields should be meaningful to make it very clear what data is kept there. The data type is defined so that the database can store the data in the most effective way.

Use of indexes and key field to organise data

Indexes can be defined to remember different **sequences** for a table. These are useful in large databases with thousands or millions of records (rows) that need to be seen in different ways, e.g. by surname order or by date order. Setting the index property to 'Yes' for these fields means the database can re-sequence the table very quickly.

A table should have one or more key fields to:

- organise the data by making sure each record has a different **identifier** to the other records
- give a **default sequence** to the records in a table.

1.2 Field characteristics

When designing your database you will need to describe the field characteristics data required. This will also help with the data entry and reject bad data.

Some field characteristics are essential as the field cannot be set up otherwise. Other field characteristics are optional and can be set to help reject bad data or to improve the appearance of the data.

Key terms

Sequences – are different orders that data can be arranged in such as A–Z.
Identifier – is a field (or fields) different for each record, such as a reference number.
Default sequence – is how a table automatically sorts a new record into place.

A field must have these characteristics:	
Field name	Used by queries, forms, reports and other places in the database.
Data type	Makes best use of memory to store data and to reject bad data accidentally typed into the field.
A field can also have other optional characteristics:	
Field size	To reject bad data with a different number of characters to that set by the field size.
Format	To control how data looks, e.g. upper case, date/time format or a custom format of your choice.
Validation rule	Can be used to reject any data typed into a field that does not match the rule.
Primary key	Is when one or more fields are set to be the key field(s). The table will reject any record with the same **primary key** data as in another record. The table also uses the primary key to automatically move any new record to the right place by keeping the order of the key field. (See section 1.4 *Ways to maintain data integrity, page 112*, for more information on primary keys.)

Table 8.2: Required and optional characteristics for a field

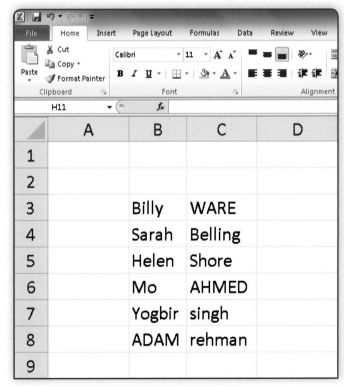

Key term

Data validation rule – used in a table to reject data entries that are obviously wrong.

Data validation and consistency, completeness and accuracy

A **data validation rule** can be set to reject bad data being typed into a field. Validation rules test the data; for example, by making sure a date of birth is before a set date to check that the person is old enough.

To ensure data integrity, information in tables must be:

- **Consistent**. Data needs to look as though it belongs together. A list of dates would look wrong if some of them were just numbers while others were a mixture of numbers and the names of months. People's names would look wrong if some were all upper case while others were a mixture of upper and lower case.
- **Complete**. The records in a table need to have all their fields filled with good information and no gaps.
- **Accurate**. Once data has been accepted into a table it should be trusted.

Most of the validation and other checks take place when the data is entered. Once the data is in the table further checks are not usually made.

Figure 8.1: Inconsistent data looks unprofessional and is hard to read

Effect of malicious or accidental alteration

Sometimes good data may be changed into bad data. This may be accidental – it could be as a result of a typing error or the wrong record is changed.

Records can also be deliberately, or maliciously, altered to turn them into bad data. For example, an employee who is very upset with their employer could make changes to company data with the intention of damaging their employer's business. This type of alteration can be difficult to find and correct.

IT systems, including databases, should be regularly backed up. This can be useful if the integrity of any data is in doubt as it can then be checked against a previous version.

Methods for maintaining integrity of existing data in a single table non-relational database

Every database needs to have good and accurate data held in the tables. When bad data is allowed into the database data integrity is broken. It is also important to maintain the integrity of data once it is held in a table. The three main ways to maintain integrity of existing data are:

- input masks
- default value
- validation rules.

Input masks

Input masks can be set on a field to control what can be typed into it. This is very powerful for fields which have a set structure, such as a National Insurance number which consists of two upper case letters, followed by six digits and one upper case letter.

The input mask for this would be:
>LL000000L

Input mask characters include:	
0	User must enter a digit (0 to 9).
9	User can enter a digit (0 to 9).
#	User can enter a digit, space, plus or minus sign. If skipped, Microsoft® Access® enters a blank space.
L	User must enter a letter.
?	User can enter a letter.
A	User must enter a letter or a digit.
A	User can enter a letter or a digit.
&	User must enter either a character or a space.
C	User can enter characters or spaces.
>	Changes all characters that follow to upper case.
<	Changes all characters that follow to lower case.
!	Causes the input mask to fill from left to right instead of from right to left.

Default value

Default values can be used to pre-fill a field in a new record with valid data such as pre-filling the 'City' field of an address table.

Validation rules

A validation rule can be used to keep out bad data and allow in good data. It is a powerful tool in helping to maintain data integrity. Validation rules can be complex and need to be tested thoroughly to ensure that they work correctly.

> A validation rule to make sure only dates after 1/1/2000 would be:
>
> >=#01/01/2000#
>
> A validation rule to make sure only dates after 1/1/2000 or before 1/1/1990 would be:
>
> >=#01/01/2007# Or <=#01/01/1990#
>
> If only EB or CL or GT are allowed in a field, the validation rule would be:
>
> "EB" Or "CL" Or "GT"

Validation rules can be combined with input masks, so data entry into this field could also be forced into two upper case characters with an input mask of:

>LL.

The field properties also allow for **validation text.** This will show if the validation rule is broken and data is rejected. The user can then read the validation text to understand why the data was not allowed and what needs to be done differently to make the data entry good so as to allow it into the table.

How field characteristics contribute to data validation

Setting the field characteristics can help to:

- control data being entered into the table
- prevent bad data being typed in.

An example of a field characteristic is an input mask which can be used to make sure text and numbers are entered into the right place. We have already seen how an organisation storing employee National Insurance numbers in a database can use an input mask of >LL000000L, ensuring data entered is two letters then six numbers followed by a letter which are forced to upper case.

1.3 Create and modify database tables

As you use your database you may want to change the information it holds. You may also decide to alter the field characteristics to make the table easier to use.

In this section you will create a database, and you will then make a series of alternations to it. The database will contain the names of your friends and family, which you can use to print out envelope labels for birthday and occassion cards.

To begin, you will need to create your database and add in the relevant fields for peoples' names and addresses.

> **Key term**
>
> **Validation text** – shows when a validation rule is broken. This needs to clearly explain what the rule will allow so the user can get their data entry accepted.

How to create an address list

1. Create a database in Microsoft® Access®. Name the database **Address List**.

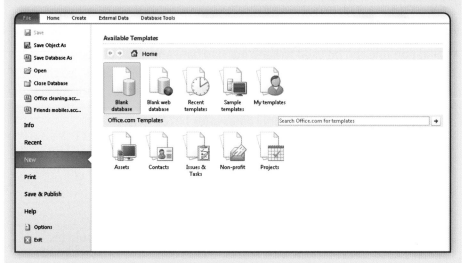

Figure 8.2: Select Blank database to create your new database

2. Click the **Table** icon in the **Create** toolbar to create a table in your database.

3. Click the **Table** icon in the **Create** toolbar to create a table in your database.

4. Click the **Design view** option. In the **Save as** dialog box that appears type **tblNames** then click the **OK** button.

Figure 8.3: Select Design view and save the table tblNames in the Save as dialog box

5. Create the following fields in your table by typing them into the **Design view**. (See Figure 8.4.)

• Title	• Postcode
• First name	• Date of birth
• Surname	• Gender
• Road	• Hat size
• District	• Birthday list
• Town	• Close friend
• County	

continued

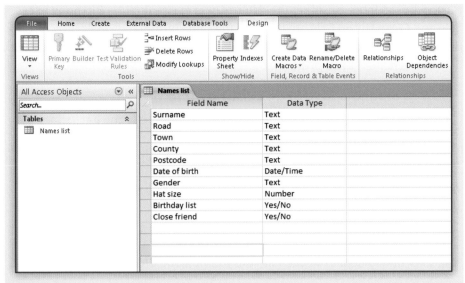

Figure 8.4: Create these fields in the table

6. Use the **View** button to change to the **Datasheet view** and save the table.

Add, amend and delete fields

Once you have created a database, it is very easy to make changes to it.

You have decided you would also like the database to contain people's phone numbers. To do this you need to add in a field.

How to add a field to an existing table

1. Right click on **tblNames** to select **Design view**.

2. Add a field named **Phone** with text data type and length of 11 characters.

3. Set format of the **Phone** field so that brackets are around the area code. This is the first four characters of the phone number.

4. The @ represents where the user can type a character, so the format for this field will be: (@@@@) @@@@@@@

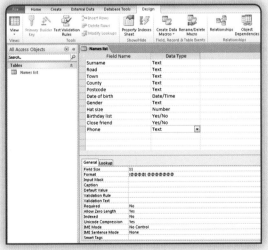

Figure 8.5: Add a field for a phone number and format as (0117) 9654325

Having looked more closely at the databse, you realise that the **Birthday list** field and **Close friend** field are there for the same purpose – to select records for printing for birthday card address labels. You decide to amend the **Birthday list** field so it is named **Card print**.

How to amend a field in an existing table

1. Double click your mouse in the **Birthday list** field. Use the **backspace** key to delete the text.

2. Type in **Card print**. Press the **Return** key.

You can also delete fields from a database. See the 'How to delete a fied in an existing table' guide below.

How to delete a field in an existing table

1. Click on the field to select it. (In this example the **Close friend** field has been highlighted.)

2. Press the **Delete** key to delete the field from the table.

Click here to select the field

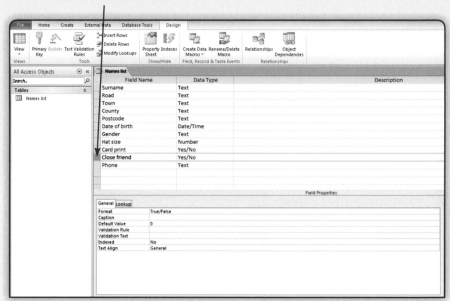

Figure 8.6: The field needs to be selected before it can be deleted

Modify field characteristics

Once you have created a database, you can modify the field characteristics.

You would like to change the **'County'** field characteristics to upper case. You also decide to reduce the size of this field to 30 characters. The 'County' field already has a text data type.

How to change the County *field characteristics to upper case*

1. Select the table.
2. Enter **Design** view.
3. Select the **County** field.
4. Type > into the **Format** property.
5. Then click **OK**.

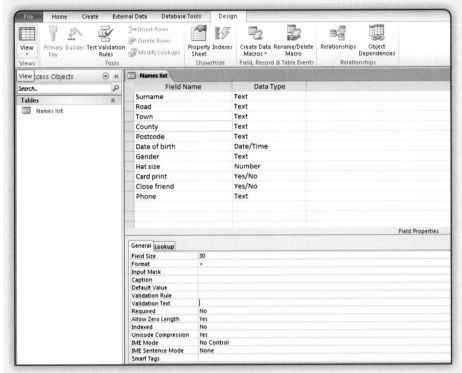

Figure 8.7: Change the County field characteristics to format it to upper case

How to change the County *field characteristics to 30 characters*

1. Select the table.
2. Enter **Design** view.
3. Select the **County** field.
4. Type 30 into the **Field size** property.
5. Then click **OK**.

Activity: Populate the modifed table.

Add the details for an additional six people to the table.

1.4 Ways to maintain data integrity

Data integrity refers to the quality and accuracy of the data is in a database. If you put wrong data into a database then the integrity is broken. This could result in reports or queries appearing as inaccurate.

Data integrity is very important. It is easy for data entry mistakes to happen so organisations then to use a number of methods to prevent this. They include:

- setting a primary key
- setting field characteristics
- validating data as it is entered.

Not null primary key

The **primary key** can be used to make sure each record is unique. It prevents the same record appearing more than once and so helps to preserve data integrity.

The primary key should be set to **not null** so that it cannot be empty which helps to ensure data integrity.

1.5 Problems with database tables

You need to be able to respond to any problems found in your database tables such as:

- redundant data
- duplication
- table structure
- field characteristics
- validation.

Redundant data

Redundant data is when the same data is held in two or more different fields. This is usually a problem in relational databases where it is possible to have the same data in more than one table. For example, a customer sales database which includes a field for customers' addresses have might this data stored in a table of customer details and in a table for sales data.

A single table database could also contain redundant data if two different fields in the table contain the same information. For example, date of birth in one field and age in another field. However, this is less likely with single table databases.

Duplication

Duplication is where the same data appears in two or more records. The primary key should prevent this, but this will depend on how the primary key has been set up.

If you let Access® automatically add a primary key named ID to your table this will give each record a different number. Although this will make the **Primary key** field unique, other fields could easily duplicate another record.

A primary key which uses two or more fields can be a very powerful way of avoiding duplicated data. For example, a table containing data relating to people could use the 'Surname', 'First name' and 'Date of birth' fields as a **composite primary key**. This would also keep the table in 'Surname', then 'First name' order.

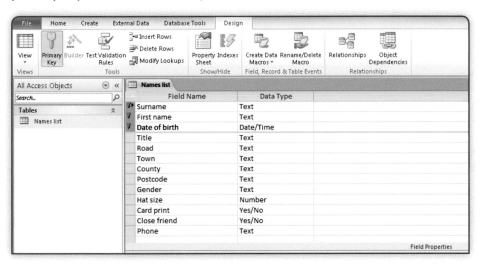

Figure 8.8: Using three fields as a composite primary key

Table structure

The way the table is structured may cause a problem if there are mistakes in the design. The structure should consist of:

- fields
- field names
- field validations and checks
- primary key
- indexes (if any).

A poor choice of primary key could stop new records which contain good data from being entered if they duplicate the 'Primary key' field. Setting the 'Surname' field as the primary key seems like a good choice as the table will automatically order itself based on the surnames and will always be in alphabetical order. This will become a problem though when you try to enter another person with the same surname – as the new data will be rejected.

To solve this problem you could set the primary key using both the 'Surname' and 'First name' fields. This will order the table by surname, then first name. However, this could also cause a problem if there are two people with the same surname and first name. A better solution would be to use a **composite primary key** using the 'Surname', 'First name' and 'Date of birth' fields.

Sources of help

If you have a problem when using a database table, then you can access support through the following ways:

- Via Access®. Use the **F1** key to start the online Help function
- Books about databases. Professional database developers use books to help them when they get stuck. Look through a book's contents pages or search the index to find what you are looking for, then scan the pages for the information you need.
- The Internet. Many websites offer help and advice and these are easily found by using search engines such as Google™ or Yahoo!.

Activity: Creating a database of books

A local charity which provides support for carers requires your help to set up a database for its library of 50 books. The database needs to hold the following information:

- book title
- author
- year of publication
- type of book (comedy, cookery, detective, hobby, thriller)
- name of borrower
- date book lent.

Carry out these tasks for the charity.

1 Create a new database named 'Charity Books'.
2 Create a new table database named 'Loans'.
3 Create fields in your table to meet the needs of the charity with appropriate names and data types.
4 Add a look-up facility to the 'Type of book' field. (See section *Look-ups*, page 128 for more information on look-ups.)
5 Add a look-up facility to the 'Name of borrower' field using five names of people you know.
6 Enter five records into your table.
7 Print the table.

Check your understanding

1 What is a non-relational database?
2 How is the primary key set and what is its purpose?
3 Identify three possible problems that may arise because of poor database design or set up.

2 Enter, edit and organise structured information in a database

Case study: Employees' database

A local cleaning company employs ten part-time staff to clean office premises. Every morning, the staff gather in the company's office and the cleaning jobs are then allocated. This information is then recorded on a piece of paper.

The Office Manager would like you to produce a database which can be used to record on a daily basis which staff member cleans which premises.

2.1 Create forms to enter, edit and organise data in a database

Many databases use forms to enter, edit and organise data.

- Forms can hold buttons that can be used to run reports or bring up other forms for data entry.
- Forms can show one record at a time, thus making data entry easier. Users can enter data into a form rather than directly into a table to make it easier for the user to see what they are doing.
- There may also be additional error checking and data validation on data that is typed into the form.

Edit data

You can use forms or type directly into the table to enter new data. You create a new record by entering new data into the fields. You can then change any data by selecting and then editing it.

> #### How to edit or change data to update a field
> 1. Select the field you want to edit. (It will become highlighted.)
> 2. To remove the highlight, either **click** again on the field or use the **F2** key.
> 3. You can now edit the data.
> 4. Use the mouse or the ⇧/⇩ key to complete the edit by selecting another field which updates the field you changed.

Organise data

A database can help to organise data by sorting a table into a different sequence or by using the **Filter** button to show the records you want.

How to organise data using Sort

1. Select the field you want to sort on.
2. Either click on either the **Ascending** or **Descending** button in the **Home** toolbar.

How to organise data using Filter

1. Select the field you want to filter.
2. Click the **Filter** button.
3. A pop-up menu appears by the field.
4. Choose what you want to see in the filtered field.

How to create a data entry form

1. Open the database **Address List** that you created earlier in this unit.
2. Go to the **Create** toolbar and click the **Form** button. This will make a data entry form based on your table.

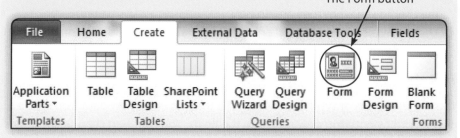

Figure 8.9: The Form button

3. Close the new form by pressing **Ctrl+F4** or click the **x** on the top right corner of the form.
4. Click the **Yes** button to save changes.
5. In the **Save as** dialog box that appears, type **frmDataEntry**, then click the **OK** button.

Access® allows you to save forms, tables and other objects, such as queries, using any name you wish. It also allows you to include spaces between letters or numbers.

Many IT professionals will name objects with a shortened file name. For example, a form may be saved as 'frm'. In the example, we named the object **frmDataEntry** as it is a form that will be used for data entry.

You can use your data entry form to view, edit and create new records. Double-click on the form to open it. You should see one of the records you entered in Activity: Creating a database of books on page 114 in your form. To see the other records, either:

- Click the **Record navigation** buttons on the bottom left of the form.
- Press the **Page Up** or **Page Down** keys.

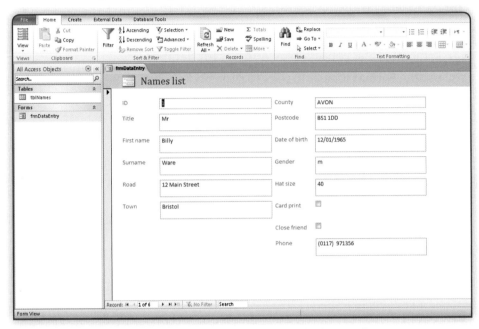

Figure 8.10: Your data entry form can be used to view and edit records

You will use this form when the database starts and to move around the various parts of the database using buttons.

How to add a label to a form

1. On the **Create** toolbar click the **Blank form** button to start the form.

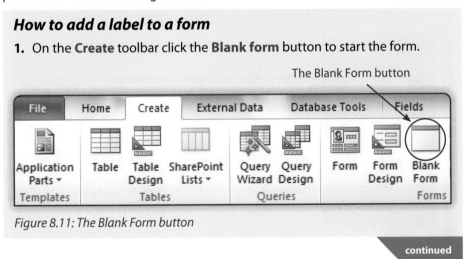

Figure 8.11: The Blank Form button

continued

2. Click the **Label** button to add a label to your form.

The Label button

Figure 8.12: The Label button

3. In the label that appears, type **Address list database**.
4. Use the **Format** toolbar to select a larger font.
5. Use the **Format** toolbar to centre the text using the button.

How to place a button on a data entry form

1. Click the **Button** button in the **Design** toolbar. This starts a wizard which will help you set up what happens when the button is used.

The Button button

Figure 8.13: The Button button

2. In the first **Command Button Wizard** dialog box select both **Form operations** and **Open form**. (See Figure 8.14.)
3. Click **Next** to move to the second **Command Button Wizard** dialog box.

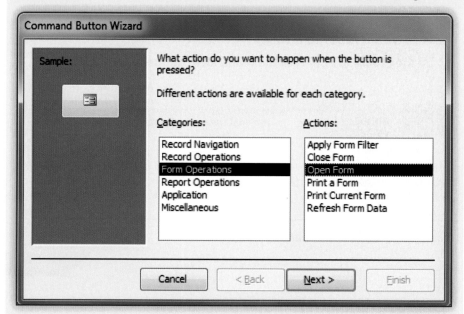

Figure 8.14: On the first Command Button Wizard dialog box select Form operations and Open form

continued

4. In the second **Command Button Wizard** dialog box select **frmDataEntry**, which is the name of the form that will open when the button is clicked. (See Figure 8.15.)

5. Click **Next** to move to the third **Command Button Wizard** dialog box.

Figure 8.15: On the second Command Button Wizard dialog box select the name of the form to open

6. In the third **Command Button Wizard** dialog box select the option to see all the records when the form is opened.

7. Click **Next** to move to the fourth **Command Button Wizard** dialog box.

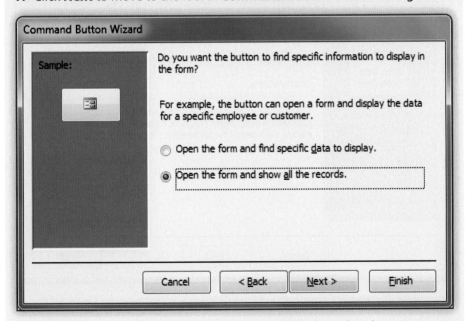

Figure 8.16: On the third Command Button Wizard dialog box select the option to see all the records

continued

8. In the fourth **Command Button Wizard** dialog box select text and re-type what is already there with Next.

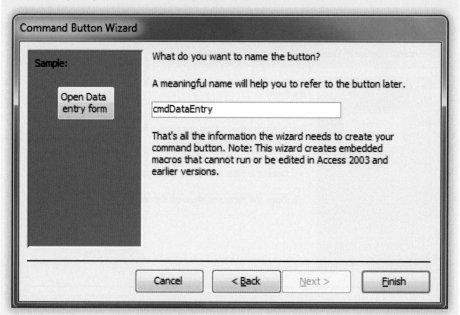

Figure 8.17: On the fourth Command Button Wizard dialog box select text for the button

9. Click **Next** to move to the final **Command Button Wizard** dialog box.

10. In the final **Command Button Wizard** dialog box type the name for the button. Do not include spaces. The first three letters should be lower case (cmd) as this is a command button.

Command Button Wizard

Sample:

Open Data entry form

What do you want to name the button?

A meaningful name will help you to refer to the button later.

cmdDataEntry

That's all the information the wizard needs to create your command button. Note: This wizard creates embedded macros that cannot run or be edited in Access 2003 and earlier versions.

Cancel   < Back   Next >   Finish

Figure 8.18: On the last Command Button Wizard dialog box type the name for the button

continued

11. Click **Next** to see the button and label which have been connected together in the layout.

Figure 8.19: The form now has a label and a button

12. Right click on the button and select **Layout**. Select **Remove layout** from the menu to break the connection between label and button.

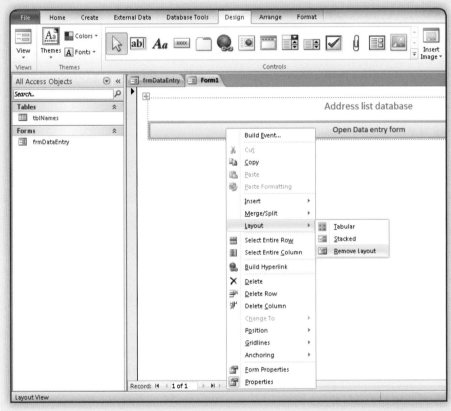

Figure 8.20: Select Remove layout to break connection between label and button

continued

13. Drag the button to another part of the form and resize the button.

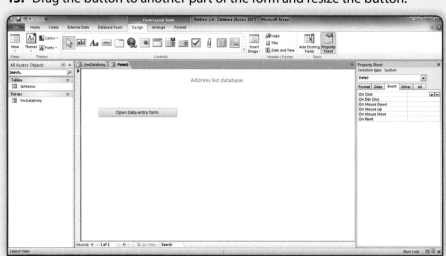

Figure 8.21: The button can be placed on the form and resized.

14. Click the **View** button to move from **Design view** to **Form view**. The form button should now work. Click the **Open data entry form** button to check it opens the first form you created.

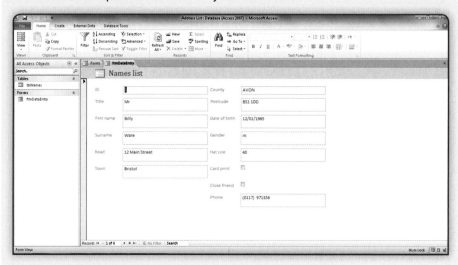

Figure 8.22: The button can be used to show the data entry form

15. Close the data entry form by pressing **Ctrl+F4** or click the **x** on the top right corner of the form.

16. Close your new form by pressing **Ctrl+F4** or click the **x** on the top right corner of the form. In the **Save as** dialog box that appears, type **frmMain** then click the **OK** button.

Earlier in this unit you entered new records directly into the **Address List** table (see Activity: Populate the modified table on page 111). You can use the **New (blank) record** button at the bottom left of the form to start a new record or you could press the **Page Down** key to move through the records to the last one, then start a new record.

When you move to another record, each new record is saved automatically.

Moving around a table will select the fields in turn. When a field is selected, anything you type will replace what is already there.

You can select and update a field to make a small change by clicking on the field with the mouse. You could also use the **F2** key when a field is selected to remove the highlight so you can edit it.

Activity: Address list data entry form

The *How to place a button on a data entry form* step-by-step guide (pages 118–122) will help you with this activity.

1 Right click on **frmDataEntry** to select **Design view**.

   a Add a button to the form which:

      • carries out a form operation to **Close form**

      • uses **Quit** as text on the button

      • is named **cmdQuit**.

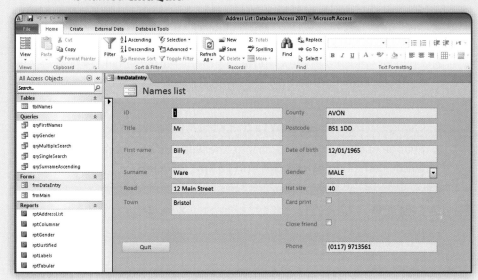

Figure 8.23: Design view of frmDataEntry with a button to close the form

   b Close the data entry form by pressing **Ctrl+F4** or click the **x** on the top right corner of the form and save the changes.

   c Place a button named **cmdQuit** on your **frmMain** to close the form. Close and save **frmMain**.

   d Double-click on **frmMain** to open this form.

   e Click the **Open data entry form** button to open this form, then use the **Quit** button to check it closes the data entry form.

   f Use the **Quit** button on the main form to check that it also works to close **frmMain**.

2 Open the data entry form and enter another three records.

3 Edit two of your records directly into the **tblNames** (without using the forms). You can double click on the table to open it, then make the changes before closing the table.

Locate and amend records

Access® can help you to locate records using the search box. The search facility will highlight anything in the table or data entry form that matches what you type into the search box. To jump to the next place in the data where there is a match, press the **Enter** key.

The search box is similar to the **Find** button in the **Home** toolbar which allows you to select the fields Access® will search for a match.

Using wildcards

You can also use the * and **?** wildcards in searches using either the search box or the **Find** button.

* represents any combination of characters. For example, 'He*' will find anything starting with 'He'. This is the same as simply typing 'He' which will also find anything starting with these letters.

? represents any single character. For example, 'He??o' will find anything starting with 'He' which then has two characters followed by 'o', such as 'Hello'.

> ### How to search a database using wildcards
>
> 1. Double-click **qrySingleSearch** to open it.
> 2. Use a **H*** wildcard in the **Criteria** row of the Surname field to find everyone whose surname begins with H.
> 3. The wildcard query changes when you move away from the field.
> 4. Change to **Datasheet view** to check the wildcard search has worked.
> 5. Change to **Design view** to change the wildcard to search for everyone whose name begins with **Sm** using a **Sm*** wildcard .
>
>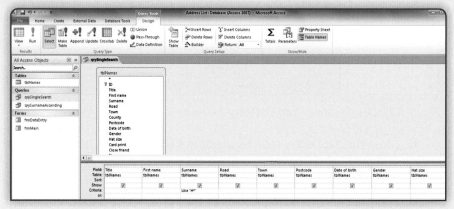
>
> Figure 8.24: Use the * wildcard in a query to find records where the field data starts with H
>
> 6. Close the query, and save your changes.

Using search operators

Search operators can be found by using the **Filter** button. The choices you see here depend upon the field that is selected when the **Filter** button is used. The **Text filters** option shows a choice of which data can be seen in your filter (refer to Figure 8.25). The text filter will operate on the currently selected field.

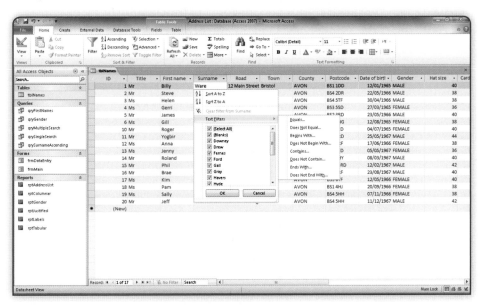

Figure 8.25: Text filters give good search options

Error checking

Error checking can prevent a lot of bad data going into the database. Errors can be checked by code written by IT professionals to work with the form to reject bad data.

You can check for errors by carefully proof-reading any data you enter into your table. For further information on error checking refer to section 2.3 *Check data entry*, pages 130–133.

Data validation

Data validation is where only data selected from given choices can be entered. The choices are set in the field properties or on the form. As the data that can go into the field has to come from the choices available, the data entered has to be valid. For further information on data validation, refer to section 2.4 *Responding to data entry errors* on pages 133–135.

2.2 Format data entry forms

Formatting data entry forms and other forms helps to make the database look more professional and can also make data entry easier.

Field characteristics and layout

The field characteristics can be set on the form. In **frmDataEntry**, for example, you could select the 'Gender' field and use the **properties sheet** to change the format to upper case.

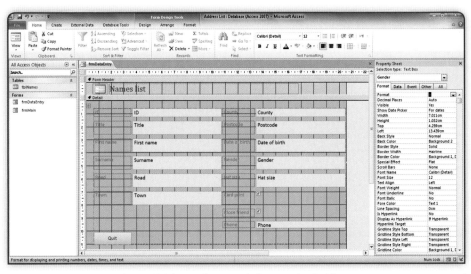

Figure 8.26: You can select a field on a form and change the field properties

You have a choice of three views when editing and working with forms.

- **Form**
- **Design**
- **Layout**.

The **Form** view shows the finished form with the data to allow you to edit and add records to the database. The **Design** and **Layout** views enable you to make changes to the form. These views offer similar functionality. The main difference is that **Layout** view shows a set of data on the form while you edit the form design.

You can change the layout of the form to move fields and other objects, such as buttons, to resize and then move them to where you think they look best and are easiest to use.

See section 1.2 *Field characteristics*, pages 104–107, for more information on field characteristics.

Tables

Most forms have a table as the record source. The record source is where the fields on the form link to and where the information shown on the form and changed by the form is kept.

How to view the record source of a form

1. Right click on the form.

2. Select **Form properties**.

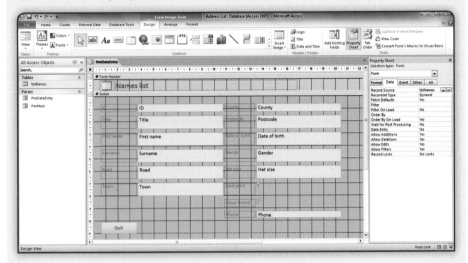

Figure 8.27: The form properties shows the record source

Colour

You can use colour tools such as **Shape fill** or **Font color** to change the colours of different parts of your form.

How to use the colour tools for an object

1. Select an object.

2. In the **Format** toolbar use the **Font color** icon to select a colour for the text.

3. In the **Format** toolbar use the **Background color** icon to select a background colour for the object.

4. To change several objects, e.g. text boxes, at the same time, select them by holding the **Shift** key as you click on each object to add it to the selection. You can now change them all at once.

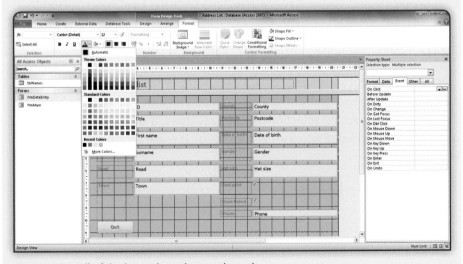

Figure 8.28: All of the boxes have been selected

How to use the colour tools for a text box

1. Select a text box.

2. In the **Format** toolbar select the **Font color** icon.

3. To change the colour of part of the form background, select the band at the top of the form section. Right click then select the **Fill/ Backcolor** menu option. (See Figure 8.29.)

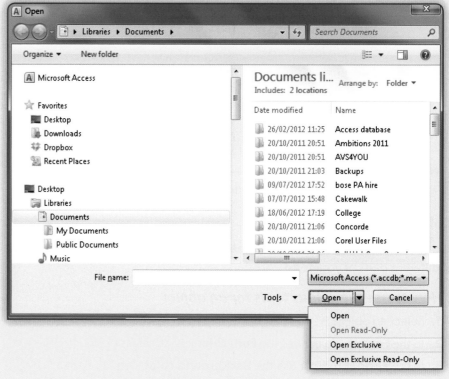

Figure 8.29: Select the form band then use the Background colour tool

4. To change the colour of several objects at the same time, select your chosen field text boxes together by holding the **Shift** key as you click on each object to add it to the selection. Click the **Font color** button to change the colour of all the objects.

Look-ups

Look-ups are useful for quick, accurate data entry. When the user clicks on a field a **combo box** appears giving a range of values. The user simply clicks a value instead of typing. As the selections are already there, it is impossible to mistype or enter an invalid value into the field, although it is still possible to select the wrong value.

For a look-up to work in a form, it needs to be defined first in the table to set the look-up property of a field. In your **Address List** data entry form, follow the instructions in the 'How to set up a combo box in a data entry form' guide below to set the 'Gender' field to offer a choice of 'M' (male) or 'F' (female) in a combo box.

The data entry form needs to be closed before working on the table design. This is because this form is built on the table and they cannot both be open for editing at the same time.

How to set up a combo box in a data entry form

1. Make sure **frmDataEntry** is not open.

2. Open **tblDataEntry** in **Design view**.

3. Select the 'Gender field' and click the **Lookup** tab at the bottom of the screen.

4. Set the **Lookup** to:

   - **Combo box** for the appearance of the lookup

   - **Value list** for where the data in the lookup comes from

   - **F;M** to give the choice of 'F' or 'M'. The semi-colon (;) is used to separate values to be shown in the combo box. (See Figure 8.30.)

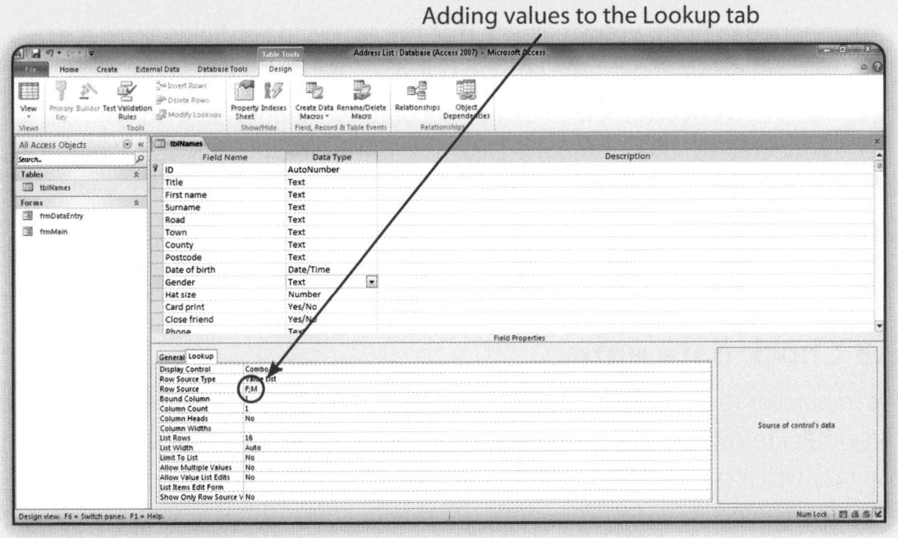

Figure 8.30: You can set a field to lookup values in a combo box

5. Change the view of the table to **Datasheet** and save your changes to make sure the combo box shows when you click on the 'Gender' field of a record.

6. Close the table.

7. Open **frmDataEntry** into **Form view**. The 'Gender' field should be as it was before you made changes to the table. This field needs to be replaced with the current lookup version.

continued

8. Change to **Layout view**. Click the **Field list** icon to show all the current fields for the table. Double-click 'Gender' in the field list to add the current version of this field to your form.

9. You now have two 'Gender' fields, as shown in Figure 8.31.

Figure 8.31: Use the Field list to add a current version of a field

10. Change to **Form view** to check that the two 'Gender' fields show the same data. Changing the combo box also changes the 'Gender' text box.

11. Return to **Layout view** to delete the original 'Gender' text box by selecting this then using the **Delete** key, thus leaving the newer combo box for the 'Gender' field.

12. Move the fields around to tidy up the layout before closing and saving the form.

2.3 Check data entry

It is important to check that the data you enter into your database is correct. You can either look at the screen to compare it with a paper copy of the original or you may find it quicker and easier to print the database entries. You can then place the original data and your print out side by side – this is a better and more accurate way to make your checks.

Spell check

Access® has a **Spelling** icon on the **Home** toolbar. Click the icon to start checking your data for spelling errors as in other Microsoft® products. When a mis-spelt word is found you will be given the option to add it to the dictionary (if you think it is spelt correctly) or to ignore it. You can also set the spell check program to ignore a field with mis-spelt data.

Format

You will need to check the format of the data to make sure it uses upper/lower case letters consistently in each field. Data looks very unprofessional if there is a mixture of upper and lower case, such as the surname appearing as Smith in some places and SMITH elsewhere. Inconsistent formatting also makes it more difficult to spot errors in the data.

The **field format** property can be set to force data into a mixture of upper and lower case. For further information see the section *Input masks* on page 106.

Accuracy

The data in your database must be accurate. You will need to check the data regularly to make sure it is correct. Remember the importance of **GIGO** – it is essential to input correct data.

All fields should be completed for all records, as appropriate. Databases work best when all the data is there and accurate. Data missing from a field could mean that an important record is not found by a search.

Consistency

As with the format of data, consistency is important to ensure that the data in a field matches other data in the field. For example, a database about people might include a field for their initials. Data could be typed in as RJ or R.J. or RJ. or R J – which would make the data inconsistent.

Validity

The validity of data entered can be checked using validation rules in the field properties. See the section *How field characteristics contribute to data validation* on page 107. It is also easier for the database to check validity if the fields are correctly formatted.

Security

The security of information stored in a database is always important.

- There should be no opportunities for any unauthorised access that may damage data integrity.
- Sensitive information must be kept confidential and only viewed by authorised people.

You can include a password to prevent others from accessing it. The password also **encrypts** the database so that it is even harder to see the data inside. See pages 132–133 for more information on how to encrypt a database.

Key terms

GIGO – Garbage In Garbage Out. This term is used to show how important it is to input good data into an IT system as bad data will always produce bad results.

Encrypts – encryption is a technique used by a computer system to scramble a file or document so that if it is opened by someone who is not authorised to use it they will see only random characters with no meaning. Encrypting data needs a password, which is also used to decrypt the data.

How to encrypt an Access® database

1. Open the database from the **File** toolbar but instead of double-clicking on the database name or clicking the **Open** icon, click on the **downward arrow** to the right of this icon to see the ways the database can be opened.

2. In the options that appear, select **Open Exclusive** .

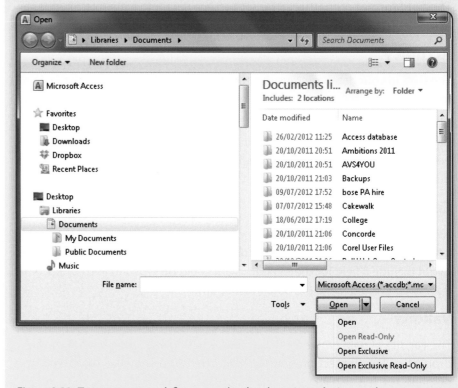

Figure 8.32: To set a password, first open the database in exclusive mode

3. Click the **File** toolbar.

4. Select **Info**.

5. Click the **Encrypt with password** option.

6. Type your surname twice into the **Set database password** dialog box then click the **OK** button. Your surname is now the password.

continued

7. You will now be asked for this password every time you want to open the database.

Figure 8.33: To set a password, use the File menu to select Info then Encrypt with Password

2.4 Responding to data entry errors

When a database has been set up properly there will be a lot of built-in checks which will help to reject bad data from data entry errors. Data may be rejected because:

- it is too long to fit into the field size
- it is the wrong data type
- it fails a validation check.

If any of these checks identifies a problem, a data entry error message will appear on the screen. The error message should give the user information to help them understand what is wrong with the data they tried to enter. A validation rule should also have validation text for the user to read if the rule is broken. A field description can contain useful help such as the number of characters allowed in the field.

Tables and forms may give different error messages for the same error. The error messages for entering the wrong data type give a lot more detail when typing into the table than when typing into a table field on a form.

You will need to show you can deal with situations when the database rejects data entry errors you make and to solve data entry problems so you get good and valid data into your database. This may involve:

- changing bad data into good data so the database will accept it
- modifying the database to allow such data to be entered.

Errors due to field size

The **Field size** sets how many characters can be entered into a field. If your entry is too large for the field you will need to enter a shortened version of the data or modify the field design.

Sometimes when entering data you recognise that the table design is wrong and that a field needs to be able to handle larger data entries than you planned. In this situation you will need to enter the **Design view** and change the field property. Refer to the the *Modify field characteristics* section, page 110.

The field size can also be limited by an input mask which forces the user to enter a set number of letters or numbers. If this has been designed so that good data cannot be entered it will need to be changed (see the section on *Input masks* on page 106).

Errors due to data type

Data entry errors from trying to enter the wrong data type are easy to identify and remedy. Mistyping part of a number with a letter into a number field, perhaps with the letter O instead of the number 0 is an example of a data type error. Access® will give a very clear error message if this happens, explaining the type of data expected and what you need to do to correct the problem.

Validation checks

Validation checks make sure that anything which gets typed into a field is within the set rules. You must be able to deal with data entry errors from validation checks. This will be a lot easier if the validation text has been set as well as the check to explain to the user what the data should look like and why the check is there. Validation text should remind the user of what data is expected to be entered into the field as it appears as part of the onscreen error message.

There are two possibilities if a validation check identifies a problem.

- The data is wrong.
- The validation check is wrong.

If the data is wrong, it simply needs to be retyped.

There is always a possibility that the validation check is wrong as validation rules can be complicated. This is why databases should be thoroughly tested before the user gets delivery. When a validation check alerts the user to a problem with data entry, if the data looks correct the rule will need to be checked and might need to be modified.

Using Help

Access® has a lot of built in help to guide you through setting up and using your databases.

To start Access® **Help** , press the **F1** key which should bring up a help page to assist with whatever you are doing. (See Figure 8.34.)

The help also has a search box where you can type anything you are interested in.

Problems with forms

Any of these data entry errors can occur using a table or a form. Most problems with forms used for data entry can be resolved by changing the table behind the form. Other form problems can be fixed by entering the design view and changing the field properties.

Figure 8.34: Use F1 to get help about using Access

Activity: Creating an employees' database

You have been asked by a local cleaning company to produce a database to record which employees clean which premises on specific days.

Carry out these tasks.

1   Create a new database named 'Cleaning jobs'.
2   Create a new table named 'Allocations'.
3   Create these fields in your table with appropriate data types:
   - 'Job date' – which automatically shows today's date.
   - 'Client' – to hold the name of the office to be cleaned.
   - 'Employee' – to hold the name of the person who is allocated to the office.
   - 'Job hours' – to record how long the office cleaning took to do.
4   Add a look-up facility to the 'Client' field with the names of ten clients.
5   Add a look-up facility to the 'Employee' field with the names of ten people you know.
6   Enter ten records into your table to allocate an employee to each client.
7   Print the table.
8   Enter ten records into your table to check the 'Job date' automatically shows the current date.
9   Print the table.

3 Use database software tools to run queries and produce reports

Case study: Steam train club database

You like to spend some of your weekends helping out at a steam train club where members bring along their model steam engines. Members of the public are encouraged to come along and enjoy free rides on the trains,

The Club Secretary has asked you to create a database for that can be used to record which trains are running each weekend and how long each journey will take.

Did you know?

A relational database with more than one table depends upon queries to join the tables together to make datasets that can then be used by reports and forms.

3.1 Create and run database queries

Queries can carry out many different actions on data in the tables of a database to arrange the data so it's ready to be used by a form or report.

A query can reduce the number of fields you see, bringing only those needed into the dataset.

You will need to create queries to:

- sort your table into different sequences
- filter the data in your table on both single and multiple criteria.

You will also save your queries into the database so they can be easily used again.

The output from a query can be seen onscreen via the **Datasheet view**, which looks similar to a table. Query output can also be used by a report or form to show the data.

Alphanumeric sort

You can use a query to sort the data in a table, either into alphabetical order (A-Z) or numerical order.

The 'How to sort data in a table' guide (pages 137–139), shows you how to sort data alphabetically. You can also sort data for other queries using similar methods.

How to sort data in a table

1. Open the **Address List** database.

2. On the **Create** toolbar click the **Query Design** option to start a new query. (See Figure 8.35.)

Figure 8.35: Use the Create toolbar to start a new query with the Query Design button

3. In the **Show Table** dialog box that appears, your table will be selected as your database only has one table. Click the **Add** button so the query can use this table (see Figure 8.36) then click the **Close** button.

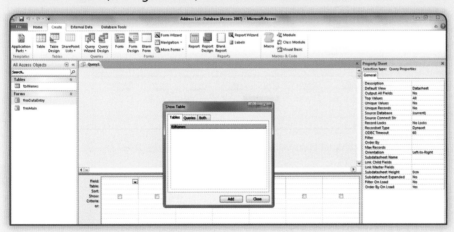

Figure 8.36: Press the Add button to use your table in the query

continued

4. Double-click each field where you want the query to show. In this example, double-click every field apart from the **ID** field. (See Figure 8.37)

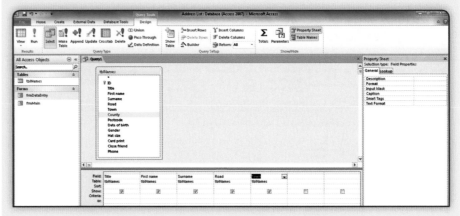

Figure 8.37: Double-click on the fields you want the query to show

5. Under the **Surname** field, click the row **Sort**.

6. In the combo box that appears, select **Ascending** , as shown in Figure 8.38. This will sort the table on the **Surname** field from A to Z.

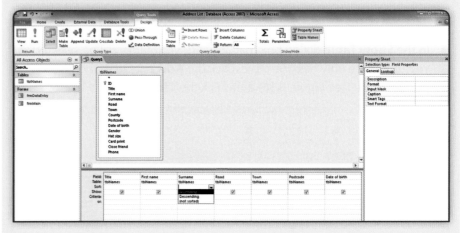

Figure 8.38: You can sort your data to appear in ascending order (A–Z)

continued

7. Click the **View** icon to switch to **Datasheet view**. (See Figure 8.39.) The table sorted on the Surname appears.

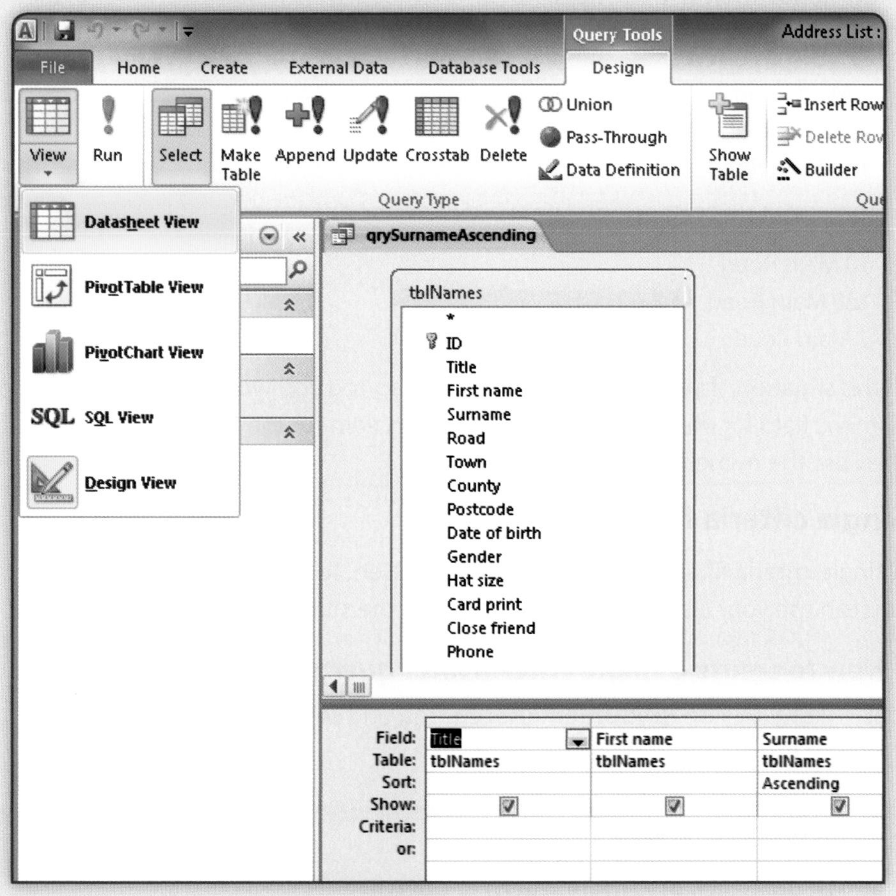

Figure 8.39: Use the View button to move between Datasheet and Design view

8. Click the **View** option to return to the **Design view**.

9. In the combo box select **Descending** to change the sort on the **Surname** field from Z to A.

10. Switch to **Datasheet view** to see the table sorted from Z to A.

11. Click the **View** option to return to the **Design view**. In the combo box select **(not sorted)** to remove the Surname sort.

12. Switch to **Datasheet view** to see the table is now not sorted

13. Set the ascending sort back to Surname. Switch to **Datasheet view** to check the sort works. Use the (not sorted) option to remove the Surname sort.

14. Press **Ctrl+F4** or click **x** on the top right corner of the query to close and save the query as **qrySurnameAscending**.

In similar ways, the query could sort on **Date of birth**, **Hat size** or any of the fields.

A sort can be alphanumeric or numeric, depending upon the data type in the field. You do not need to do anything to specify the type of sort as the query understands what is in the field.

An alphanumeric sort treats numbers as words, so for addresses of:

- 2 Main Road
- 10 Main Road
- 120 Main Road

a query would sort them into:

- 10 Main Road
- 120 Main Road
- 2 Main Road.

In this situation, if you wanted the addresses sorted you would need two fields: a numeric field for the house number and a text field for the road. The query could then use the numeric field to sort.

Single criteria filter

A single criteria filter reduces the records you see. To create a single criteria filter, you can use your alphanumeric sort query as the starting point of a new query.

How to create a single criteria filter query

1. Right click on **qrySurnameAscending** and select **Copy** .

2. Right click again and select **Paste** .

3. In the **Paste as** dialog box that appears, type **qrySingleSearch** then click the **OK** button.

4. Double-click **qrySingleSearch** to open it.

5. Click the **View** option to enter the **Design view** and select (**not sorted**) to remove the sort.

6. Type **M** into the **Criteria** row of the **Gender** field. Access® shows you several functions that can be used here which you do not want. Press the **Esc** key to remove the list of functions. **M** stays in the **Gender criteria** box.

7. Change to **Datasheet view** to check that only the male records are shown.

8. Return to **Design view** and set the sort on Surname. Switch to **Datasheet view** to see the effect with the records filtered on **M** and sorted by **Surname**.

9. Delete the **M** in the **Gender** criteria.

10. Close and save the query.

Queries allow as many filters and sorts as you want. Filter queries can also use the **:*** and **?** wildcards. For more information on this refer to the section *Using wildcards* on page 124).

Multiple criteria filter

You can now create a multiple criteria filter query. In this example, this will be a query to find all the males with names beginning with H.

This time you will use another technique for creating a new query based upon an existing query. This method uses **qrySingleSearch** as the starting point of the new query.

How to create a multiple criteria filter query

1. Select **qrySingleSearch**.
2. On the **File** toolbar click the **Save Object as** option.

Figure 8.40: You can save a query with a different name

3. In the **Save as** dialog box that appears, edit the name to **qryMultipleSearch**. Click the **OK** button.

4. Open **qryMultipleSearch** in **Design view**.

5. Type **M** into the **Criteria** row of the **Gender** field to edit the query into showing all the people whose surname begins with H and are male. (See Figure 8.41.)

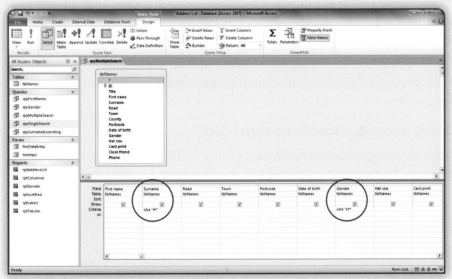

Figure 8.41: A query to show all the people whose names begin with H and are male

continued

6. Switch to the **Datasheet view** to check this works.

7. Delete the **Surname** criteria.

8. Add the criteria **>1/1/1966** to Date of birth field criteria to show everyone born after this date.

9. Switch to the **Datasheet** view to check this works.

10. Close your query, saving the changes.

The output from a query depends upon the data in the table so will quite likely be different when a query is re-run.

The output from a particular query can be kept by copying then pasting to another application such as Excel®.

3.2 Plan and produce database reports

Reports are the best way of getting the data from your table into a printed format. You can print a table or query when they are open, but the result from this is similar to an unformatted spreadsheet.

Database reports will give you much more control over how the data is presented and displayed. Large databases can have millions of records, and printing out all of this data would make it very difficult to sort and search through. A report can be produced from a table, but a query is a better option. A query can prepare a dataset from the table which is very useful if you just want particular fields.

Most IT professionals plan a database report before they actually produce it. Planning a report takes time, but is usually quicker in the long run as the report is more likely to be correct first-time round and contain all the needed information. Planning also involves looking at the best way to lay out the information on a printed page.

You will need to produce a drawing or sketch of the report to show what the report will look like and where the fields will be printed. The drawing could be created using a software application such as Microsoft® Paint® but it is generally better to use pencil and paper. Pencil is preferred to ink as you can rub out a small mistake.

Planning should include a list of the fields required in the report and any sorting that is required. This can be annotated on your sketch or shown in a separate document.

Using menus, wizards or shortcuts

There are several ways of creating a report in Access® using menus, wizards and shortcuts. These are all started by selecting the table or query the report will show, and then using the **Create** toolbar.

The options for starting a new report using the **Create** toolbar include:

- **Report** – which is a shortcut to producing an instant tabular report
- **Report design** – to create an empty report where you need to add your own fields
- **Labels** – to start a wizard to create a report for printed labels
- **Report wizard** – for creating other reports.

In this section, you will use the **Report wizard** or **Label** buttons to start your reports.

There are three types of report layout offered by the Access® Report Wizard:

- **Columnar** with each record grouped together
- **Tabular** showing records with a row for each
- **Justified** similar to columnar but with records filling the page width.

The Report Wizard will help you to create a report, but you will need to edit the report yourself to complete it.

You are now going to create an address list report which will show a list of the addresses in your **Address List** database in first name order with their telephone numbers. First, you will need to create a query.

How to create a query to sort a table

1. Click the **Query design** option.

2. In the **Show Table** dialog box that appears, your table will be selected as your database only has one table. Click the **Add** button so the query can use this table, then click the **Close** button.

3. Double click each of these fields to include them in the query:
   - First name
   - Surname
   - Road
   - Town
   - County
   - Postcode
   - Phone

   The query should be similar to Figure 8.42.

4. Click the **View** option then click **Datasheet view** to check the query shows all these fields in the order of first names from low to high.

5. Close the query and save it as **qryFirstNames**.

Figure 8.42: The Design View of qryFirstNames

How to create an address list report

1. Select **qryFirstNames**.

2. Click the **Report Wizard** option on the **Create** toolbar.

3. The wizard starts using this query as the data source.

4. On the first **Report Wizard** dialog box click the >> button to select all the fields. (See Figure 8.43.)

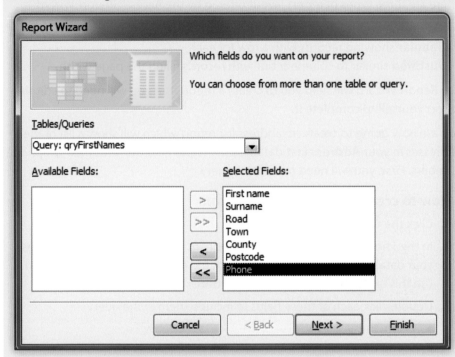

Figure 8.43: Select the fields you want to include in your report

5. Click **Next** to move to the second **Report Wizard** dialog box. This is for report subheadings, which are not needed.

6. Click **Next** to move to the third **Report Wizard** dialog box. This is to select a different sorting for your dataset.

continued

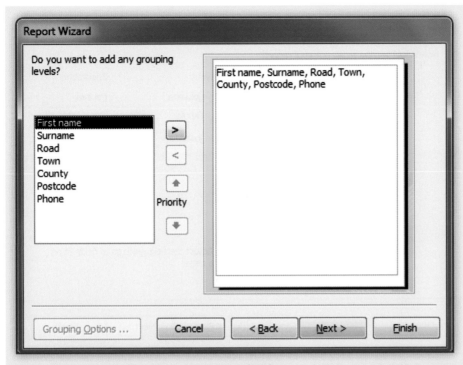

Figure 8.44: You can choose to add grouping levels

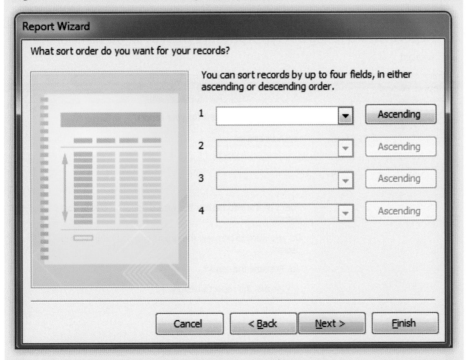

Figure 8.45: You can choose how to sort your records

7. Click **Next** to move to the fourth **Report Wizard** dialog box. On the fourth **Report Wizard** dialog box select the **Tabular** with **Landscape orientation** layout for your report.

continued

145

Figure 8.46: Select the Tabular with landscape orientation options

8. Click **Next** to move to the fifth **Report Wizard** dialog box. On the fifth **Report Wizard** dialog box type **rptAddressList** as for the name of the report.

Figure 8.47: Give your report a title

continued

9. Click the **Finish** button to complete the report and show a preview of your report.

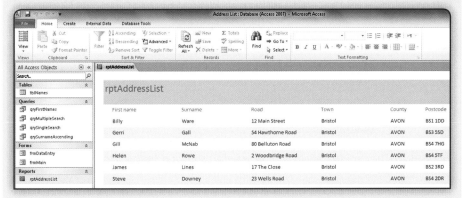

Figure 8.48: The print preview screen shows how your report will look when printed

Check your preview carefully to see if there any problems by comparing it to your planning sketch. You might need the report header re-typed and fields adjusted so the phone number is shown properly.

If you need to edit the address list report, refer to the 'How to edit the address list report' guide below.

How to edit the address list report

1. Select **rptAddressList**.

2. Right click to select **Design View** where you can edit the report to correct these problems.

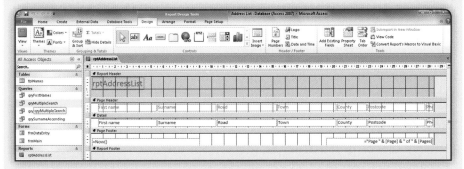

Figure 8.49: The Design View of your new report

3. Click twice in the text label in the report header to edit **rptAddressList** into **Address list**.

4. Change the sizes of the **Postcode** label in the Page header and the **Postcode** field in the Detail to make them smaller.

5. Change the sizes of the **Phone** label in the Page header and the **Phone** field in the Detail to make them larger so all the digits of the phone numbers can be seen in the report.

6. The **Design View** should now be similar to Figure 8.50.

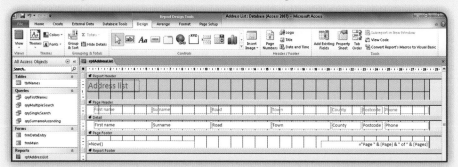

Figure 8.50: The Design View of your new report showing changes to the Postcode and Phone fields

7. Click the **View** option to show **Print Preview** to check your changes worked as expected.

8. Click the **Close Print Preview** button to exit print preview.

9. Close and save your report changes.

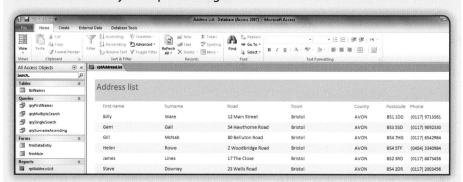

Figure 8.51: Print preview of your report with the corrections

You will now be able to produce a report by 'Gender', using grouping to include subheadings for males and females in your report.

How to produce the query for a report by gender

1. Right click on **qryFirstNames**, choose copy then paste a copy back named **qryGender**.

2. Right click **qryGender** to open into **Design View**.

3. Double click on 'Gender' to add this to the fields.

continued

148

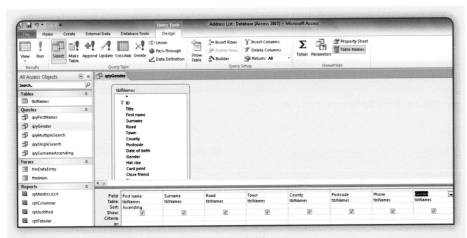

Figure 8.52: qryGender showing the Gender field

4. Click on the **View** option to enter **Datasheet View** to confirm the gender shows.

5. Close the query and save changes.

How to produce a report by gender

1. You have already followed the 'How to produce a the query for a report by gender' step-by-step to produce **qryGender**.

2. Select **qryGender** then click the **Report Wizard** in the **Create** toolbar.

3. Click **Next** to move to the second **Report Wizard** dialog box.

4. On the second **Report Wizard** dialog box select the **Gender field** for grouping the records by gender.

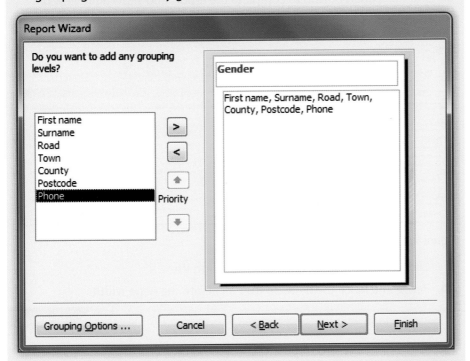

Figure 8.53: qryGender showing the Gender field for grouping the records by gender

continued

5. Click **Next** to move to the third and fourth **Report Wizard** dialog boxes.

6. On the fourth **Report Wizard** dialog box select **Stepped** for the layout.

Figure 8.54: Select the Stepped layout option

7. Click the **Next** button on each **Report Wizard** dialog box until you reach the last one where you name the report **rptGender**.

8. Click the **Finish** button to complete the report and show a preview of your report.

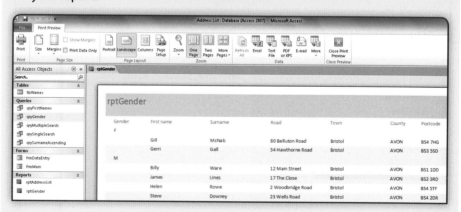

Figure 8.55: A preview of your report

9. Click the **View** option to enter the **Design View**.

10. Resize and place the fields so they all fit into the page width.

continued

11. The report shows M as the subheading for the males and F as the subheading for females. This would be a lot better with the words as shown in the next steps. Close your report and save the changes.

12. Open **tblNames** then select the **Gender** field.

13. Click the **Replace** option in the **Home** toolbar to bring up the **Find and Replace** dialog box.

14. In the **Find and Replace** dialog box search for M and replace with Male.

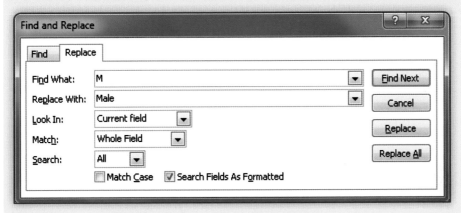

Figure 8.56: Use Find and Replace to change data in a field

15. Click the **Replace All** button to change every M record to Male.

16. Repeat with steps 13-15, changing F to Female.

17. Save and close the table.

18. Preview **rptGender**, your completed report.

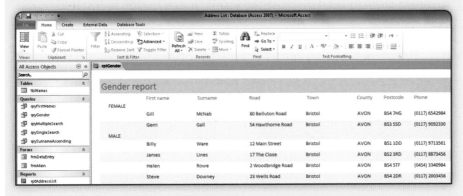

Figure 8.57: Preview your completed report

How to adjust page and section layout to add text and an image to a report

1. Return to the **Design View** of **rptGender**.

2. Use the mouse to drag down the **Gender** header bar to make the **Page Header** band taller. This will give some room for an image to be placed in this band.

3. Select the field names (First name, Surname, etc.) in the **Page Header** band to drag them down to the bottom of this band.

Drag the Gender header band down to make the Page Header band larger

Use the Insert Image button then browse for an image

Drag the field names down to just above the Gender Header band

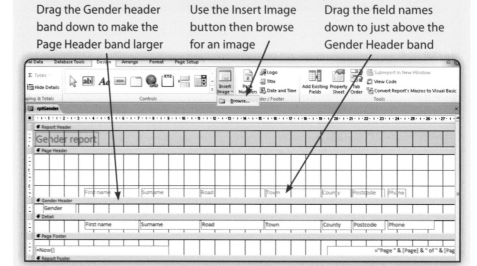

Figure 8.58: The Page Header band can be made deeper to allow room for an image

4. Select an image and then use the **Insert Image** button to insert it.

Use the Label tool to add words

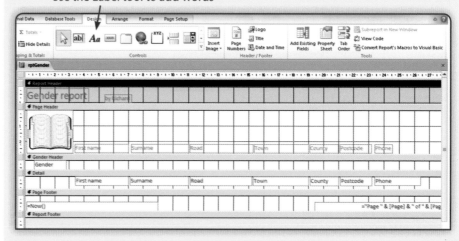

Figure 8.59: The Label tool can be used to add words to a report

5. Use the **Label** option to add your name to the **Report Header** band.

6. Return to the preview to see the effects of your editing.

You can produce an address labels report which will be able to print out sticky address labels using the **qrySurnameAscending** query you made earlier.

How to produce an address labels report

1. Select **qrySurnameAscending** then click the **Labels Wizard** icon in the **Create** toolbar. The wizard will start with this query as the data source.

2. On the first **Label Wizard** dialog box accept the default for the type of labels that the report will use (unless you have some label paper, needing you to change this dialog box).

3. Click **Next** to move to the second **Label Wizard** dialog box.

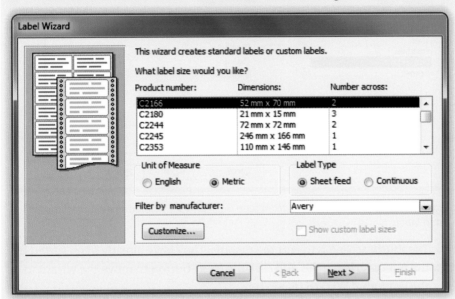

Figure 8.60: *This Label Wizard screen is used to select the type of sticky label paper*

4. The second screen is to select the font and font size. The defaults are fine here, so click **Next** to move to the third **Label Wizard** dialog box.

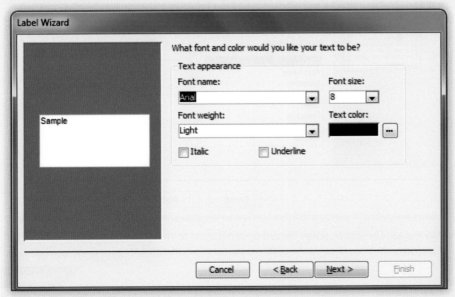

Figure 8.61: *The second Label Wizard screen is used to select the font and font size*

continued

5. The third **Label Wizard** dialog box is to select fields and where they are to be placed on labels. Use the > button to place each field onto the label.

6. Use the **Enter** key to start each new line, arranging your label.

7. Click **Next** to move to the fourth **Label Wizard** dialog box.

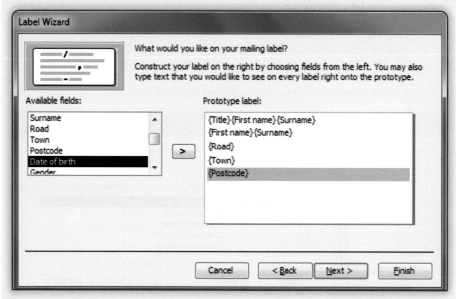

Figure 8.62: The third Label Wizard screen is used to set where the fields are used in each label

8. The fourth screen is to sort the records. They have already been sorted by the query, so leave this and click the **Next** button to move the wizard to the last **Label Wizard** dialog box.

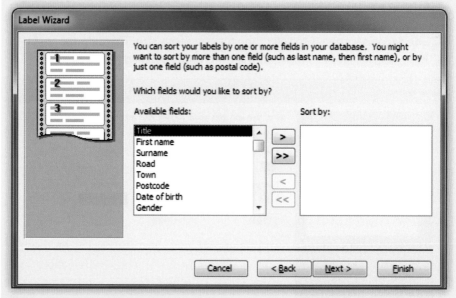

Figure 8.63: The fourth Label Wizard screen is used to sort the records into a different sequence

continued

9. On the last **Label Wizard** dialog box name your report **rptLabels**.

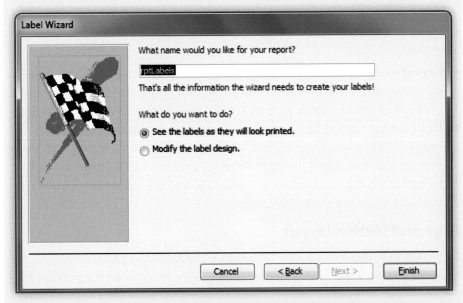

Figure 8.64: The last Label Wizard screen is used to name the report

10. Click the **Finish** button to complete the wizard and show the preview.

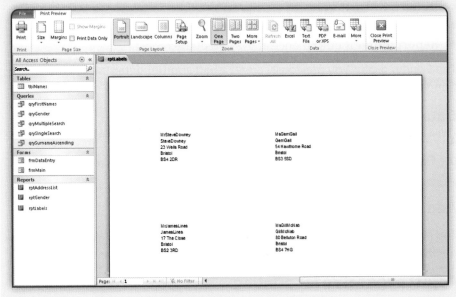

Figure 8.65: This label report preview should look like this

Selected fields and records

To use selected fields in a report, you can create a query. The **Report Wizard** can then create a report from the query. You can select records in a table by dragging the **Record** buttons at the left of the table using the mouse.

There is an option in the **Print** dialog box where you can choose to only print records currently selected in a table.

3.3 Formatting database reports

To format a database report you need to be in the **Layout** or **Design** view. Here you can move fields around, change their size and add or edit any fixed text in the report.

- **Layout view** is good for final formatting, such as font size, as you can see some sample data in the report you are working on. Data field properties are best edited in this view as you can instantly see the effects of your changes.
- **Design view** is good for more major changes such as adding text or an image to the report. The page and section layout is clearly shown in this view, making it easy to adjust the page setup for printing such as page headers, footers at the top and bottom of every page and the report header which is printed once at the start of the report.

Page and section layout

Each page in a report has the sections layout controlled by bands across the report in **Design View** to show where the headers, footers and data details will be output by the report:

- **Report header** is output once at the beginning of the report
- **Page header** is output at the top of every page
- **Detail** is where the records are shown
- **Page footer** is at the bottom of each page
- **Report footer** is output once at the end of the report

The Gender report you previously created had another detail band for the Gender header section.

Data fields

Any data field in a report can be easily formatted by selecting it then using the **Format** toolbar in much the same way as for the other Microsoft® Office® software applications.

Add text or images

You can add text and images to a report as you would for a form using a **label** or the **Insert image** icon. See page 152 for more information on inserting images.

Adjust page setup for printing

There are icons in the **Page setup** toolbar where you can adjust how the report will print. These give you control over the page size, orientation, numbering and margins.

Headers are in the **Page header** band of the report and footers in the **Page footer** band.

Did you know?

The report header is used to give a name and description to the report as well as other details, such as the print date and time, so the report can easily be identified when it is printed from the first page.

3.4 Check reports meet needs

You will need to check the reports you write for:

- completeness
- accuracy
- security
- sorting
- formatting
- layout.

Completeness and accuracy

It is important to make sure that everything that is required is included in the report. You should always check reports against the original requirements.

As a report uses the data in the table or query behind it, this should be accurate. Any text used to label a field in the report must accurately describe the data shown there.

Security

If the database requires a password to enter it, you will need to check that it works. It is possible to password protect objects such as reports inside a database, but that involves writing program code and is beyond the scope of this unit.

Sorting

The sorting or sequence of a report needs to be checked against the original requirements. Sorting can be set in the query or the report. If there is a problem with the sorting you will need to check whether the report is carrying out a different sort to the query.

Formatting and layout

The fields in the report should be formatted to show data in the most easily understood way, such as for dates, telephone numbers and the number of decimal places set for numerical data.

The layout needs to ensure all data in the report is easy to read. Fields should not overlap. Similar information should be kept together and well spaced from other information.

Activity: Creating a database for a local steam train club

You have been asked to create a database for a steam train club to record which trains are running each weekend and how long each journey will take.

The database needs to include following information:

- today's date
- name (or number) of the steam train engine
- time it starts running on the track
- time it finishes running on the track.

Carry out these tasks for the club.

1. Create a new database named 'Steam train club'.
2. Create a new table named 'Track times'.
3. Create fields to meet the needs of the club with appropriate field names, data types and lookups.
4. Add 20 records to your table.
5. Create a query to find out how long each engine has been on the track.
6. Create a query to sequence the data, grouping each engine together and then showing date order of days the engine was out on the track.
7. Create a query to sequence the data by days, most recent first then showing time order of the engines out on the track.

Check your understanding

1 Identify four uses for a query.
2 Explain how tables, queries, forms and reports can be used by a database.
3 Describe two formatting actions that could be applied to a report.

ASSESSMENT ACTIVITY

You run a small part-time business which specialises in buying and selling musical instruments, amplification and effects. You mainly buy items from websites like eBay™ and you tend to buy cheapish items which are geographically close enough to your house so that you can collect them.

All the items you buy, you then sell on for a small profit. You then to advertise these items on websites including Gumtree, Craigslist and eBay™.

You have decided to set up a database to keep track of your purchases and sales. You would like to be able to create and print out reports to track how well or badly items have sold.

The database requires two forms: one to navigate around the database; the other for data entry.

The database will have reports to:

- print all the current stock
- print all the sold stock in the order of the fastest sales to the slowest
- print all the sold stock in the order of the quickest sales to the slowest
- print all the sold stock in the order of how much profit was made
- print all the sold stock in alphabetical order
- print all the sold and unsold stock in the order of the purchase dates
- print all the sold and unsold stock in alphabetical order
- print of all the sold stock grouped by how they were sold.

The table will need to include fields to store:
- the name or short description of the item
- the purchase date
- the sold date
- the purchase price
- the sale price
- the website you purchased the item from
- the website you sold the item on.
-

(Turn to page 160 to complete this Assessment activity.)

Tasks

1 Produce a design for the database including: the types of information to be stored; the data entry form and any other forms you will create; the routine queries; how the data will be structured into fields in a single table database; any indexes and key fields you plan to use to organise the data.

2 Add the field characteristics for the fields you will use in your table.

3 Create the table you have designed.

4 Explain what you can do with your table design to help keep the data accurate.

5 Record in your documentation any problems you meet and solve when creating the data entry checks for your fields and testing them.

6 Implement the data integrity checks you previously described and check they work as expected.

7 Create the form you planned to allow data entry into your table.

8 Make sure your forms meet your planning guidelines and look professional.

9 Plan and create some test data for your database. This should be around 20 records providing a good variety of data which can be used to check that the database can produce the reports identified in the scenario.

10 Enter your test data from Step 9 and document how you sorted any data entry errors you found when you typed this data into the table.

11 Use your planning from Step 1 to implement and run the database queries needed to provide the datasets for your planned reports.

12 Use your Step 1 planning to create and run the database reports using the queries to provide the datasets to meet the needs of the scenario.

13 Print your reports to see how they look on paper. Modify the designs of the reports to make them look more professional.

14 Print the reports again and check them against the Assessment activity scenario (page 159) and your planning. Annotate the printouts to identify where they have met the requirements. Make any corrections required to meet the original needs.

Imaging software

This unit is about creating and editing digital images. Digital images are all around us on websites, posters, magazines, books and even T-shirts. Digital images can either be based on a digital photograph which is edited in some way to make it suitable for its intended purpose, or they are drawn on the computer. Some images can be a combination of both of these.

In this unit you will learn how to obtain images from different sources, combine and edit them. You will also look at how to choose suitable file formats for different applications and to be aware of copyright issues.

Learning outcomes

After completing this unit you should be able to achieve the following learning outcomes.

» **LO1** Obtain, insert and combine information for images

» **LO2** Use imaging software tools to create, manipulate and edit images

1 Obtain, insert and combine information for images

1.1 Types of images

Before you create (design) or obtain an image, the first thing to consider is the type of image you need. This will vary depending on its purpose. The image may be used on its own, but it is more likely to be part of something else, like a poster, web page or presentation. You will need to consider these questions.

- Who is the intended audience for the image? For example, are you advertising a product? Are you targeting a certain age group or a particular group of people? You will need to create or select an image that will appeal to the audience you have in mind.
- What is the purpose of the image? It may be just to add interest to the document it is to be included in, or it may need to put across important information such as a diagram in an instruction leaflet.
- What **medium** will be used to present the image or the document it is included in? For example, the image might be printed on a colour or black and white printer, it might be included on a web page so will be viewed on a computer screen, or it could be part of a presentation which will be shown on a screen.

The two main images that you will use are:

- **Bitmap images** – these usually come from a digital camera or a scanner and are made up of millions of dots, known as pixels. Bitmaps are used for realistic images like photos (see Figure 9.1).
- **Vector images** – these are drawn on a computer and are made up of objects such as circles, lines and boxes rather than pixels. Vector images are used for diagrams, cartoons and other non-lifelike images (see Figure 9.2).

Table 9.1 shows the differences between bitmap and vector images. Some images combine bitmap and vector images. For example, if you add some text to a digital photo, the text will normally be added as a vector image to the bitmap photo.

Key terms

Medium – in this context the medium is how the image will be presented. Paper, a computer monitor and a HD (High Definition) projector are all examples of mediums through which the image might be viewed.

Bitmap image – made up of dots know as pixels. Millions of different colour pixels make a lifelike image.

Vector image – made up of objects such as circles and rectangles. Used for diagrams, cartoons and non-lifelike images.

Figure 9.1: A bitmap image

Figure 9.2: A vector image

Characteristic	Bitmap	Vector
Made up of	Pixels	Drawing objects
Used for	Photos – realistic images	Diagrams, cartoons
File size	Larger	Smaller
Scaling	If enlarged too much the individual pixels can be seen and the image loses quality	Can be enlarged without loss of quality

Table 9.1: The differences between bitmap and vector images

Bitmap and vector images are used for different purposes and each type has its own advantages. In this unit, we will be using Adobe® Photoshop®, the best known image editing software. Photoshop® is mainly a bitmap editing application, but it can also create and edit vector images.

Case study: The Green Veterinary Centre (1)

The Green Veterinary Centre is a local veterinary surgery. They look after all sorts of different pets, from hamsters to horses. You work in the office there as an administrator, dealing with a range of tasks on the surgery computer system. Quite a lot of your work involves working with images to create posters and fact sheets for the surgery's customers.

1.2 Obtaining images

There are many different ways of obtaining images.

Photos from a digital camera

Photos taken with a digital camera can be uploaded to a computer and loaded into imaging software. Images input from a digital camera will be bitmap images.

Scanned images

Existing artwork or other documents, such as photos or hand-drawn pictures or paintings, can be input to the computer using a scanner. Images input from a scanner will be bitmap images.

Graphic elements

Imaging software can be used to create drawings directly on the computer, using the mouse or a **graphics tablet**. They can be either vector or bitmap images.

Clip art

Clip art refers to a bank of images which already exist. They are usually vector images provided by a number of sources. The Microsoft® Office® suite comes with an extensive library of ClipArt images and many websites provide clip art. Some clip art, such as the images supplied by the Microsoft® library, is royalty free and you can use it freely in your projects.

> **Key term**
>
> **Graphics tablet** – also known as a digitising tablet. This is an input device which allows you to draw images just as you would using a pen and paper. You can also trace over an existing piece of artwork by taping it to the top of the tablet.

1.3 Preparing images

Once you have obtained or created an image, you need to make it suitable for its intended use. This includes:

- changing the image's size to fit the document
- cropping any parts of the image you do not want
- positioning the image within the document.

Size

An image's size can be measured in three different ways.

1. Its actual size is its width and height in centimetres. These are the image's dimensions. This is sometimes called the **canvas size**.

2. The file size of the image is measured in **kilobytes** (KB) or **megabytes** (MB).

3. The **pixel dimensions** or **resolution** of the image is the number of pixels in the image, horizontally (width) and vertically (height). Resolution is closely linked to file size. The higher the resolution of an image, the larger the size of the file. Also, the higher the number of pixels per square inch or centimetre – its pixel density – the better quality the image is likely to be.

How to adjust the size of an image

1. You can see the **canvas size**, **pixel dimensions** and resolution of an image in Photoshop® by clicking on the **Image** menu and choosing **Image Size**.

2. This will display the **Image Size** dialog box. (See Figure 9.3.)

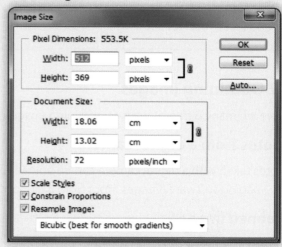

Figure 9.3: The Image Size dialog box

3. You can adjust the **canvas size**, **pixel dimensions** and resolution from this dialog box. If you change the **pixel dimensions** the **canvas size** will automatically change, and vice versa.

When an image is created on a digital camera or scanner, the resolution is fixed. You will not be able to improve the quality using Photoshop® even if you increase the resolution of the image.

When resizing an image you will normally want to keep it in proportion. The height and width of an image (its aspect ratio) are linked – if you increase the size of the height, the width will increase, or if you reduce the size of the height, the width will get smaller. Photoshop® locks the width and height of your image so if you change one, the other will change in proportion. In the **Image Size** dialog box, the link next to **Canvas Size** and **Pixel Dimensions** shows that they are linked and will change in proportion (see Figure 9.3). If you uncheck the **Constrain Proportions** check box, the link will disappear and you can change the width or height individually, but this will affect the image's **aspect ratio**.

For more information on canvas size, pixel dimensions and resolution, *see section 2.1 on page 172.*

Cropping

This involves removing parts of the image which are not required. Unwanted detail may need to be removed from images such as photos, so that the audience only sees the important parts of the image.

How to crop an image using the Crop tool

1. Click the **Crop tool** in the toolbar on the left side of the screen.
2. Then drag out a marquee over the area of the image you want to keep, as shown in Figure 9.4.

The 'Crop' tool   The 'Crop' box

Figure 9.4: The Crop box

continued

3. Right click the image and choose **Crop**. Only the parts of the image that were inside the crop marquee will be kept.

4. If you decide you have made a mistake and want to go back to the original image, choose **Edit** from the menu. Then choose **Undo crop**.

Figure 9.5: Example of a cropped image

How to crop an image using Copy and Paste

1. An alternative to using the **Crop tool** is to use **Copy** and **Paste**. A benefit of this is that the original image is retained, rather than lost as it is with **Crop**.

2. To use this method, select the rectangular marquee tool and drag it over the area of the image you want to keep. Then, from the **Edit** menu, choose **Copy**.

3. Now go to the **File** menu and choose **New**. Click **OK** on the **New** dialog box and you will get an empty image, the size of the image you copied.

4. Go to the **Edit** menu and choose **Paste**, and the part of the image you copied from the original will appear in the new image.

Position

You can also make an image larger than the section of the original image that you cropped or copied. You might need to do this if you're creating a montage of several different images. When you create a new file, select a size for the canvas that is larger than the image you've copied. (See the 'How to crop an image using Copy and Paste' guide.) When you paste the copied image into the new file, you can position the image within the canvas by selecting the **Move** tool in the toolbar (top one) and dragging the image to the desired position.

1.4 Context in which images will be used

Where the image is to appear (e.g. on a web page or in a slide presentation) will affect how you create and prepare it. *See section 2.1 on page 172* for more information.

Onscreen display

Images such as those included on a web page will only be displayed on a computer screen and are often quite small.

Computer monitors have a limited resolution, so it is not necessary to use very high resolution images. Most computer monitors are limited to about 100 pixels per inch (40 pixels per cm) or less, so it is important to consider the size and resolution of images. A large image file will take time to download and make the web page slow to load.

Hard copy printout

When preparing an image that is to be printed, you need to consider:

- whether it is to be printed in colour or black and white
- the size that the image will be printed at.

When using bitmap images, the larger the size of the image in the final document, the higher the resolution needs to be. This is important on posters (A3 size or larger) where the image may be very large.

If you resize a bitmap image larger than its original canvas size, the number of pixels remains the same. This means that the number of pixels per centimetre will reduce and the individual pixels may become visible. This effect is known as pixelation (see Figure 9.6).

Figure 9.6: The increase in size has reduced the quality of the image

Digital files

Some images, such as those included in a PowerPoint® slide shows may be displayed using a projector at quite a large size (a metre or more wide). Like computer monitors, projectors have a limited resolution, so it is not necessary to use a very high resolution image. Unlike web pages, a PowerPoint® slide show is not affected by download speed or file size, so you will not need to reduce the resolution or the size of the file.

1.5 Organise and combine information

So far, you have looked at how to prepare a single image for use in a document. Now you will look at combining different types of information, such as vector and bitmap images and text.

To create a document which consists of combined text, images and other elements, you first need to create a canvas to work with.

How to create a new canvas

1. In Photoshop® go to the **File** menu, and choose **New**.
2. This will display the **New** dialog box.
3. For an A4-size canvas choose **International Paper** from the **Preset** drop-down box.
4. Click **OK** to create the canvas.

Insert, size and position

Having created a new canvas, you can insert, size and position images within it. The simplest way to insert images is to copy and paste them from another Photoshop® window. Once you paste them on the canvas you have created, then you can position and size them.

How to position and size images

1. Once you have pasted your image on to the canvas, select the **Move** tool in the toolbar and you will see a set of handles appear around the image.
2. You can position the image by pointing inside the image (not on the handles) and dragging the image to the desired location.
3. To size the image, drag on the handles at the corners of the image.

The manager of The Green Veterinary Centre has asked you to create the front page image for a fact sheet about caring for a puppy, which will be printed at A5 size (half A4), portrait orientation.

Find or create a suitable image for the fact sheet, and edit it so that it is suitable for the front page. Add suitable text and clip art to complete the image.

1.6 Copyright constraints

If you plan to use any images you did not create yourself, you will need to check the copyright situation. You may need to obtain the copyright holder's permission to use them and perhaps pay a royalty fee. As previously mentioned, some clip art (such as images from the Microsoft® library) can be used freely in your projects.

Remember, you cannot copy and paste images from websites. This is regarded as **plagiarism** and breaks copyright rules. Unless an image specifically says it is copyright free, then you should assume you cannot use it without permission.

Copyright is also covered in *Unit 1 Improving productivity using IT* (*page 7*).

1.7 File formats for saving images

Method of compression

Some file formats such as JPEG and GIF use techniques to compress (make smaller) the size of the file. JPEG, for example, reduces the amount of data in an image file by discarding those aspects of the image that the human eye is not likely to notice. This is known as **lossy compression** because part of the original data is discarded (lost) during the compression process. **Non-lossy** or **loss-less compression techniques** do not discard any of the original data. If you compress a Windows® folder, loss-less compression is used.

Images can be supplied, used and saved in a wide variety of formats. Table 9.2 lists the different formats and illustrates how a particular format can be identified via its file extension.

Format	Type	Commonly used for	Compressed?	File extension	Comments
JPEG: (Joint Photographic Experts' Group)	Bitmap	Photos	Yes – lossy	.JPG	Widely used and supported for photographic images
GIF: (Graphics Interchange Format)	Bitmap	Non-photographic images	Yes – loss-less	.GIF	Best suited to non-photographic images (e.g. cartoons or other drawings with areas of the same colour rather than the continuous variations in colour that you typically get in a photograph)
PNG: (Portable Network Graphics)	Bitmap	Non-photographic images	Yes – loss-less	.PNG	Best suited to non-photographic images; with photographic images it creates much larger file sizes than JPEG due to loss-less compression
SVG: (Scalable Vector Graphics)	Vector	Combinations of text and vector graphics	No	.SVG	–
PSD: (Photoshop document)	Bitmap	Adobe® Photoshop® files	No	.PSD	Proprietary format used by Photoshop®
BMP: (Bitmap)	Bitmap	Simple bitmap images	No	.BMP	Widely supported but creates large files as it is uncompressed
WMF: (Windows® Meta-File)	Bitmap and vector	Images which contain a combination of vector and bitmap elements	No	.WMF	Microsoft® developed graphics format for Windows®
EPS: (Encapsulated PostScript)	Vector	Graphics to be printed on a PostScript printer	No	.eps	Largely replaced by the PDF format
PDF: (Portable Document Format)	Vector and bitmap	Documents which can contain both text and images	No	.pdf	Very widely used format developed by Adobe® for storing documents

Table 9.2: Key information about different image formats

1.8 Store and retrieve files effectively

Storing and retrieving image files is much the same as it is in other applications. You should apply the same good practice with regard to choosing meaningful file names and keeping back-up copies.

Files

When you create a new Photoshop® file, you need to make some choices in the **New** dialog box. As mentioned earlier, you need to select the canvas size and resolution. These issues are covered in more detail in section 1.3, page 164.

When you save a Photoshop® file, you need to select the format for the file. The default format is the Photoshop® proprietary format, PSD. This is a good choice if you are planning to carry on editing the file in Photoshop®. However, if you want to use the image in other applications (e.g. insert it in a Word® document or use it within a web page), then a widely supported non-proprietary format, such as JPEG or PNG, would be a better choice.

File size

File size is an important issue in image creation and editing, which is covered in detail in the following section. When you create a new file, Photoshop® shows you the size of the image in the **New** dialog box on the right.

Version control

Creating complex images can be an involved process and it may take many attempts to achieve a result that you are happy with. You may also want to try several different ideas and techniques before arriving at the end result. It is therefore often wise to keep several different versions of the image you are working on. You can do this by using **Save As** when you save the file rather than **Save** (which will save the image, overwriting the original). Save As gives you an opportunity to say what file name you want to use to save the file, thereby allowing you to create a copy of the image. You can keep track of different versions of your work by adding version numbers to the file name. So, for example, if you create a new version of a file, you might call it 'PuppyFactSheet V2'.

Import data

Photoshop® can import a wide range of image files in different formats. Supported import formats are listed on the **Open** dialog box under the **Files of Type** drop-down box.

Folders

It is wise to keep image files in a separate folder from other files. Creating a folder can be done using the Windows® documents display or the **Create New Folder** icon at the top of the **Save** dialog box. Remember to give your image folder a meaningful name.

Check your understanding

1 Which type of graphic image can be scaled up (enlarged) without loss of quality, bitmap or vector?
2 What is the difference between lossy and loss-less compression?
3 Explain the term 'resolution'.
4 Give an example of what you might use a scanner for.

2 Use imaging software tools to create, manipulate and edit images

Developing the skills to create and edit images is key for this unit. You will need to practise to become proficient. There are also technical factors which affect images, and you need to be aware of these.

Case study: The Green Veterinary Centre (2)

You work as an administrator for The Green Veterinary Centre.

The Centre is keen to improve its presence in the local community and is planning a new marketing campaign, involving both print and online media. You have been asked to handle the campaign and take charge of choosing images and making them fit for purpose for both mediums.

2.1 Technical factors affecting images

There are a number of quite complex technical factors that affect graphic images. You need to understand these factors because they have an impact on how you create, edit and use images.

Page or canvas size

When selecting images, you need to consider:

- the size the image will be used at
- how it will be used, especially if it is to appear on a website.

Earlier in the unit, you saw that the pixel dimensions of a bitmap image are set when the image is created by a digital camera or scanner. Dimensions are measured in terms of the number of horizontal and vertical pixels in the image.

Did you know?

The resolution of modern digital cameras is usually quoted in mega pixels or MP, such as 5 MP. A mega pixel is equal to 1 million pixels. A camera with an image sensor with 2048 x 1536 elements would be described as a 3.1 MP camera, since 2048 x 1536 = 3,145,728.

Let's look at an example. Suppose you take a digital photo with a 6 mega pixel camera. Each image the camera takes will be made up of around 3,000 pixels horizontally and 2,000 vertically. Each image will have a file size of about 3 MB and a physical size of about 25 cm x 17 cm.

It would not be a good idea to use an image of this file size on a website. Such a large file would take a long time to download. The web page containing the image would appear slow to load. Before using a large image in a web page, you need to change its pixel dimensions using Photoshop®. This will reduce the file size of the image and its canvas size, but its resolution and quality will stay the same.

Let's look at a second example. Suppose you need a large image which is around 20 cm high and 15 cm wide for a poster. The image from a 6 mega pixel digital camera would be fine for this, but you want to use a low resolution image taken on a mobile phone and emailed to you by a friend. The email software in the mobile phone has reduced the size of the file to make it quicker to send. The file size is only 42 KB, the canvas size of the image is 8 cm x 11 cm and the resolution is 72 pixels per inch (see Figure 9.7) If you insert this image into a word-processing program to create the poster and **scale** it up to the required size, it becomes pixelated and loses quality. To use an image at this size, you need to start off with a larger and/or higher resolution image in the first place.

Key term

Scale – scaling an image means increasing or decreasing its size.

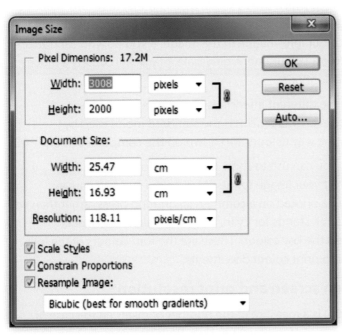

Figure 9.7: Locating the image size

Colour mode

Another technical factor that affects images is **colour mode** or colour depth.

A bitmap image is made up of pixels. The colour mode of an image defines how many bits are used to make up each pixel. This then defines how many different colours each pixel can represent. If each pixel is only represented by a single bit (which can only be 1 or 0) an image can only have pixels of pure black or pure white.

Colour images are made up of red, green and blue. The three colours are often called **colour channels**. Most digital cameras use 8 bits for each channel – 8 bits can represent 256 different values. For each colour channel there are 256 different levels of **intensity** available to make up different colours. The three channels provide a total of over 16 million different colours. 8 bits per channel is sometimes called 24 bit colour (8 x 3 = 24) or true colour. Higher quality cameras sometimes use 36 bit colour (12 bits per pixel).

You can see the colour mode an image uses in Photoshop® by choosing the **Mode** option under the **Image** menu. The larger the number of bits per channel, the larger the size of file the image will occupy. You can reduce the number of bits per channel by selecting a lower quality mode, but once you do this you cannot return to the higher quality colour mode, so you should take a backup of the original image before you do this. You can also convert the image to greyscale (black and white), which uses a single 8 bit channel to record shades of grey, by selecting the **Greyscale** option on the Mode menu. Photoshop® will ask if you want to discard colour information in the image. If you do, you cannot later change the image back to a colour one. A greyscale image will occupy a much smaller file size than a colour one.

RGB colour mode uses the different intensities of red, green and blue to represent the colours in an image. This is the standard mode used by Photoshop® and is also the way colours are shown on the computer screen.

There are other modes you can use to show the colours in an image. For example, you can convert your image to the CMYK colour mode if you are producing an image to be printed on a commercial printing press rather than an inkjet or laser printer. CMYK stands for Cyan, Magenta, Yellow and Black (K because Black is called the key colour). These are the four colours of the inks used in a printing press to print colour documents.

Difference between screen and print resolution

Resolution (see page 106) is a measure of the number of pixels (in the case of monitors) or dots (in the case of printers) per inch. Printers generally have the ability to reproduce images at a higher resolution than monitors. Most printers can print 300 dots per inch and photo quality ink jet printers often have the ability to print up to 4,800 dots per inch. The resolution, in pixels per inch (PPI), of a computer monitor depends on the size of the monitor and the number of horizontal and vertical pixels. So a 15" monitor with 1,024 pixels horizontally and 768 vertically will have a PPI of 85.

Resolution (see page 106)

Key term

Intensity – in this context intensity refers to the brightness of the individual coloured pixels. By varying the brightness of the red, green and blue pixels, a range of different colours can be reproduced.

2.2 Create images

You can create images by drawing them on the computer using graphics editing software. This section covers the basic skills of computer drawing.

Draw basic shapes and adjust properties

You can create an image using Photoshop's® drawing tools. These allow you to create shapes and freehand drawings.

> #### How to create drawings
>
> 1. Create an empty file of suitable dimensions (go to **File**, choose **New** and then select the size you want), although you could also add a drawing to an existing file.
>
> 2. Before you draw a shape, choose the colour it will be filled with. Click the **Set Foreground colour** tool on the left and the **Color Picker** will appear (see Figure 9.8).
>
> The 'Color Picker' tool
>
>
>
> *Figure 9.8: The Color Picker*
>
> 3. Use the slide in the middle to select the general colour and then click in the panel on the left to choose the exact colour you require.
>
> 4. Then select the **Shape** tool on the left of the window. The **Shape** tool options bar will then appear across the top and you can choose the type of shape, colour and other settings.

continued

175

5. Drawing shapes is best done using vector graphics rather than bitmap, as vector shapes are easier to edit after you have drawn them. So make sure you have the **Shape Layers** option selected in the **Shape** tool options bar. Photoshop® adds vector shapes to your image on a different layer than bitmaps. Think of layers like transparent sheets on top of each other.

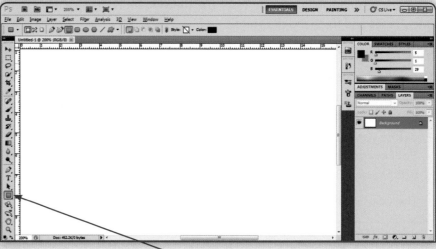

Figure 9.9: The Shape tool   The 'Shape' tool

6. Now you can drag out a rectangle shape with your mouse. You can change the colour of the rectangle after you have drawn it by clicking the **Color box** in the **Shape** options bar.

7. You can add another vector shape to your image, either to the same layer or a new one (although if you add the shapes to the same layer you cannot edit them separately).

8. To add another shape to the same layer as the existing one, click the **Add to shape area** icon, or to add each shape to a different layer click the **Create new shape layer** icon.

9. To see the **layers** you have created, click the **Layers** button in the option panel on the right and the **Layers** window will pop out (see Figure 9.10).

The 'Layers' tool   The 'Layers' window

Figure 9.10: The Layers tool and Layers window

continued

10. To move, rotate or size a shape, first select the layer it is on by clicking on it in the **Layer** window. Then click the **Move** icon in the toolbar on the left. This will make small handles appear around the shape. You can move the shape by dragging in the middle of it, or resize it by dragging on one of the handles around the outside of the shape.

11. You can draw other shapes including circles, ellipses, polygons and lines by clicking the appropriate icon in the **Shape** options bar.

Photoshop® is primarily a bitmap editing application. The facilities provided for editing vector graphics are rather limited.

You cannot use bitmap drawing tools such as the painting brush on the vector shape layers. You must first use the **Layers** menu to select the background layer. Once you have done this, choose the **Set foreground colour** tool to choose the colour you want to draw with, then choose the **Brush** tool on the left. The **Brush** options bar will appear across the top where you can choose different brush options. You can then drag the mouse over the drawing area to paint freehand (see Figure 9.11).

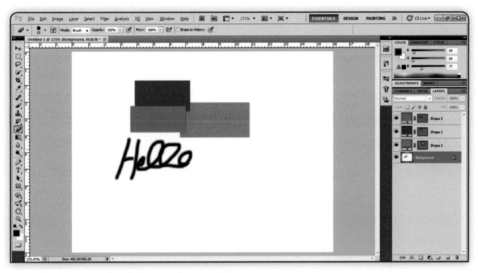

Figure 9.11: Example of drawing freehand

Activity: Freehand drawing

Freehand drawing with a mouse takes practice to achieve good results.

Use Photoshop®, Paint® or another bitmap painting program to create a freehand image which can be used as a background to a poster you are creating for the veterinary centre.

Download digital photos from a camera

Most digital cameras can be connected to your computer using a USB cable. When you attach a camera, your computer will recognise the camera and display a window (see Figure 9.12).

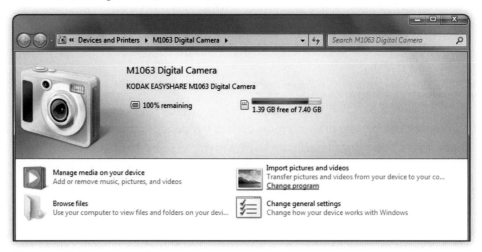

Figure 9.12: The camera window

From here you can browse through all the photos on the camera, or import them to your **Pictures** folder. Most mobile phones can also be connected to a computer using a USB cable – they will be listed in the computer window like any other USB storage device. You can then navigate to the folder where the photos are stored – usually a folder called DCIM – and copy them to your **Pictures** folder.

Scan images

Scanning an existing piece of artwork, a photo or other item is one way of obtaining an image.

How to scan an item

1. Place the item in the scanner, following the instructions that come with the scanner.

2. In Photoshop® go to the **File** menu and choose **Import**.

3. From the pop-up menu that appears, choose **WIA-*scanner name*** (the scanner name will depend on the make of scanner you have). You should see the **Scan** dialog box (see Figure 9.13).

continued

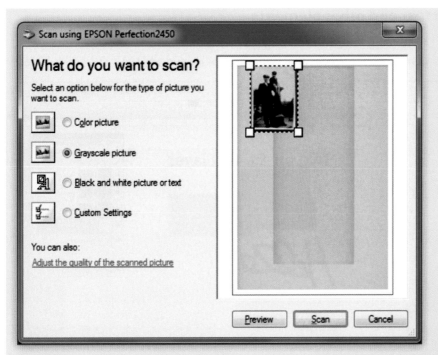

Figure 9.13: The Scan dialog box

4. Choose the type of item you want to scan by clicking one of the buttons on the right.

5. Click the **Preview** button to see a preview of the item to be scanned.

6. Use the selection handles in the **Preview** window to select the area you want to scan.

7. Now click the **Scan** button. The scanner will then scan the item and after a few seconds the result will be displayed in Photoshop®.

8. You can now edit the image as required.

Resizing images is covered on *page 164*.

Activity: Scanning images

Find some hand drawn artwork that you or a friend have created. It could be a drawing, diagram, painting or traditional photographic print. It should be no larger than A4 size as most scanners are limited to this size. Scan the artwork into Photoshop® and save it as a digital file.

Experiment with different scanner settings such as resolution and note the effects.

Add text and other elements

When combining text with an image, it needs to be added to a separate layer (see Figure 9.14).

Figure 9.14: Adding a text layer

How to create a paragraph box

1. As with vector shapes, you must first select the text layer in the **Layer** window.

2. Choose the **Text** tool and then drag out a box on the **Image** window.

3. Choose text fonts, sizes and colours from the **Text** options bar and type your text into the box (see Figure 9.15).

Although you can edit the text as you would in a word processor, there is no spell checking facility in Photoshop®. You might find it easier to type and edit text in a word processor, then copy and paste it into a paragraph box.

You can draw lines with or without arrow heads using a similar technique to that used to draw rectangles. Click and hold the **Shape** tool, then choose the **Line** tool. The toolbar across the top will then show the options for the tool, including the thickness (weight) of the line in pixels. Clicking the drop-down box arrow will display the arrow head options. Lines, like rectangles and other shape objects, are added on separate layers.

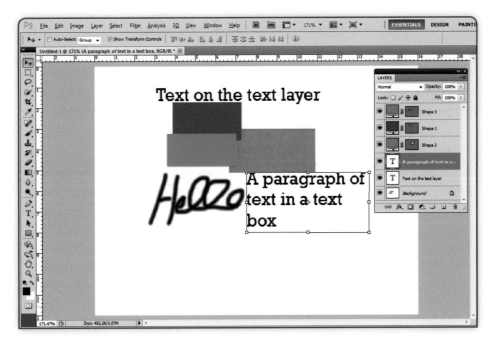

Figure 9.15: The paragraph text

Create more complicated designs using painting, drawing or image manipulation software

You can of course combine the various techniques described above to create a more complex design. You can take scanned or photographic images and combine them with freehand drawn or painted content which you create yourself in the image manipulation software.

Activity: Complex images

The manager of The Green Veterinary Centre has asked you to create a poster reminding people of the need to bring their pet in regularly for a check up and booster vaccinations. Create a poster combining text, clip art, a freehand drawn image and photographic images.

2.3 Manipulation and editing techniques

There are a wide range of tools you can use to manipulate and edit your images. Let's look at a few simple examples.

When using imaging software in the workplace, you will be expected to produce images which are accurate and precise. Creating professional-looking images takes patience and practice. Photoshop® provides a number of tools to help you improve the precision and accuracy of your images.

Photoshop® will display a horizontal and vertical ruler above and to the left of the editing window. If this is not displayed, select the **View** menu and choose the **Rulers** option, and they will appear. You can also drag horizontal and vertical guidelines from the rulers. Simply click with the mouse in one of the rulers, then drag across or down the drawing area. Guidelines do not print or save in the image file itself. They are there to help you line up objects in the image you are creating. When moving selections or vector shapes into place, they will 'snap' onto grid lines to make aligning easier.

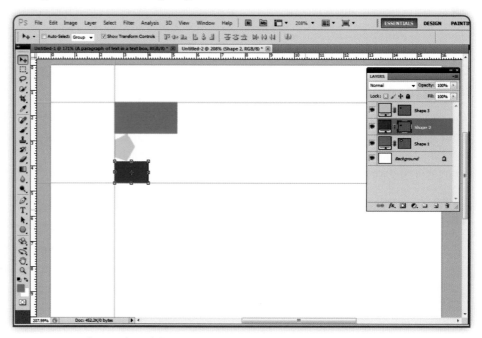

Figure 9.16: Rulers and guidelines

Align

With vector shapes there are a number of editing features you can use. For example, you can align a number of shapes. The shapes shown in Figure 9.17 have been aligned to their left edges.

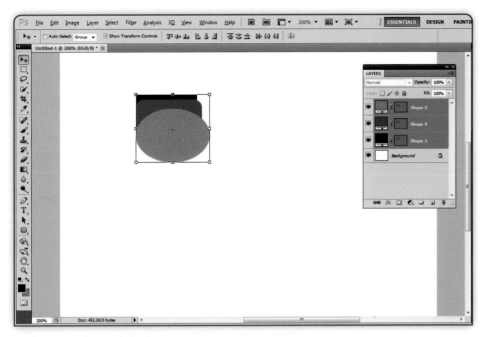

Figure 9.17: Align to left edge

How to align shapes

1. Select all the layers that contain the shapes you want to align. To do this, press and hold down the **SHIFT key**. Then click on each of the layers you want to select in the **Layers** window. These will appear highlighted.

2. Click the **Move** tool in the toolbar. The shape will appear within the same bounding box (see Figure 9.18).

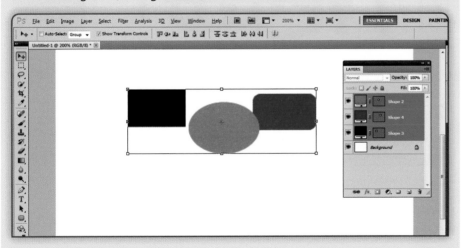

Figure 9.18: Selecting multiple layers

3. You can use the various **Align** and **Distribute** icons in the **Move** tool option bar to align the shapes with each other or distribute them evenly in various ways. If you keep your cursor steady under an icon, a message will pop up explaining what the icon does.

Rotate, flip and arrange

You can rotate an image or part of an image.

How to rotate an image

1. To rotate the whole image, go to the **Image** menu and choose **Image Rotation**. Then choose the option you want: **CW** stands for clockwise; **CCW** stands for counter-clockwise. The **Arbitrary** option lets you choose any angle of rotation.

2. You can also flip the whole drawing canvas vertically or horizontally. If you want to rotate just part of the image use the **Rectangular marquee** tool to select the part of the image you want to rotate. Go to the **Edit** menu, select **Transform** and from the pop-up menu choose **Rotate**.

3. Handles will then appear around the selection marquee. You can rotate the selection to any angle using the mouse (see Figure 9.19).

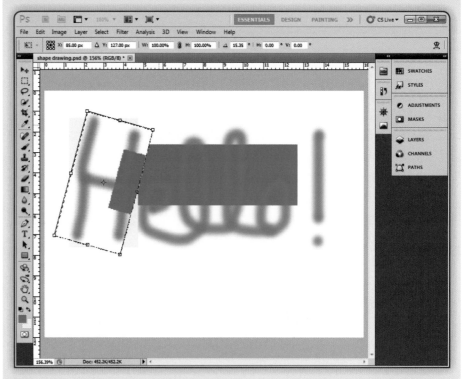

Figure 9.19: Rotating a selection

With vector shapes you need to select the vector layer that the shape is on before you can transform it.

The **Transform** pop-up menu gives you many other options for transforming a selection, including resizing.

Activity: Editing an image

1   Find the image you scanned or the freehand drawing you created in earlier activities. Practise using image rotation and other options on the **Transform** menu to manipulate the image.

2   Add some vector shapes and text to the image and investigate the use of layers.

Change font, text and colour

You may also need to change the colour balance of an image, especially a digital photograph. Colour digital images are made up of red, green and blue, which are combined in different intensities to give different colours. When you adjust the colour balance of an image it changes the amount of red, green or blue in the picture. Usually, you want a photo to have a natural look but sometimes you can create a special effect by adjusting **colour balance**.

Let's look at an example. The image of the dog shown in Figure 9.20 has too much green in it and looks unnatural.

Key term

Colour balance – sometimes called white balance of an image, colour balance is the intensity of the pixels of each of the three primary colours (red, green and blue) that make up the image.

How to adjust colour balance

1.   Select the **Image** menu. Then choose the **Adjustments** option.

2.   Choose **Color Balance**.

Figure 9.20: Colour balance

continued

3. The sliders on the **Color Balance** dialog box allow you to adjust the amount of cyan or red, magenta or green, and yellow or blue in the image. In this case there is too much green, so moving the magenta/green slider towards magenta will reduce the amount of green. Moving the slider to **-63** makes the colours look more natural (see Figure 9.21).

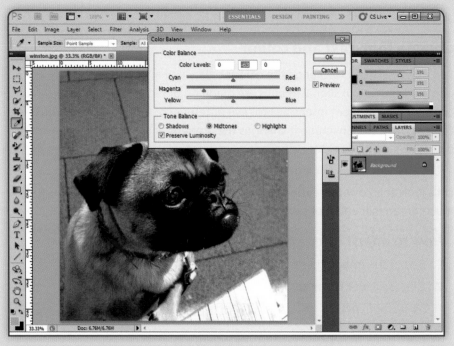

Figure 9.21: Adjusting the colour balance adjusted

With images such as digital photos, you may need to improve them by adjusting the brightness and/or contrast of the image.

How to adjust the brightness/contrast

1. Go to the **Image** menu and choose **Adjustments**.

2. Then choose **Brightness/Contrast**.

3. The **Brightness/Contrast** dialog box will appear. In this case, increasing the brightness to about 70 improves the image quite a lot (see Figure 9.22).

continued

Figure 9.22: An image of an apple with the brightness adjusted to 71

Adjusting the **contrast** will make little difference to this image. The image shown in Figure 9.23 shows the difference between low and high contrast.

Figure 9.23: This image has had the left half darkened, showing the contrast with the brighter right hand side

Photoshop® has a number of automatic **optimising features**. These features are useful if you are in a hurry, but they may not always significantly improve the image quality.

In the **Image** menu in Photoshop®, you can find **Auto Contrast** and **Auto Color** options. These automatically adjust the contrast and colour balance of an image. There is also an **Auto Tone** option, which adjusts the level of black and white in an image, and generally this increases the contrast of the image.

Group and ungroup

When you are making a complex image from vector shapes, it can be helpful to group together layers so you can deal with them as a single object.

> #### How to create a group
> 1. Click the **Create a new group** icon at the bottom of the **Layers** window.
> 2. The group will appear at the top of the **Layers** window and be called Group 1. (If you double click on the Group 1 name, you can change it to something more meaningful if you wish.)
> 3. Drag the layers you want to include in the group into the group name. They will then appear indented, indicating they are part of this group.
> 4. You can still select and edit the layers individually, but now if you click the group name to select it you can move and resize all the shapes in the group together. (See Figure 9.24.)
>
>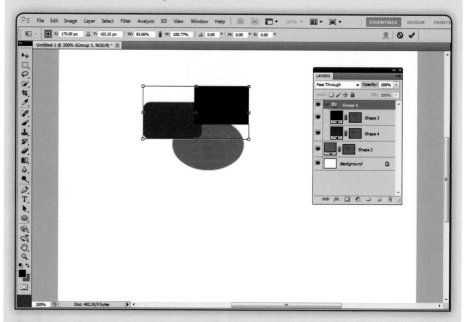
>
> Figure 9.24: Grouping layers
>
> 5. You can also remove the group, but leave the layers as they were. To do this, right click on the group in the **Layers** window and then choose **Ungroup layers** from the menu that appears.

Filters to create special effects

Photoshop® provides a range of filters you can apply to images to give special effects. These can be applied from the **Filter** menu. Each type of filter listed (artistic, blur, distort, etc.) has a submenu that lists the individual filters of that type. When you select an individual filter, a dialog box will open where you can select various options and see a preview of how the filter will look when applied.

Orders and layers

You will have seen how shapes sit on top of each other. The order is controlled by the layers, with the top-most layer listed in the **Layer** window on top of the others. You can drag the layers in the Layer window so they are in a different order and the shapes will rearrange their order likewise.

2.4 Check images

Once you think you have completed an image you should check it carefully, both to make sure it is technically accurate and correct, and also that it meets the requirements and is suitable for its intended purpose.

Size, alignment and orientation

As mentioned earlier, the physical size of an image is important. You need to check that the image you have created is suitable for the size at which it will be displayed or printed. If the image is larger than the physical size at which it will be used, it will require a larger than necessary file to store it and this can cause problems with download speeds on websites. However, it is not difficult to reduce the physical size of the image. If the physical size of the image you have created is smaller than the size at which it will be used, you have a problem. This is because you cannot scale up a bitmap image without losing quality.

You should also check the orientation of the image, or its aspect ratio. Generally, most images are either square (equal height and width), portrait orientation (higher than wide) or landscape orientation (wider than high). You need to compare the aspect ratio of the image to how it will be used. For example, if an image is being used to illustrate the front cover of an A4 portrait-orientation booklet, then it should have a matching orientation. You may be able to resolve this by cropping the image.

Suitability of file format

As explained earlier, there are many different graphics file formats. You need to check that your file is saved in one that matches the type of graphic you have created and how it will be used. For example, if a graphic is to be displayed on a website, you must choose a file format that is supported by common web browsers such as Microsoft® Internet Explorer® and Google™ Chrome™.

Appropriate choice of colour mode and use of filters

The colour mode, as described earlier (*see page 174*), defines the number of colours that can be displayed in an image. Colour photographs normally use 8 bit colour but if an image is only going to be printed in black and white it may be converted to greyscale.

Filters are mostly used for artistic effects and they should not be used where it would not be appropriate. For example, in a product brochure people will want to see how the product looks in reality.

Fitness for purpose of image resolution

The resolution of an image needs to be suitable for the medium that will be used to display the image. As explained earlier, for onscreen display (such as on a website) 100 dpi will be sufficient. If the image is to be printed, then a higher resolution such as 300 dpi or higher will be beneficial in terms of image quality. Where images are to be used on a website, file sizes need to be minimised to reduce download times. So making sure that the image is not a higher resolution than necessary is important.

2.5 Quality problems with images

Images may suffer from a number of problems which affect their quality and make them unsuitable for their intended use. It may be possible to correct some of the problems using the features of Photoshop®. Other problems cannot be corrected and the image will need to be recreated. Table 9.3 lists some common quality problems.

Problem	Solution
Image is pixelated (individual pixels visible)	The image resolution is too low for it to be displayed at its current size without pixelation. Either use the image at a smaller size, or obtain a higher resolution image.
Image is dark	The brightness can be adjusted in Photoshop®.
Image lacks contrast	The contrast can be adjusted in Photoshop®.
Image is fuzzy (out of focus)	You cannot adjust this in Photoshop®. You need to obtain an image which is in focus.
Image has unnatural colours	The colour balance of the image can be adjusted in Photoshop®.

Table 9.3: Common quality problems with images

Check your understanding

1   Which medium will benefit from higher resolution images (300 dpi or over): print or onscreen display?
2   Colour images created on a digital camera are made up of which primary colours?
3   How many pixels does a 1 MP digital camera have?
4   Why is it a bad idea to use high resolution images on a website?

ASSESSMENT ACTIVITY

You have been asked to provide some art work for a booklet about all the different services provided at The Green Veterinary Centre. In particular, you have been asked to produce:

- a front cover image for the booklet which combines photographs and some text. Prepare two versions of this image: one suitable for print, the other for use on a website.
- a back page for the booklet which will include a map of how to find the surgery. It should include both a diagram of the location of the surgery and an image of the surgery.

The booklet is aimed at pet owners who might be interested in using the surgery to look after their pet.

Task 1 – Obtain information for images

Make a list of the images you will need. You might find it helpful to hand draw a mock-up of the front and back pages of the booklet. Your list should identify the context in which the images will be used and describe the copyright constraints that apply to each image.

Task 2 – Insert information for images

Having identified what you need, you can now move on to collecting the various required images and preparing them as required (e.g. resizing them, cropping, adjusting, etc.). You should take screenshots of this process. Also show that you have chosen a suitable file format to save the files in and have saved them regularly.

Task 3 – Combine information for images

Combine, edit and manipulate the images you have collected to make the two composite images for the front and back covers of the booklet. As before, take screenshots of the process to use as evidence for your portfolio.

Task 4 –use imaging software to create, manipulate and edit images

Write an explanation of how and why you modified the print version of the front page image for use on the website.

Task 5 – Use imaging software to create, maniplate and edit images

Swap draft versions of the images you have created with a colleague and check that the colleague's work is suitable for the required purpose. Identify quality problems with the images and suggest how the problems might be overcome. As evidence for this task, you should submit an annotated version of your colleague's work, explaining how the work does or doesn't meet needs, and what quality problems you have identified.

Presentation software

Presentations often combine a range of media, such as text, images, video and sound. They are used in education, training, business and entertainment.

In this unit you will look at how to create presentations that suit particular needs and audiences. The unit will help you to select and use a wide range of presentation software tools and techniques, such as slide animations and slide transition options. You will have the opportunity to plan, input, structure and edit a presentation, as well as review it and then prepare your slideshow for use.

Learning outcomes

After completing this unit you should be able to achieve the following learning outcomes.

» **LO1** Input and combine text and other information within presentation slides

» **LO2** Use presentation software tools to structure, edit and format slide sequences

» **LO3** Prepare slideshow for presentation

1 Input and combine text and other information within presentation slides

In this unit you will be using Microsoft® PowerPoint® to create your presentation. PowerPoint® is part of the Microsoft® Office® suite of programs, and has many of the same features as Microsoft® Word® and Microsoft® Excel®. If you have used either of these software applications, you will already be familiar with many of the techniques used below.

1.1 Types of information

Before you start to gather information for your presentation, you need to know:

- the purpose of the presentation
- who the presentation is aimed at (i.e. the audience)
- how it will be presented.

This knowledge will help you to decide on the types of information you need.

There are several options you can choose from, including:

- text
- numbers
- images (including **graphics** or animation)
- sound (audio) and video.

However, if you use too many different types of information in the same presentation, you may distract the viewer from the message you are trying to communicate.

Once you have decided what to include in your presentation, you need to know how to create it. This unit will show you how to do just that.

1.2 Entering text and selecting appropriate layouts

Presentation software shares many features with other programs. In this unit you will be working with Microsoft® PowerPoint®, which is the most commonly used presentation software.

Use of text boxes

To enter text into a presentation slide, you need to use a text box. The slide may already have a text box which you can enter information into. If it does, then move your cursor into the text box, click the left mouse button and start typing.

If you want to enter text into a blank area of the slide, you first need to insert a text box.

> ### How to insert a text box
> 1. Select the **Insert** menu and click the **Text Box** icon.
> 2. Click on the slide where you would like the text box to be. Then hold down the left mouse button and drag the mouse to draw a text box.
> 3. A text box appears with a flashing **I-bar**.

Key term

Graphics – a general term used to describe pictures, photos, clip art, SmartArt, charts, diagrams, and individual shapes such as arrows or boxes. In Microsoft® PowerPoint®, graphics may also be referred to vas illustrations.

You can resize a text box by clicking on one of the sizing handles and holding down the left mouse button while you drag the mouse.

Activity: Adding and editing slides

In this activity you will create a new presentation and practise adding slides and entering text.

1 Open Microsoft® PowerPoint®. A new blank presentation will be created automatically. The presentation contains one slide only (this is shown in the window on the left-hand side of the screen), with the **Title Slide** layout.

2 Click in the box that says 'Click to add title' and type the following text:

'Understanding the reasons why organisations use ICT'.

Then add your name to the sub-title box.

3 Click on **New Slide** and then **Title** and **Content layout**.

4 On your slide, add the information below. Put the title into the **Title** box and the rest in the main window area.

> Organisations use ICT to:
> - present information
> - manipulate information
> - make decisions
> - communicate
> - manage information.

5 Insert three more similar slides and add the information given below.

> The reasons why organisations use ICT can be divided into:
> - external factors
> - internal factors
>
> **External factors**
> - Organisations need to exploit new technologies
> - Suppliers change their expectations
> - Changing customer or market demands
> - Increased competition
> - New laws
>
> **Internal factors**
> - Increased cost-effectiveness (often the main reason)
> - To improve quality control procedures, in order to comply with legal requirements that relate to employees
> - To get better information in order to make better decisions

6 **Save** the presentation, using an appropriate name. The saving process is essentially the same as in other Microsoft® software – select **File** from the main menu and then **Save As** and follow instructions.

Borders

How your presentation looks visually is also important, as you want it to appeal to the audience. Different types of borders (outlines) can be applied around the outside of placeholders and other objects, in order to make them stand out from the rest of the content.

How to apply a border

1. Highlight the object or placeholder.
2. Select **Shape Outline** from the **Format** menu.

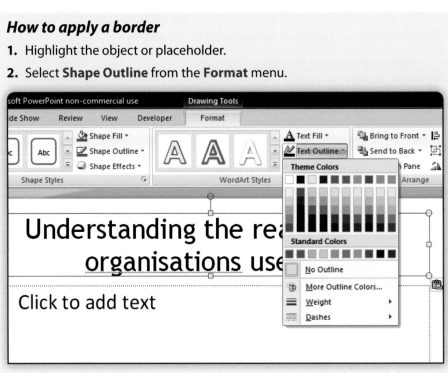

Figure 10.1: Adding a border

3. Then select the options you need. You can change the colour of the border and also the thickness (weight) of the line used.

Create diagrams or graphics

Sometimes it is easier or clearer to use a diagram or graphic to illustrate a point. You can use graphics software to do this but PowerPoint® has a range of options.

Click the **Insert** tab and you will find the:

- **Images** section – Picture, ClipArt, Screenshot, Photo Album
- **Illustrations** section – Shapes, SmartArt, Chart.

See *section 1.3 on page 140* for information on diagrams and graphics.

1.3 Charts and tables for presentation

Tables and charts can either be created within the presentation software or imported from other sources, such as Microsoft® Word® or Excel®.

Tables

Structured information that is naturally divided into a series of rows and columns is typically best presented in a table. Figure 10.2 shows a table that details the sales of the different items in a garden centre both as a column chart and table.

Item group	Month 1	Month 2
Trees	£3,3033.33	£2,365.99
Shrubs	£1,256.79	£1,293.41
Vegetable plants	£125.53	£166.09
Flowering plants – perennials	£704.11	£1,296.61
Flowering plants – annuals	£387.74	£324.22
Bulbs	£125.90	£105.74
TOTAL	£5,903.41	£5,552.06

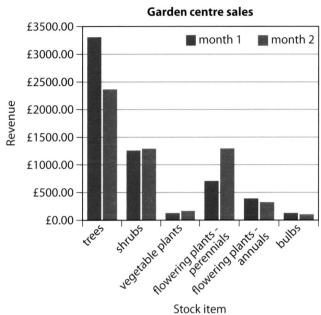

Figure 10.2: Complete slide showing table and chart

Pie charts

Pie charts are particularly useful if you want to show the proportions of different parts of a whole. For example, if you are talking about the different items sold by a garden centre, you might show the sales of each item as a proportion of the total sales. This allows you to see which items are most popular. For example, in Figure 10.3 you can see that over half of the items sold by the garden centre are trees.

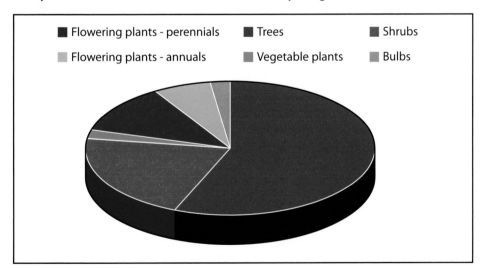

Figure 10.3: A pie chart showing sales values as a proportion of the total sales

Organisational charts

Organisational charts show the management structure in an organisation. PowerPoint® provides a template for organisational charts in the SmartArt library.

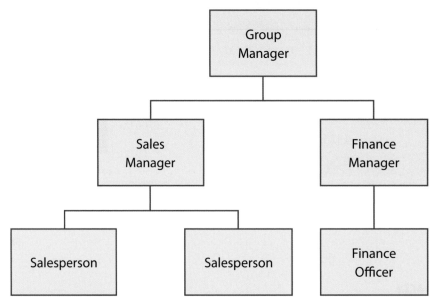

Figure 10.4: An example of an organisational chart

Flowcharts

A flowchart shows how information or processes flow through a system. Flowcharts are often used to show the consequences of Yes/No decisions in a logical process. There is a range of flowchart templates available in the SmartArt library in PowerPoint®. Alternatively – if none of these templates is suitable – you can create your own flowchart. To do this, use the **Insert Shapes** option in the **Insert** menu to add shapes and arrows to your slide.

Graphs

Graphs can be used to find or show the relationship between two variables (often referred to as the x and y variables). Some people refer to bar charts as bar graphs.

Diagrams

The word 'diagram' is used to describe a variety of non-standard graphic images. A diagram may be used to describe a scientific process or show how something works. For example, doctors may use a diagram of how blood flows around the body if they are giving a presentation on this topic.

Activity: Inserting tables and charts

Create one slide that includes text, tables and charts. This slide will include a table that shows the products sold by a small IT company.

1 Open Microsoft® PowerPoint®. A new presentation will open automatically.
2 Add an appropriate title to the first slide (e.g. Monthly Report – June 2012). Add your name to the second box.
3 Insert one new slide and select the **Two Content** layout.
4 In the title box insert a title: 'Products, stock and sales'.
5 In the box on the left of the slide, select the **Table** icon, choose three columns and rows, and then enter the following details.

Product reference	Description	Stock at 31 June
BH61	Network card	100
BR45	LAN kit	200
BR51	LAN board	75
BV22	Workstation	9
CS03	Mouse adapter	90
DF61	Pen drive	230
DS12	Mouse mat	53
DW01	Floor stand	9

Figure 10.5: Inserting a table

6 Now click on the **Chart** icon in the box on the right of the slide. A new window will appear, giving you a number of choices. Choose an appropriate chart type, e.g. **Column**.
7 A spreadsheet will be displayed in a new window. Delete the **Example category** and **Series data** displayed and enter the following.

Product	Sales
BH61	340
BR45	123
BR51	250
BV22	70
CS03	90
DF61	100
DS12	55
DW01	34

Figure 10.6: Inserting a chart

continued

8 Close the spreadsheet window and the slide will display both the earlier table and the chart. Change the size and the position of the graph accordingly.

Product reference	Description	Stock
BH61	Network card	100
BR45	LAN kit	200
BR51	LAN board	75
BV22	Workstation	9
CS03	Mouse adapter	90
DF61	Pen drive	230
DS12	Mouse mat	53
DW01	Floor stand	9

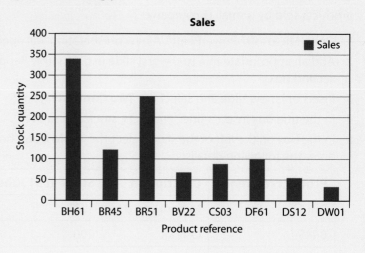

Figure 10.7: A table and column chart

9 **Save** the presentation. The saving process is essentially the same as in other Microsoft software – select **File** from the main menu and then **Save As** and follow instructions.

10 Look at the chart style choice and consider the other options (line, pie, etc.). Note one further style that would be appropriate for this type of information. Explain your reasoning.

1.4 Images, video or sound for presentations

In some presentations you will need to use images, video and sound elements; for example, if you are trying to explain how to use or repair a machine. Even where this type of information is not essential, images and sound can help to engage the audience.

Image formats

The four commonly used image file formats are:

- TIF
- JPG
- PNG
- GIF.

TIF and PNG are very high quality, but TIF cannot be used in Internet browsers.

JPG images are often the best choice for web pages and presentations because they compress easily without significant loss of quality and have one of the smallest file sizes. The overall file size becomes more of a problem if the file is going to be emailed.

When adding images to a presentation you need to decide whether to:

- create your own
- scan an image taken by someone else
- use a piece of **clip art** or **SmartArt** . Microsoft® PowerPoint® has a library of images which you can insert into your presentation quickly and easily.

Images can be inserted into a PowerPoint® slide using the **Insert** menu.

How to insert a picture into a placeholder

1. Position the cursor in the **placeholder** and click the mouse button.
2. Select the **Insert** menu and click the **Picture** icon.
3. In the **Insert Picture** dialog box that appears, find the picture you would like to insert and double click on it.
4. The picture appears in the placeholder.

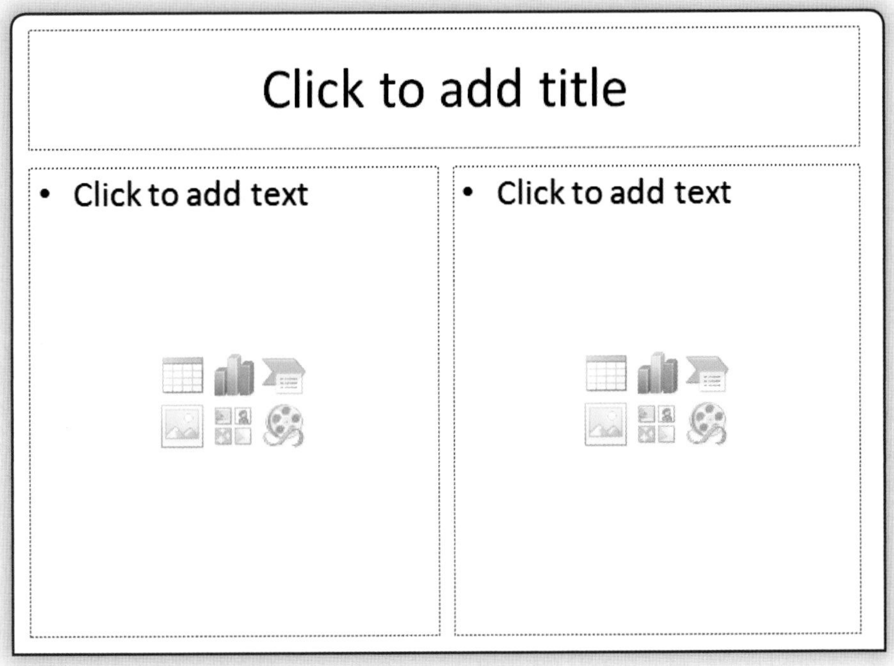
Click to add title
• Click to add text
• Click to add text

Figure 10.8: A standard slide ***template*** *showing three placeholders*

Images can also be inserted into blank slides.

Once you have inserted a picture you can resize and move it. *See Unit 9 Section 1.3 on page 164* for more information on how to resize and move pictures.

Key terms

Clip art – this is a single piece of ready-made art, often appearing as a bitmap or a combination of drawn shapes.

SmartArt – this is a series of specialist graphics available with Microsoft® software that allow you to create a variety of effective diagrams, e.g. cycles, processes, organisational structures, and many more. They can be adapted for particular purposes.

Template – a standard slide layout. Once chosen for a new slide, however, placeholders can be adapted and new ones added.

Placeholder – a box with dotted borders in a slide layout that shows where content can be placed.

Figure 10.9: The Media clip icon

Inserting audio/video clips

You may want to include sound (audio) and video clips. Sometimes you may be able to use pre-recorded clips, or you might decide to record your own.

You cannot create or alter video or audio files using PowerPoint®. If you wish to create your own clips, you need to use specialist software and then **import** the finished files into PowerPoint®.

Audio and video clips can be inserted into a slide template using the **Media clip** icon (see Figure 10.9).

How to insert a video

1. If inserting into a placeholder, click on the **Media clip** icon.

Figure 10.10: Selecting a video to insert

2. Click on the video you wish to insert. Then click on the **Insert** button. If the video is not in the **Videos library**, navigate through the folders until it is visible.

3. The video will be inserted into the placeholder box.

4. When viewed as a slideshow, the slide will appear (see Figure 10.10) with control buttons and a progress bar.

continued

The progress bar   The audio controls

Figure 10.11: A video viewed in Slideshow mode

To insert a video without using a placeholder, select the **Insert Video** icon from the **Insert** menu. You will probably need to resize the video after insertion.

Working with sound

The use of sound (audio) clips is different to video because you can record sound clips directly within PowerPoint®. There are a number of tools available that will, for example, allow the sound to be trimmed and faded in or out. In addition, the volume can be controlled within PowerPoint®.

How to insert an audio clip

1. Go to the **Insert** tab and select the **Audio** icon. Then select the **Audio from File** option. (See Figure 10.12.)

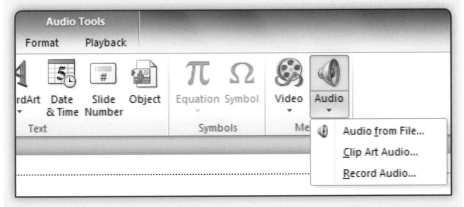

Figure 10.12: Inserting an audio clip

2. A window will be displayed, allowing you to find the audio clip you wish to use.

continued

3. Click on the audio clip you wish to insert and click on the **Insert** button.

4. The sound will be inserted.

5. When viewed as a slideshow, the slide will appear (see Figure 10.13) with control buttons and a progress bar.

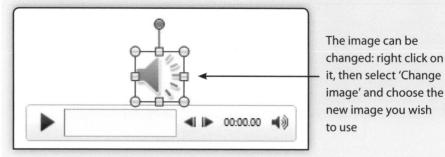

The image can be changed: right click on it, then select 'Change image' and choose the new image you wish to use

Figure 10.13: An inserted sound clip when viewed in slideshow mode

Further audio options are available in the **Playback** section of the **Audio Tools** menu, which is displayed when you highlight the inserted clip (see Figure 10.14).

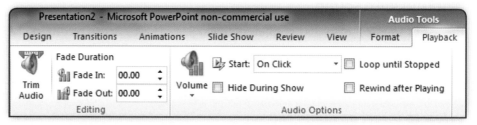

Figure 10.14: Additional audio tools

Audio and video formats

A range of video formats are available, including AVI (Windows® video file), WMV (Windows® Media file), MPEG (Movie Pictures Expert Group) and Adobe® Flash® Media. MPEG is generally recognised as being the most useful format for presentations as it is recognised by a wide variety of systems and computers. AVI files tend to be larger than other formats, and of relatively poor quality, but they do have some advantages, they can be used without problems on Mac computers.

The most commonly used audio files are mp3, wav (Windows® audio wave file) and WMA Windows® media audio file. mp3 files are known to be useful for presentations because they are good quality and generally have a small file size.

It is likely that the software used to create an audio or video clip will determine the format of any source file. However, file conversion software is commonly available. The situation you intend to use the clips in will also influence your choice. If, for example, you intend to give the presentation on a large screen, or you are showing very detailed visual instructions, then you may need to choose a file format that provides high-quality definition, even though this is likely to increase the file size.

Activity: Choosing content

1   For each of the following situations, decide what types of information you might want to use in a presentation. Be prepared to explain your answers.

   a   A college wishes to use a presentation to inform potential applicants about the facilities available at the campus and also to invite current students to provide their opinions on these facilities.

   b   A manufacturer wishes to put a presentation together for people who have bought one of their chainsaws. The presentation is designed to help them use the chainsaw safely.

2   For each of the two examples, describe the potential sources of the content that might be needed.

1.5 Combine information for presentations

You have looked at how to *insert* different types of information in a presentation. The next step is to understand how to *combine* different types of information in a presentation.

Combine information by inserting, resizing and positioning

Most documents contain several different types of information. Typically, a text document is created first and other details are inserted later (e.g. charts, tables and images). These details will often need repositioning or resizing after they have been added to the text document.

Import information produced using other software

If you want to use text, images or charts from another document, you need to import them into your presentation. The quality of imported graphics may be quite low, because they have been copied and converted from one format to another. In this case, it may be better to find the original source of the image, or choose an alternative.

Did you know?

When creating a presentation you must be aware of copyright laws. It is illegal to reproduce another person's work, such as images, text or music, in your presentation without first getting the permission of the copyright holder.

Activity: Why import?

As you are importing some text from a Word® report into a presentation, a colleague queries your actions and suggests that you ought to print out the text and then type it in again to the slide.

1   Identify two disadvantages of not importing.

2   Identify a situation where it might be sensible to manually re-enter the information.

Key term

Hyperlink – a graphic or piece of text which, when clicked on, takes the user to another slide or website. Text hyperlinks are usually underlined.

Reference external information with hyperlinks

When creating your presentation, you can insert **hyperlinks** which will take the user to another location – for example, an email address, a web page or another slide within the presentation. If the hyperlink leads to a web page, the user will need to be working on a computer which is connected to the Internet. You may need to link to the Internet if you wish to use a video clip in your presentation: there may not be room to save the clip as part of your presentation but, if the video is online, you can link to it and play it during your presentation.

How to insert a hyperlink into a presentation

1. Select the **Insert** menu and click the **Hyperlink** icon.

2. In the **Insert Hyperlink** dialog window that opens, select one of the options on the left of the screen (see Figure 10.15):

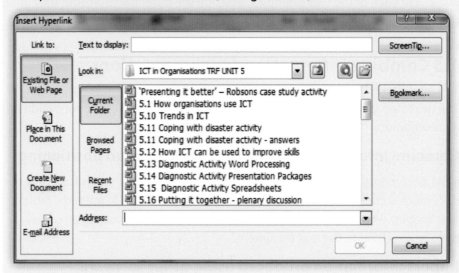

Figure 10.15: A hyperlink dialogue window

- **Existing File or Web Page** – use this to link to any kind of file within a folder, or to a full web address.

- **Place in This Document** – this is a good option to use if you wish to provide a menu at the start of a presentation. Hyperlinks to each of the slides or main sections can be placed in a menu slide at the start of a presentation. You would need to consider how the user can return to the menu option.

- **Create New Document** – use this to place the hyperlink in a new document.

- **E-mail Address** – an email address can be added. As long as an email client is installed and active on the computer, clicking on the link will open a new blank email to that address.

Hyperlinks can be deleted in the same way that text is deleted – highlight the hyperlink and press the **Delete** key.

Did you know?

If you have already written your text in another software application (such as Microsoft® Word®), you can switch to the other program, highlight and copy the text, then switch back to Microsoft® PowerPoint® and paste the text into your slide. When you copy or cut information from any Microsoft® application, it is transferred to a temporary storage area called the clipboard. Information on the clipboard is available in any Microsoft® application. However, the clipboard can usually only store one piece of information at a time, so you must paste one item before you copy or cut another.

1.6 Constraints

When you are creating a presentation, there will always be limits to what you can achieve. You must always consider your audience and the purpose of the presentation, but you must also be aware of copyright issues and wider requirements, such as equal opportunities regulations.

Constraints on content

Copyright law

When finding information for your presentation, you need to be aware of copyright law. You should never reproduce someone else's work without their permission. This applies to:

- text, such as from a book or magazine
- images, such as photos, drawings or cartoons
- music.

You may be able to download music or pictures from the Internet but unless you have permission to do this, you will be breaking the law. Your local library may have bought sets of images which you can use freely.

Acknowledgement of sources and avoiding plagiarism

When you use someone else's work you must always acknowledge the source. Plagiarism is when you use someone else's work and pretend it is your own. This is taken very seriously and can lead to poor marks, or even expulsion from college courses. You could also be sued by the owner of the work. Even accidental plagiarism could have serious consequences.

Equal opportunities and other local guidelines

If you are working for an organisation, make sure you know about any company guidelines you have to follow. These guidelines may require you to be careful about equal opportunities. For example, in a slide designed for new employees, you must make sure you do not disadvantage, exclude or unfairly represent any groups of people. A simple example might be the choice of font size or particular combinations of colour that might make material difficult to read by some.

Constraints on delivery

Some other constraints will depend on:

- where you are going to deliver the presentation and the facilities there
- timing (*see pages 216–217*).

In the workplace, presentations are sometimes given in special rooms set up to help with their delivery. Other presentations will be more informal. They may be given on individual desktop computers or laptops, or people may print out the presentations and talk through them in a meeting room.

> **Did you know?**
>
> The term 'equal opportunities' refers to the Equality Act 2010, which aims to make the workplace a fair environment. You must not discriminate against people on the grounds of their age, disability, race, religion or belief, or sexual orientation.

> **Did you know?**
>
> How you present work –so the size of font, type of font, font colour, background colour, etc – is very important. You need to ensure printed and electronic formats are accessible to everybody and that documents or presentations meet specific accessibility guidelines.

If someone else is delivering a presentation that you have written, it is important to make sure that you have fully covered the content. Slides should be simple and uncluttered. You may wish to give additional information to the presenter to help them.

If the presentation is to be given in an open environment, such as a shopping centre, you need to make sure that each slide stands alone with a short, simple message, as the audience may not see the whole presentation.

You will need to test the presentation in the environment before you deliver it to an audience. In many cases, presentations are prepared locally, stored on a **memory stick** and taken to an event where individual facilities such as sound systems can be fully tested. The computer to be used is also important, and the person presenting needs to be sure that all drivers, fonts and so on are installed and working.

1.7 Store and retrieve files effectively

If you have saved and opened files in other Microsoft® packages such as Excel®, you should find that the process in PowerPoint® is very similar. Before you save your files, ask your tutor or supervisor where on the **network** you are expected to store them. You may be allocated space on a network or asked to use the main hard drive, or perhaps an external drive.

The Save As function

The first time you save your presentation, use the **Save As** function. This will allow you to give your presentation a name and select where you'd like to save it.

If you're creating a presentation at work, find out about naming protocols. These are guidelines to use when creating a file name for a document. Many organisations create their own naming protocols so that files can be identified easily. For example, a file name may need to include the initials of the person who created it and the version number of the document. If the work relates to a series of different projects, a project reference code might be included.

The Find function

If you cannot find a file, you can use the **Search** option in either Windows® Explorer® or within the **Open** dialog box in the **File** menu of the presentation software itself.

To search using the **Open** dialog box, type the name of the file you are looking for in the box in the top right-hand corner of the **Open** window. You can search for all or part of a file name, or you can search for a word or phrase in the file itself.

Reduce file size

There are a number of other file types, or formats, that you could choose to save your presentation. The three below are the ones you are likely to find most useful. They all reduce the file size.

- **Presentation Show** – saving the file as a show creates one of the smallest files and allows the presentation to be given on a machine that does not have the software loaded. Shows cannot, however, be changed, so this format is useful when you do not want people to be able to change the content.
- **PDF** (portable document format) – this is a commonly used format and the software needed to view it is on most machines. Although it uses less space than the Presentation format, the difference is small.
- **Windows® Media Video** – this is likely to be the largest file of the three mentioned here but it is smaller than most video formats. It may be suitable if a video format is required, but the quality may be poor compared with most other video formats.

If you want to save the file as a normal **Presentation** file, but you need to reduce the size, you could save it as a **zip file**.

> **Key term**
>
> **Zip file** – contains one or more files that have been compressed to reduce their file size. Zip files usually use the .zip extension and can be unzipped using many freely available utility programs.

Activity: Save options and file sizes

1 Find or create a simple, short text-based presentation.
2 Save the presentation in four different formats in the same directory.
3 Switch to Windows® Explorer® and find out the size of the different files. List them in order of size in a table.
4 Repeat the activity for a more complex presentation that includes graphics, sound or video.
5 Summarise what you find.

Check your understanding

1 What is a placeholder? What is it used for?
2 What types of files can you insert into a presentation?
3 Give an example of when you would use a chart to present information.
4 Give an example of when you would use a table to present information.

2 Use presentation software tools to structure, edit and format slide sequences

2.1 Slide structure

When preparing a presentation, you need to choose a suitable structure. The four key areas to consider are:

- the layout of your slides
- whether to use an existing template, or adapt or create a template
- designs and styles
- any organisational guidelines you have to meet.

Slide layout

Slide layouts contain formatting, positioning and placeholders for different types of information.

Placeholders are like containers that you can put information into, such as:

- text and bulleted lists
- tables
- charts
- SmartArt graphics
- video
- sounds
- pictures and clip art.

Use existing templates

When you open PowerPoint®, a new presentation is created automatically. You can then create your own presentation file by selecting from nine different slide layouts (see Figure 10.16). These slide layouts are known as **templates**. Choosing the best template for the types of information you are using can save a lot of time and trouble. You can change a template if you cannot find one that exactly meets your needs. Templates will help make your slides look consistent and your presentation look professional.

> ### How to create a presentation file and choose a template
>
> **1.** Open the **File** menu and select **New** from the main menu.
>
> **2.** Select a template (e.g. **Blank** presentation) from the templates offered.

How to insert a slide template into your presentation

1. In the **Home** menu, click **New Slide**.
2. From the drop-down menu (see Figure 10.16), choose a template and click on it.

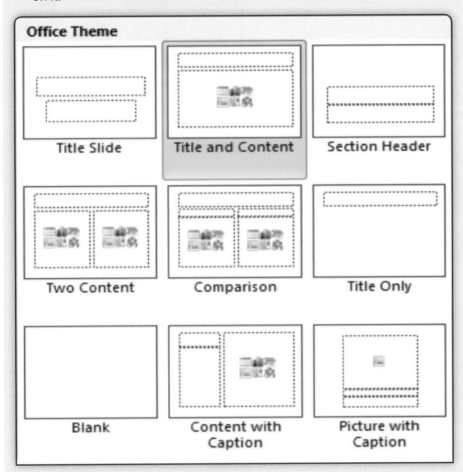

Figure 10.16: Existing templates in Microsoft® PowerPoint®

3. A new slide will appear in your presentation.

In the centre of some of the templates are six icons which show the types of information that can be added to your slides (see Figure 10.17). They are:

- table
- chart
- SmartArt graphic
- picture
- ClipArt
- media clip.

Table 10.1 will help you to decide which template to use.

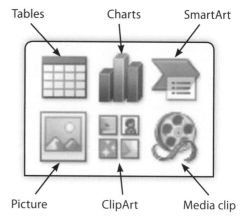

Figure 10.17: Types of information that can be added to slides

Template	Description
Title slide	This is usually used once at the beginning of the presentation. There is very little space for text, although there is a subtitle box.
Title and content	This layout is used where the slide is about one item or topic. Underneath the title you can add a bulleted list or a graphic.
Section header	If your presentation has a number of different parts you can use the section header layout to give a clear structure.
Two content	Use this layout if you want to show two or more different aspects of the same topic, for example a bulleted list of information and a photo.
Comparison	This layout is similar to 'Two content', but above each of the content boxes there is space for a heading. The layout is suitable to make comparisons.
Title only	This slide only has a title box. You can then choose to add other content as required.
Blank	This is the most flexible layout. No structure is given and you can add whatever content you like.
Content with caption	This is a more complex version of the 'Title and content' layout, with an additional caption box.
Picture with caption	This allows you to display one large graphic image per slide, with two boxes below the image where you can give a title and a brief description.

Table 10.1: PowerPoint® templates

Activity: Choosing a layout

Many of the National Parks have decided to install the equipment needed to show presentations in their visitor buildings.

1 One of the presentations to be created is called 'Birds and Bird Song' and there will be a series of slides, one for each bird. Select which one of the nine layouts will be the most appropriate for there slides. On an example slide or on paper, describe what types of information might be stored where, and what variations on the slide layout you might consider.

2 Explain the advantages and disadvantages of using exactly the same layout for each bird slide.

Activity: Choosing a set of layouts

Prior to committing to the use of slide presentations in National Park buildings, the managers wish to put together a presentation to senior directors that explains what the project is about, using the 'Birds' presentation as an example. There will be a number of different types of slides.

1 Consider which layout you would use for each of the following slides:

   a Front slide, to give the name and date of the project

   b Purpose of the project

   c Example bird slides

   d Project team members

   e Project stages

   f Potential costs.

2 Copy and complete the table below. Within the table, note the layout you have chosen for each slide and explain your choices.

Slide reference	Layout chosen	Reasons for choice
a		
b		
c		
<add in additional rows yourself to cover all the slide references>		

Adapt or create new templates

If none of the templates are suitable for a particular slide, you can adapt one of the templates or create a new layout. To create a new layout, select **Blank** from the drop-down **Layout** menu. You can add text boxes and insert objects such as images, charts and graphs to the slide.

How to adapt a template

Although you choose a template when you start a new presentation, you can change this later.

1. Load an existing presentation.

2. Choose the **Design** menu and consider the options.

3. Firstly, view the range of themes and select the most appropriate one to begin with.

4. Experiment with different colours and fonts, as well as the background styles, until you have the best look and feel for the presentation being created.

5. Investigate the possible **Page Setup** and **Slide Orientation** changes. The defaults are appropriate for an onscreen show.

6. **Save** the presentation.

7. To save a template that could be used for other similar presentations:

   a. remove any content that is specific only to the presentation but leave examples of the different types of slides and content

   b. use **Save As** but choose to save the file as a PowerPoint® template.

   c. select an appropriate name and click **Save**.

Designs and styles

Most presentations will use a consistent design and style for all of the slides. PowerPoint® provides several different design templates for you to use (see Figure 10.18).

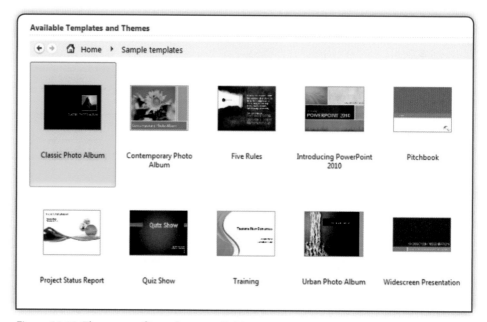

Figure 10.18: The range of templates available

How to open a sample template

1. Select the **File** menu and click **New**.
2. In the **Available Templates and Themes** window that opens, select **Sample templates**.
3. From the set of templates that appears, select and click **Create**.
4. A presentation will then open.

A **Sample template** includes:

- layouts
- colours
- fonts
- effects
- background styles
- content.

Organisational guidelines

Many organisations provide templates for different tasks which employees are expected to use. These templates may include the company logo or use the company colours. This helps the organisation to present a professional and consistent image to its customers.

You may find that your tutor has provided a set of templates for you that you can explore.

2.2 Presentation effects

You can use a variety of effects in your presentation to get information across to your audience. They include:

- video
- sound
- animation
- slide transitions
- visual and sound effects
- hyperlinks.

See Table 10.2 for a list of guidelines to apply when preparing your presentation.

> **Did you know?**
>
> Some design templates will be included in the presentation software you are using. Others can be downloaded for free or bought online. You can also create your own templates using the design options in PowerPoint®.

Do	Don't
✓ Use animation, video and sound to catch the attention of your audience. ✓ Use graphics to emphasise key points or important messages. ✓ Use SmartArt graphics to make diagrams look professional and communicate difficult ideas. ✓ Use a consistent approach when using transitions and animations.	✗ Include too many different effects, as this can be distracting for your audience. ✗ Overuse effects. The message and information in your presentation must be clear for the audience.

Table 10.2: Guidelines on using effects in a presentation

Animation

In presentation software, **animation** means the way that slides are presented, for example the way one slide disappears and the next one appears. You can use animation to make each slide, or parts of it, dissolve or bounce in and out. You can also use animation to control the timing of the presentation and emphasise certain slides or pieces of information.

Once you have prepared the content for your presentation, you must think about how you are going to move from one slide to the next. There are two ways of doing this: manually or using timings.

Manually

This means that the person giving the presentation chooses when to show the next slide. To move on to the next slide, you can:

- press the **space bar**
- click the left **mouse button**
- use the → or ↓ arrow keys on the keyboard.

Using timings

This means that each slide will be shown for a set length of time, before the next slide is shown automatically. You will need to think carefully about how much time to allow between slides. You need to give the audience enough time to read the information on the slide, but not so long that they get bored and lose interest before the slide changes.

You would use 'Manually' if you were giving a presentation in person. You can never be sure how much time people will need to look at a slide, and if someone stops you to ask a question you do not want your presentation to carry on without you.

You would use 'Using timings' for a presentation such as the one described in the Activity: Choosing a layout on page 213. Visitors (the audience) would be passing the exhibit throughout the day and it would not be possible for a member of staff to stand beside the presentation all day and click through the slides. In this situation, you would probably want to run your presentation on a loop – this means that it would restart automatically each time it finishes.

You can set the timings for your slides using the **Transitions** menu.

How to set slide timings

1. Open your presentation and run through the slides in order. Write down how long (in seconds) you think it will take someone to read each slide.
2. Select the **Transitions** menu.
3. Select each slide in turn, check the **After** box and set how long that slide should be shown for (see Figure 10.19).

continued

4. To show all slides for the same length of time, set the timing for the first slide and click **Apply To All**.

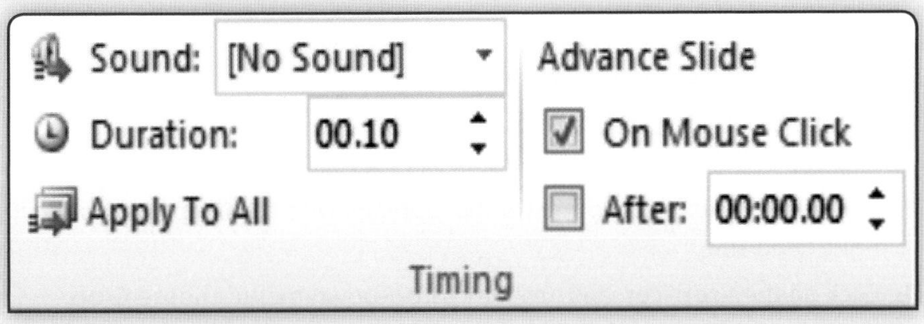

Figure 10.19: Transition timings

Slide transitions

The **Transitions** menu also allows you to control how one slide changes to the next. As with timings, you can have a different transition time for every slide or you can set the transition time for the first slide and then click **Apply To All**.

Experiment with different transitions to see what each one does. Remember that complicated transitions can be distracting or even annoying. It may draw the audience's attention away from the content of your presentation.

Activity: Setting timings

1 Add timings to an example presentation and set it to run automatically. Set all slides to display for 3 seconds, except the first and last slide; set these slides to display for 8 seconds.
2 View the presentation and test the timings.
3 Add transitions between the slides if you wish. Experiment with a few different ones before deciding which one to choose.

2.3 Edit slides

The text content in slides can be altered using similar techniques to those found in word-processing programs.

If you open the **Home** menu, you will see a range of useful icons and functions. To format a section of text, highlight it using the mouse. You can then move text around (using the mouse to 'drag and drop' it, or using **Copy** or **Cut** and **Paste**), or alter the font, colour, size or alignment as needed.

You can also use **Find** and **Replace**, **Undo** and **Redo** – these functions are available in the **Editing** section within the **Home** menu.

Size, crop and position objects

You can also crop images. The term 'cropping' applies to pictures and allows you to use just a part of a picture.

How to use the cropping tool

1. Double click in the middle of the picture and the **Picture Tools** menu appears at the top of the screen.

2. Click on **Format** and another toolbar appears with the **Crop** icon on the right-hand side.

3. Click on the **Crop** icon and, from the drop-down menu, choose **Crop**. You will notice that different handles appear around the image.

Figure 10.20: The location of the cropping handles

continued

4. Click and drag on the cropping handles until you have selected the part of the image you wish to crop.

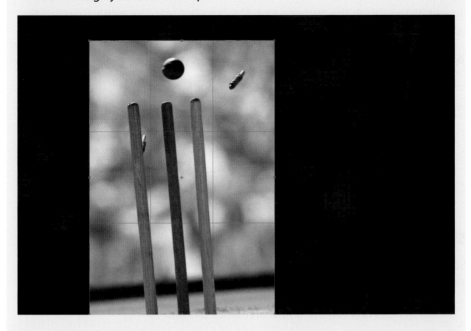

Figure 10.21: Selecting the part of the image to be cropped

5. Now click anywhere outside the picture and only the smaller image will display. The rest has been cropped.

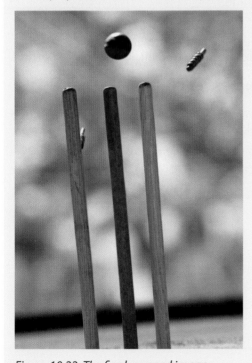

Figure 10.22: The final cropped image

Wrap text

As in word processors, text added to a text box will naturally run onto the next line when you reach the end of a line. This is called text wrapping. See *Unit 13 Word-processing software, page 302* for more information on text wrapping.

Add captions and graphic elements

You can add additional lines and shapes to your presentation.

How to add lines and shapes to your presentation

1. Open the **Insert** menu and select **Shapes**.
2. Click on the shape you would like.
3. Position your mouse cursor on the slide, then click and hold down the left mouse button while you drag the mouse to insert your shape.

Slide order

Sometimes you will need to change the order of the slides in your presentation. The easiest way to do this is to open the **Slide Sorter View**.

1. Open the **View** toolbar and select **Slide Sorter**.
2. Click the **Slide Sorter** icon in the bottom right-hand corner of the screen.

When you open **Slide Sorter**, small images of all of the slides will be displayed on screen. To move a slide, simply click on it and hold down the left mouse button while you drag it to a new position.

Change orientation

You can change the orientation of slides from the default, landscape, to portrait.

How to change the orientation of slides from landscape to portrait

1. Select the **Design** menu and click **Page Setup**.
2. In the **Page Setup** dialog box that appears (see Figure 10.23), click the **Portrait** button in the **Slides** section.
3. The slide orientation changes to portrait.

continued

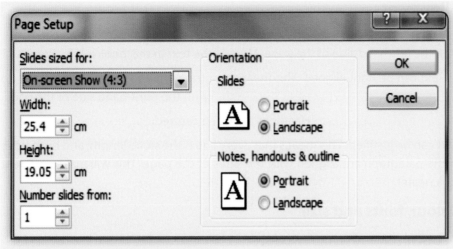

Figure 10.23: The Page Setup dialog box

In the **Page Setup** dialog box, you can also change the actual sizes of the slides to meet any particular needs. The default sizes offered are for onscreen shows.

Bullets and numbering

Bullet points and numbered lists have been used a lot in this textbook. They can be used to:

- break up paragraphs of text
- show important information in simple lists.

Presentation slides often contain a limited amount of text, showing only the most important information. For this reason, bullet points or numbered lists are used a lot in presentations.

You may find that the system indents the text a little when it applies the bullet points. This effect will help to separate the bullet points from the rest of the text.

To apply bullets or numbering to a list, highlight your text. In the **Home** menu, click on the **Bullets** icon or the **Numbering** icon and select the style you would like from the drop-down menu that appears.

Line spacing

You will not usually need to think about line spacing, because the software you are using will choose a sensible spacing. If you wish to change the line spacing, highlight the paragraph you want to change, click on the **Line spacing** icon in the **Home** menu, and choose the appropriate line spacing from the drop-down menu that appears.

Alignment

Usually, text is left aligned. This means that the left end of each line is lined up with the left-hand side of the page. Most of the text in this book is left aligned.

Text can be right aligned. This means that the right end of each line is lined up with the right-hand side of the page.

Headings are often centred.

Text can be justified. This means that every line is the same length, and both sides of the paragraph are aligned with the sides of the page. This will make your text look neater.

Colour, fonts and size

Individual characters, words or sections of text can be formatted in a number of different ways. This will help you to communicate the meaning of the text through emphasis.

To format a word or a section of text, you must first highlight it using the mouse. You can then click on the appropriate icon in the **Home** menu.

You could use formatting to pick out the words that you would emphasise if you were speaking. For example, you could make words or phrases **bold**, use a **different font colour**, or change the font or size. You can also make sections of text superscript or subscript.

Backgrounds

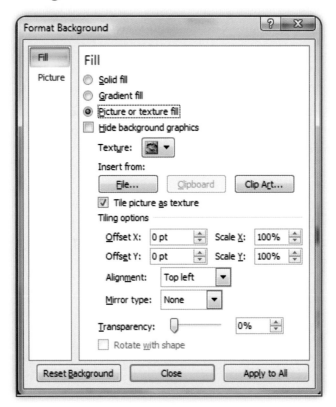

Figure 10.24: The Format Background window

You can change the background of each slide. There are a number of standard background styles you can use, or you can design your own background using a picture or a piece of clip art.

To use one of the standard background styles, select **Background Styles** from the **Design** menu. Alternatively, select **Format Background** (see Figure 10.24) to design your own background style.

Figure 10.25 shows a range of background styles applied to the same slide. If the background colour or image is strong (e.g. brightly coloured), you may need to increase the transparency of the background. This will make it easier to read the text on the slides. You can change the transparency using the **Format Background** menu.

Figure 10.25: Different backgrounds applied to the same slide

Master slides

A master slide stores information about the design and style of slides and slide layouts in a presentation, including the background, colours, fonts and other effects.

If you change a master slide, those changes will be applied to every slide in the presentation. Using a master slide can save a lot of time, because information on the master slide will appear automatically on each new slide. This means that you do not have to type it over and over again.

The **Slide Master** can be found in the **View** menu in the **Master Views** area.

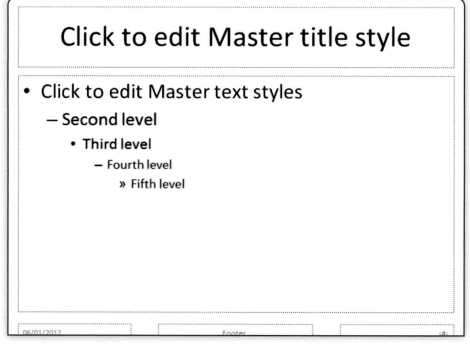

Figure 10.26: The Master Views

Activity: Adding a logo to the master slide

1 Select **Slide Master**. From the set of master slides, choose the top one which will apply to all slides.

2 Adding a logo to this slide will add the logo to all slides in the presentation. Use the **Insert Picture** process (*see page 201*) and choose your logo. Put the graphic logo in an appropriate position, remembering the range of slides that you might be using.

3 Close the **Master Views** menu using the icon on the right.

Themes

Themes offer a set of colours, graphics and fonts that work together to create an overall style for your presentation. PowerPoint® has a large number of themes that you can use, but you can also change the colour and fonts to suit your needs.

The **Themes** toolbar is shown in Figure 10.27. Themes can be shared across different applications such as Word®, which helps to standardise the style of a variety of documents from the same organisation or individual.

Figure 10.27: The Themes toolbar

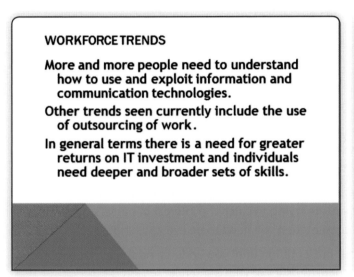

Figure 10.28: The same slide with two different themes

Colour schemes

Each theme contains its own colour schemes. However, new combinations of colour schemes can be designed and embedded in themes or templates.

Activity: Choosing a theme

Consider the two different themes applied to the Workforce Trends slide in Figure 10.28.

1   Assuming that the presentation will be given as part of a professional course to managers, choose and explain which theme might be the most appropriate.

2   If possible, recreate the slide on your own computer and apply lots of different themes to find the one you think is the best.

3 Prepare slideshow for presentation

Once you have created your slides and added information to them, you may need to undertake further work to complete your presentation.

3.1 Present slides

Organisation of information

The way in which you organise information in your presentation will depend on its purpose. For example, you may choose to divide a long or complex presentation into shorter sections, with a separate title slide for each section. This will make it easier for your audience to understand the presentation.

Audience needs and location

Everything you produce should meet the needs of your audience and the location where the presentation will be shown.

For example, if you are speaking to a group of young children, you are likely to use a brightly coloured background, with simple text and lots of pictures. If you are presenting to adults, you will be able to use more complex language, although it is still a good idea to break up the text with pictures or diagrams.

In some cases, your audience will already be interested in the topic and will want lots of information. If you are trying to catch the interest of passers-by, say in a shopping centre, the presentation will need to be eye-catching.

You cannot design your presentation until you understand the purpose of the presentation and the characteristics of your audience.

Activity: The audience

In Activity: Choosing a layout, page 213, you looked at a situation where many of the National Parks are considering showing a presentation about birds in their visitor buildings.

The management team is the client, who will pay you for the work you do. However, they will not be the audience.

1 List the types of people who might visit National Parks' visitor centres and watch the presentation.
2 Consider your answer to question 1 and make a list of your audience's needs. You must take these needs into account when designing and producing your presentation.
3 Describe the potential environment inside a visitor centre. How might this impact on design decisions?

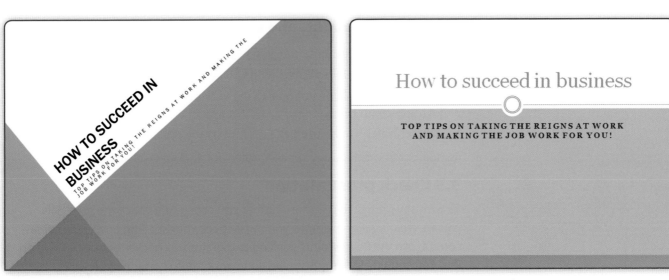

Figure 10.29: Remember that your presentation's look and feel should be suitable for your target audience

3.2 Prepare slides

View and re-order slides

To view your presentation as a **Slide Show**, open the **Slide Show** toolbar and choose one of the following options:

- **From Beginning** – this will play the slide show from the beginning.
- **From Current Slide** – this will play your slide show from the slide you are currently viewing. For example, if you are working on a slide in the middle of the presentation, the show will start from that slide.

Once you feel confident, add more slides to your presentation and try out the other options on this toolbar.

Figure 10.30: The Slide Show toolbar

Rehearse timing and effects

It is a good idea to rehearse the presentation before you show it. This will allow you to make changes if necessary. You should check the:

- volume and quality of video or sound clips
- transition timings
- presentation effects
- slide order
- room brightness.

Print slides, handouts and speaker notes

After creating your presentation, you will need to prepare any materials that you might require during the presentation. These could include:

- printouts of the slides – to give to the audience as handouts that they can take away with them
- speaker notes – to be used as a prompt by the person giving the presentation.

Remember to produce any speaker notes or handouts well in advance.

3.3 Check presentation

As with any project, it is important that you constantly check the materials you are creating. For example, you must check your spelling and grammar are correct. Use the PowerPoint® spelling and grammar checker but do not rely on this. You should always proof-read your work carefully (slide by slide, line by line, word by word) to make sure there are no errors.

It is particularly important to check numerical information as it is easy to make a mistake when you are typing numbers. Your presentation will be less effective if your information is inaccurate.

Once you have completed your presentation, refer back to the original requirements to make sure you have not missed anything or added unnecessary content.

Check the main features of your presentation, including:

- orientation
- slide layouts
- order of slides
- text alignment and formatting
- accuracy and ease of understanding
- transitions and timings.

Do	Don't
✓ Organise your ideas on paper first. ✓ Divide the content into sections. ✓ Always have opening and closing slides. ✓ Use a suitable font size – walk to the back of your presentation venue and check that you can still read the text. ✓ Keep your style the same throughout. ✓ Check that you have done what you were asked to do. ✓ Ask for help if you need it. ✓ Rehearse the presentation in the venue using the correct equipment.	✗ Forget your audience and their needs. ✗ Work on the visual parts of the presentation first – instead, focus on the content to start with. ✗ Put everything on one slide – too much text is hard to read. ✗ Simply read out the text on your slides as the audience will get bored. ✗ Use too many different colours or colours that clash. ✗ Use too many fonts and animation effects on each slide.

Table 10.3: What to do/what not to do when creating and delivering a presentation

3.4 Quality problems with presentations

You may have problems with the quality of:

- text – formatting and styles
- images – size, position and orientation
- effects – timing, brightness, contrast, sound levels and order of animations.

Many of the quality issues that need to be checked have already been covered in earlier sections of this unit. These are to do with the presentation itself. However, there are other problems relating to the environment in which you are to deliver the presentation.

- Can the room be made dark enough for the presentation?
- Does the layout of the room allow the whole audience to see the presentation screen; for example, are there pillars in the way of the screen?

It is also a good idea to show part of the presentation to someone who is going to be in the audience. You should use their comments to review the presentation and make changes.

You could track any quality issues using a test plan. This could be a table divided into three columns listing any problems you found, what you did to solve them and the date on which you did this.

Check your understanding

1 Explain why it is a good idea to use a title slide.
2 When practising your presentation, what types of things should you be considering?
3 Why is it a good idea to rehearse your presentation at the venue?

A college head of department wants a promotional presentation to help inform potential applicants about the facilities available. You are tasked with developing a draft presentation that outlines the possibilities, prior to any decision.

An initial discussion with the head of department and other senior managers has identified content that you need to take into account. In summary, this includes:

a range of courses offered

b facilities available (with images)

c key admissions staff

d details of how to apply

e video footage of some key areas in the department

f video and/or audio interviews with current students.

You are expected to make the presentation engaging, with a range of information including graphics, multimedia and tables.

You are tasked with the following.

1 Collect the information needed in relation to a department in the college.

2 Consider the requirements and write a short report identifying:

- the overall template or theme style and structure that might best communicate the information you have collected

- the types of information that are needed and how the presentation might best be structured

- the different slide layouts needed for each part of the presentation.

3 Generate some example content in your slides and use appropriate tools and techniques to enter, edit and format the slides to make the whole presentation consistent and engaging. Save the presentation at regular intervals with a file name which is both appropriate and in keeping with guidelines provided.

4 Identify any copyright issues with the material you have used. Take advice as to how any sources might be acknowledged, or whether the presentation needs amending.

5 Check that the final presentation meets the brief and adapt it as necessary.

You will be asked to meet with your tutor at intervals to discuss the report and show the presentation, and also to identify any additional skills required by the specification.

Spreadsheet software

A spreadsheet software application called Visicalc was one of the main reasons why personal computers first became popular. Managers found that they could use this application to help understand the money allocated to their department, plan budget spending, and explore pricings and other calculations. The financial control this gave managers offset the large cost of a personal computer at the time.

Today, Microsoft® Excel® is the spreadsheet of choice for most organisations and people. It still delivers the means of understanding calculations and also offers many tools to produce professional results whether onscreen or via a printed report.

This unit will build up your spreadsheet skills so you are able to create professional Excel® spreadsheets to organise data, and calculate and produce charts and other end results to help you and others understand data.

You will practise using simple formulas and Excel® functions to build models to help you plan and calculate.

The unit shows you how to choose and create charts and how to edit them so they are right for explaining the selected data.

You will also find out about Excel's® formatting and presentation tools which will help you to complete your spreadsheet and make it look professional.

Learning outcomes

After completing this unit you should be able to achieve the following learning outcomes.

- » **LO1** Use a spreadsheet to enter, edit and organise numerical and other data

- » **LO2** Select and use appropriate formulas and data analysis tools to meet requirements

- » **LO3** Select and use tools and techniques to present and format spreadsheet information

1 Select and use appropriate formulas and data analysis tools to meet requirements

You cousin, Rich, is a self-employed carpenter. His business is growing and he needs some additional help, so he has asked you to work on a part-time basis. He would like you to help him out on jobs but he'd also like you to use your IT skills to help with this side of the business.

1.1 Numerical and other information

Spreadsheets are used to hold numerical and other information which can be calculated or laid out for a particular purpose. One of the main functions of a spreadsheet is its ability to do calculations. It can do very complex calculations, such as working out interest rate payments, and other operations, such as finding out how many times a word is repeated in a block of data.

Spreadsheets can be laid out in many ways, whether giving a professional appearance to data or simply to produce a form that can be printed out for people to complete by hand.

Numbers

Numbers are an obvious use for spreadsheets as they are used in calculations. A spreadsheet can easily produce answers to calculations.

Numbers can be used in other ways such as to sequence some data so it is ordered from low to high or high to low. Spreadsheet functions can use a lot of numbers to return the highest, lowest or average value.

Charts and graphs

Charts and graphs are a very powerful way of showing information. A well-chosen chart or graph can give meaning to thousands of figures which might not otherwise be seen or understood. You can insert charts and graphs into spreadsheets.

> ### How to insert a chart
>
> It is simple to create a chart or graph using spreadsheet software such as Microsoft® Excel®.
>
> 1. Highlight the data you wish to change into a chart.
> 2. Click the **Chart** options in the **Home** menu.
>
> Sometimes inserting a chart or graph in this way produces an acceptable result, but you may need to edit it to get it just right.

A chart usually has a number-based **axis** and a text-based axis. For example, one axis of a chart showing monthly sales would be labelled January, February, and so on, and the other axis would be labelled with the number of monthly sales.

Graphs are similar to charts, but they are more number-based with both the axes representing numbers. For example, a graph showing how sales have been affected by money spent on advertising would have one axis showing numbers for the sales, and the other axis would have numbers for the amount spent on advertising.

The lines around the bottom, left and sometimes side of a chart are called axes:

- **X-axis** – this axis goes left to right and is usually along the base of the chart or graph.
- **Y-axis** – this axis goes down to up and is usually along the left of the chart or graph.
- **Z-axis** – this axis is only present in 3D charts or graphs and is usually angled from the X-axis to give an impression of depth.

See section *3.3 Format charts and graphs*, page 252, for more information on how to use charts and graphs to present information.

See section *3.3 Format charts and graphs*, page 252

> **Key term**
>
> **Axis (plural is axes)** – these are the lines running along the edge of the chart which are labelled to give meaning to the chart contents. Charts and graphs usually have two axes.

Activity: Using a spreadsheet to calculate costs

Your cousin, Rich, is a self-employed carpenter and you are working for him on a part-time basis. Rich has designed a range of garden furniture which the local farm shop has agreed to sale. He needs to work out how much he can sell the furniture for (so that he is making a profit), taking into account cost of labour and materials, and sales commission.

1 Produce a spreadsheet to calculate the basic cost of producing a piece of furniture. This needs to be designed so that it is easy to change the variable values, which work out the cost.

Variable values	
Hourly rate	£15
Hours	5
Wood	£12
Glue and nails	5% of the cost of the wood
Wood stain	20% of the cost of the wood
Additional costs	£5

Worked out costs	
Glue and nails	£0.6 from £12 * 5%
Wood stain	£2.4 from £12 * 20%
Hours	£75 from £15 * 5
Sub total	£95 from Wood + Glue and nails + Wood stain + Additional costs + hours cost.

continued

2 Work out the cost of the furniture. Use the additional variable values and worked out costs shown below to help you.

Variable values	
Profit	20%
Shop mark-up	30%

Worked out costs	
Profit cost	£19 from £95 * 20%
Pre-shop cost	£114 from £95 + £19
Shop mark-up	£34.20 from £114 * 30%
Total	£148.20 from £114 + £34.20

3 You want your spreadsheet to look professional so make sure you format it properly. Show the money entries as currency. The variable figures should be clearly labelled using text in the cell to the left of each.

Text and images

Text is any writing that is in the spreadsheet. Text is often used to describe the numbers, such as VAT next to a cell containing 20%, but can also include data, such as a list of names of people in a sports club.

Many spreadsheets are used to sort text into a sequence, such as alphabetically by surname. This makes it much easier to find names in a spreadsheet list.

Images such as a company's logo or a picture can easily be inserted into the layout of a spreadsheet using **Copy** and **Paste**. Images can also be added to charts to help represent the data.

1.2 Spreadsheet structure

The structure of a spreadsheet is how it is laid out and used to calculate results. There are usually many possible structures that can be used for a spreadsheet solution to a problem. The best structure is the one which is most easily understood and that can be adjusted if needs amending.

Spreadsheet components

The components of a spreadsheet are its parts. In very basic terms, a spreadsheet comprises cells, rows and columns. (See Figure 11.1, page 235.) Refer to Table 11.1 for a detailed breakdown of the components.

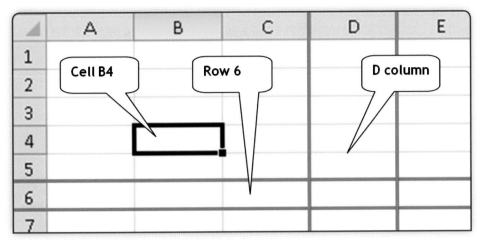

Figure 11.1: Cells, rows and columns in a spreadsheet

Component	What it is and used for
Cells	The small rectangles where information is kept. A cell always has a reference made from the column letter and row number, such as A1, which is the top-left cell in a spreadsheet.
Rows	The collections of cells in lines going down the spreadsheet. Rows are numbered with the top row 1, the row underneath this row 2 and so on.
Columns	The collections of cells in lines going across the spreadsheet. Columns are numbered with the left-most column A, the column immediately to the right of this column B and so on.
Tabs	Found at the bottom of each worksheet. The tab is used to give a name to the worksheet and can be used by the mouse to select the worksheet.
Pages	In a spreadsheet these are called worksheets. They can be selected by clicking on the tabs at the bottom of the worksheet or you can move between them by pressing the **Ctrl+PageUp** or **Ctrl+PageDown** keys.
Charts	Used to show the data in the spreadsheet in a way that makes understanding it a lot easier. Types of charts include pie charts, column charts and scatter charts.
Ranges	Collections of cells that can be selected. A range is usually rectangular and is defined as one corner to the opposite corner, for example A1:D12.
Worksheets	The pages in a spreadsheet. Each worksheet has a tab at the bottom which can be set to the name of the worksheet.
Workbook	Is a spreadsheet. It is usually made up of several worksheets, but there can be just one worksheet in a workbook.

Table 11.1: The components which make up a spreadsheet

Structure, design and layout

It is important to choose the right structure, design and layout for a spreadsheet. This helps add clarity to a spreadsheet and makes it easier to read and understand the data.

Layout refers to which cells are chosen to hold the numbers, calculations and text, as well as the many other techniques you can use to improve the appearance and readability of the spreadsheet.

A good layout will keep different parts of the spreadsheet separate; for example, by leaving some cells blank.

When thinking about the design you should consider:

- the choice of calculations and functions used
- the choice of charts to illustrate information inside the spreadsheet.

Important information can use a larger font or be set **bold** to emphasise it. Colour can be used to keep related data together and to separate different data in a range of cells. Placing lines around cell borders is another powerful layout tool that can be used to block cells together. Many people like to use a thick line around the outside of a range, with thinner lines inside to help read across and down.

When designing the structure of a spreadsheet you will also need to think about how well it will print on the page, and whether all the information prints out.

1.3 Enter and edit

You need to be able to both enter new contents into a cell and to be able to edit data that is already there, whether making small changes or corrections.

Insert data into single and multiple cells

To select a cell, either click on it or use the keyboard to move the cursor to select the cell.

The keyboard arrow keys can be used to move around the spreadsheet. There are also some shortcut keys you might like to remember.

- **Home** jumps to the beginning of the row.
- **Ctrl+Home** jumps to the top left corner of your spreadsheet.
- **Ctrl+End** jumps to the bottom right corner of your spreadsheet.

How to enter data into a single cell

1. Select the cell using the cursor. Type your data into the cell.
2. Press the **Enter** key when you're done.

Excel® allows you to insert data into multiple cells at once by typing the data directly from the keyboard. To do this, you need to highlight the cells where the data is wanted. Type the data then press **Ctrl+Shift+Enter** to insert the typed data into all the selected cells.

You can select cells by dragging the mouse over them. Selecting cells is also possible using the keyboard by holding the **Shift** key as you move through the spreadsheet using the arrow keys.

Edit cell contents

Sometimes you may want to edit a cell to make corrections rather than retype the contents.

How to edit the contents of a cell

1. Double click on the cell you want to make changes to.
2. Use the arrow keys and **Backspace** key to delete the content you no longer want and then type in the new content.
3. Click on the **Esc** key when you're finished.

Replicate data

You can **replicate** the contents of one or more cells by copying the data in the cell(s) and pasting it into a new cell or cells.

How to replicate the contents of one or more cells

1. Highlight the cells you want to replicate.
2. Use **Ctrl+C** or another copy method to copy the selected cells.
3. Select where on the worksheet you'd like to place the copied information by clicking in the desired cell.
4. Use **Ctrl+V** or another paste method to paste the copied cells.

Key term

Replicate – to copy or reproduce something.

Find and replace

Excel® spreadsheets have a **Find & Select** function, which can be used to find specific words or phrases, or to replace data.

How to use Find & Select

1. Click on the **Find & Select** icon in the **Editing** section of the **Home** tab.
2. Select **Find** if you want to find a specific word or phrase. Type it in the **Find what** box.
3. Select **Replace** if you want to replace a specific word or phrase with a revised version. Type the word or phrase you want to find in the **Find what** box and then type the revised word or phrase in the **Replace with** box.

Add and delete rows and columns

You can add in additional rows or columns to a worksheet. This is known as inserting.

How to insert a new row

In this example, we're going to add in a new row between row 5 and row 6.

1. On the left-hand side of the worksheet, right click on the number 6 (which denotes row 6).

2. From the drop-down menu which will appear, select **Insert**.

How to insert a new column

In this example we're going to add in a new column between column B and column C.

1. Along the top of the worksheet, right click on the letter C (which denotes column C).

2. From the drop-down menu which will appear, select **Insert**.

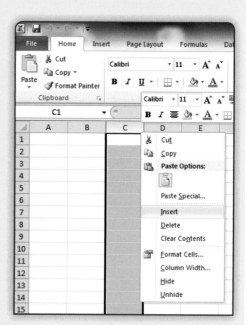

Figure 11.2: You can right click on a cell to see the Insert option

Use absolute and relative cell references

When you copy and paste information, you need to understand how to use absolute and relative cell references. These give you control over which parts of a calculation can change and which parts must stay the same.

The parts of a calculation that can change are called **relative cell references**. Parts that cannot change are **absolute cell references**.

For example, this is the calculation in cell C3: **=B3 * B1**.

B3 is a relative cell reference, whereas B1 is absolute. If this calculation is copied and pasted to C4 it will change to: **=B4 * B1**. Think of this calculation as the cell to the left multiplied by B1.

A good use for this calculation would be if B1 held a percentage discount which each of the cells in C column needs to be multiplied by.

Add data and text to a chart

Sometimes you might need to add another set of data or text to an existing chart.

How to add data or text to a chart

1. Right click on the chart. Then choose **Select data**. You will see the dialog box shown in Figure 11.3. Then select one of the following options:

   - The **Add** button allows you to insert another set of data into your chart. You can do this by typing into the range of cells to be used or by using the mouse to select them.

   - The **Edit** button allows you to change a set of data in your chart to include more or less cells than originally selected.

   - You can also change the text used to label the horizontal X-axis by selecting the cells containing the text to be used for this.

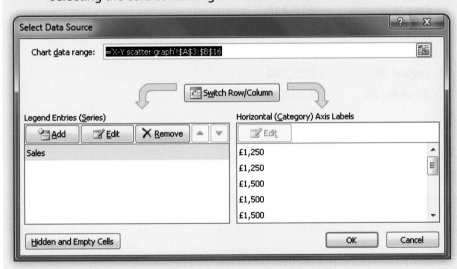

Figure 11.3: You can right click on a chart to change the data the chart uses

You can also add text to a chart by clicking once on the chart to select it then using the **Layout** toolbar that appears whilst the chart is selected. The Layout toolbar has buttons for adding a title to the chart or the axes.

Combine and link data across worksheets

When editing your spreadsheet, you might need to combine data or provide links to other data sources in different parts of the spreadsheet. For example, a spreadsheet which contains annual sales figures for a large company could contain 12 workbooks, with each workbook containing sales figures for a particular month. The information contained in the workbooks is related and you would need to use a **summary page** to show how the data is linked.

In Figure 11.4 (page 240), the total sales for January is shown in cell B13. In the workbooks for the other months (Feb–Dec), cell B13 would show that month's total sales figure.

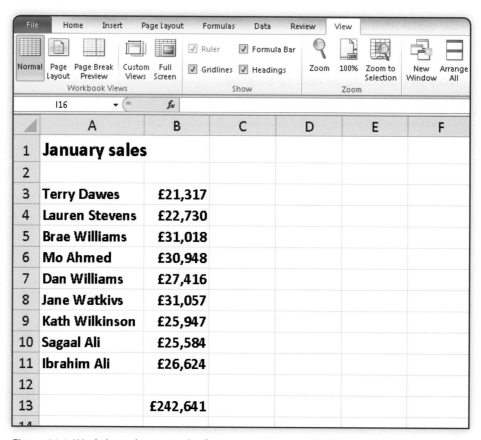

Figure 11.4: Worksheet showing sales for a month the month of January

A function can be typed into a cell in the summary sheet to add these totals together: **=Sum(Jan:Dec!B13).**

The spreadsheet is not recognising that the year starts with Jan and finishes with Dec. What it does is to start the range of cells to be summed together from the January worksheet and continues through every page until it reaches the December worksheet.

The same result could be achieved by using this function: **=Sum(Jan:Dec!B3:B11).**

The spreadsheet is now adding the D6:D18 range in the worksheets starting at the January worksheet and continuing through every page until the December worksheet.

1.4 Store and retrieve

In the workplace you are likely to have guidelines and conventions for saving documents explained to you. This will state how your documents should be named and how you should arrange and structure the folders for your work.

Storing and retrieving a spreadsheet is very similar to other application software, such as Microsoft® Word®. You should always use folders to keep your work organised and give each folder and spreadsheet a sensible and meaningful name. For example, you could create a folder named 'Course Work' with more folders within this for each one of the units that you are studying. A folder structure like this makes it very easy and quick to find saved work again. If you use a non-meaningful name such as 'Working', before very long you may forget what was in that spreadsheet. Using a meaningful name such as 'Spreadsheet assignment 2' makes it so much easier to recognise it when looking at a list of documents on the screen.

Save and Save As

Save is the quick and easy way to save the changes you have made to the spreadsheet you are working on. The **Save** option does not allow you to change the name of the spreadsheet. It simply copies the version you are working on over the previous one on the computer or network.

Many people use an existing spreadsheet as the start of a new one. They open it and then use the **Save As** option to save the spreadsheet with a different name.

Retrieving data

When you save files, spreadsheets or images, you'll more than likely want to access them again. To do this you need to know how to find, open and close files. This is also known as retrieving.

How to retrieve a spreadsheet

1. Click **File** and then select **Open**.
2. A dialog box will appear. Use the navigation options on the left-hand side to find the location of your spreadsheet. If you cannot remember the location of your spreadsheet then you can use the search box (located in the top right-hand corner) and type in the name of your spreadsheet.

How you close files is just as important as how you open or find them. There are several ways of closing a spreadsheet.

- Option 1: Use the **File** menu, select **Close**.
- Option 2: Click on **X** in top right corner to close the worksheet or workbook.
- Option 3: Use **Ctrl+ F4** to close the workbook or **Alt+ F4** to close Excel®.

If you mark any changes to a file, be sure to save the changes before you close the file.

Transferring data between applications

Sometimes you may need to transfer data between a spreadsheet and another application such as a word processing document. This may be easy if both applications can be opened at the same time on the same computer, as the data can often be copied from one application and then pasted to the other.

Transferring data between applications is more difficult if the applications are on different computers. In this situation you will need to use a file format that can be understood by both applications.

A common file format that is often used to transfer data between different applications is the **comma separated variables (CSV)** format. CSV is a simple file format that uses commas to separate out the contents of cells. Figure 11.5

shows an example of how a spreadsheet looks when saved in a CSV format, and Figure 11.6 shows a CVS file opened in an Excel® workbook.

As CSV is plain text, a CSV file will have no formatting. This means that fonts, colours, or borders won't be visible – just the text in the cells and commas.

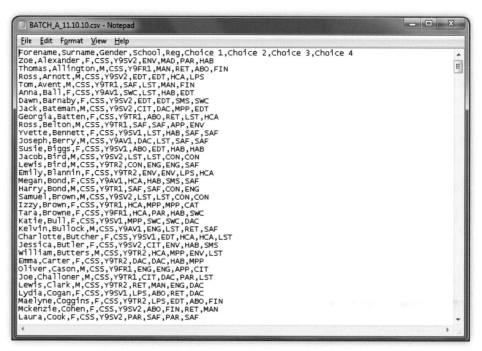

Figure 11.5: A CSV file opened in Notepad

	A	B	C	D	E	F	G	H	I
1	Forename	Surname	Gender	School	Reg	Choice 1	Choice 2	Choice 3	Choice 4
2	Zoe	Alexander	F	CSS	Y9SV2	ENV	MAD	PAR	HAB
3	Thomas	Allington	M	CSS	Y9FR1	MAN	RET	ABO	FIN
4	Ross	Arnott	M	CSS	Y9SV2	EDT	EDT	HCA	LPS
5	Tom	Avent	M	CSS	Y9TR1	SAF	LST	MAN	FIN
6	Anna	Ball	F	CSS	Y9AV1	SWC	LST	HAB	EDT
7	Dawn	Barnaby	F	CSS	Y9SV2	EDT	EDT	SMS	SWC
8	Jack	Bateman	M	CSS	Y9SV2	CIT	DAC	MPP	EDT
9	Georgia	Batten	F	CSS	Y9TR1	ABO	RET	LST	HCA
10	Ross	Belton	M	CSS	Y9TR1	SAF	SAF	APP	ENV
11	Yvette	Bennett	F	CSS	Y9SV1	LST	HAB	SAF	SAF
12	Joseph	Berry	M	CSS	Y9AV1	DAC	LST	SAF	SAF
13	Susie	Biggs	F	CSS	Y9SV1	ABO	EDT	HAB	HAB
14	Jacob	Bird	M	CSS	Y9SV2	LST	LST	CON	CON
15	Lewis	Bird	M	CSS	Y9TR2	CON	ENG	ENG	SAF
16	Emily	Blannin	F	CSS	Y9TR2	ENV	ENV	LPS	HCA

Figure 11.6: A CSV file opened in Excel®

How to save a spreadsheet file as CSV

1. Go to the **File** menu and choose **Save As**.

2. Select **CSV** (*.scv) as the file type.

3. You will then get a dialog box warning that formatting information will not be saved. Select **Yes** to this.

Templates

You can save a spreadsheet as a template so it can be used to start other similar spreadsheets. A template is different to a spreadsheet because Excel® adds a number to the name, meaning you cannot easily save over it.

How to create a template from a spreadsheet

1. Go to the **File** menu and choose **Save As**.

2. Select **CSV** as the file type. Give the file a suitable name and then click **Save**.

3. To use a template to start a new document, go to **File** and select **New**. Then select **My templates** and choose the saved template. Then click **OK**.

Check your understanding

1. Produce a diagram to show and explain the roles of cells, rows, columns and tabs in a workbook.
2. Explain what relative and absolute cell references are and provide an example of how they can be used.
3. Find examples of the different types of data which can be used in spreadsheets.

2 Select and use appropriate formulas and data analysis tools to meet requirements

This section shows you some of the options you have when creating a spreadsheet.

Case study: Building a carpentry business (2)

Your cousin, Rich, is a self-employed carpenter and you are working for him on a part-time basis. Rich spends a lot of time driving between jobs and visits to suppliers. His current van is not very fuel efficient and he is spending a lot of money on fuel every month. He thinks it is time to get a new van.

He would like your help to work out how much money he is spending each month on fuel and how much he would be spending – and potentially saving – if he buys a new van.

2.1 Analyse and manipulate

You need to be able to analyse data in your spreadsheets. This means you will have to decide which calculations, functions and sorting will be needed to change the figures and text in the original data into the outcomes that are required from your spreadsheet, such as sorting a list of names by their surname.

Manipulation could include any of the tools and techniques offered by the spreadsheet for you to arrange, calculate and format data.

Totals, sub-totals and summary data

Sub-totals are used to add up sections of numbers in your spreadsheet. Totals are used to add up sub-totals and to show the main results from calculations. Summary data can be used to bring the main results into the same part of the spreadsheet so that you can easily see everything.

Sorting and display order

Sorting and display order are useful when you have a lot of information and need to find something, such as a name or the top five in a list.

Lists and tables

Lists are good for showing lots of similar information, such as names with addresses. Tables are similar to lists but are mostly used with formatting, such as border lines.

Graphs and charts

Graphs and charts can give meaning to information. The right graph or chart needs to be carefully selected to ensure that the data can be easily understood.

Filter rows and columns

Filter rows in columns enhance lists of data by allowing the user to easily select which rows are shown. A list of names and addresses could use filtering to only show the people that live in a selected postcode or town.

> ### How to filter rows
> 1. Click on the **Data** tab. Then click on the **Filter** option in the **Sort & Filter** section.
> 2. A **drop-down combo box** will appear at the top of each column. When you click on this a menu box will appear. You can select different filtering options within this box.

Judgment of when and how to use these methods

You will need to make your own judgments on which methods can best analyse the data in your spreadsheets. To do this you will have to understand what's required and do your best to deliver this, such as sorting a list of data into the exact order that's required.

2.2 Functions and formulas

Functions and formulas are used to calculate results and other actions, such as looking up a word from a table.

Both functions and formulas start with equals (=) as this is needed for Excel® to know there is something in the cell to be worked out.

Functions are calculations using words such as average which are built into the spreadsheet. Formulas use mathematical operators such as + in their calculations.

Design of formulas to meet calculation requirements

You need to be able to design formulas to meet calculation requirements. This is usually very simple, as how you type a formula is very similar to how you would write it.

For example, if you want to type a calculation into a cell to multiply numbers in cells B3 and C3 together, the formula will be **= B3 * C3**.

Sometimes you may want to make sure part of a formula is worked out before the rest of it. In this case, use brackets () around the part of the calculation that is needed first. If you want to type a calculation into a cell to add the numbers in cells B3 and C3 together then multiply this by the number in cell D3, the formula will be **= (B3 + C3) * D3**.

If you have a complex calculation to work out you could choose to use several cells, each with a part of the calculation. This makes it a lot easier to understand what you are doing and also will show results from parts of the calculation to check they are correct.

Your cousin, Rich, would like to buy a more fuel efficient van. He would like your help in working out how much money he spends on fuel each month, and how much money he would be spending – and potentially saving – if he bought a new van.

His current van does 4.5 miles for every litre of fuel. The new van does 7.5 miles for every litre of fuel. The spreadsheet should show Rich's mileage from the previous year (shown below) and compare both vans' fuel consumption.

Jan	Feb	March	April	May	June	July	Aug	Sept	Oct	Nov	Dec
443	350	522	367	554	603	489	468	532	472	513	475

1 Create a spreadsheet showing the miles covered each month and the cost of fuel for each of the vans.

2 Find out the current cost of a litre of fuel and show how much Rich can save each month with the new van.

3 The spreadsheet should also have some analysis of the data showing the average, maximum and minimum savings.

4 There should also be some charts to clearly illustrate the meanings of your data comparing the money that can be saved.

Different types of functions

Functions can be divided into five types:

- **mathematical** to calculate results using numbers
- **statistical** to summarise lots of numbers
- **financial** for business calculations such as interest rates
- **conditional** to provide one of several results
- **logical** to compare items, returning true or false.

Any of these functions may give a **circular reference** error warning (see Figure 11.7). These errors are called circular because they try to use the cell holding the function which then tries to loop round to include the result in the calculation – this is an impossible task for the spreadsheet.

Figure 11.7: Circular reference error waning message

Mathematical

Mathematical functions that calculate results which you will find useful include:

- ABS function to make any number positive
- EVEN to round a number up to the next even integer (whole number)
- INT to round a number down to the nearest integer
- MOD to show the remainder from a division
- ODD to round a number up to the next odd integer
- RAND to produce a random number between 0 and 1
- RANDBETWEEN to produce a random number between the numbers in brackets
- ROUND to round a number to a number of digits
- ROUNDDOWN to round a number down to a number of digits
- ROUNDUP to round a number up to a number of digits
- SUM to add numbers together.

Statistical

Statistical functions to summarise which you will find useful include:

- AVERAGE to return the average of some numbers
- COUNT to count how many cells have numbers in them
- COUNTA to count how many cells have something in them
- MAX to return the maximum value in some numbers
- MEDIAN to return the middle value (median) of some numbers
- MIN to return the minimum value in some numbers.

Financial

Financial functions for business calculations which you will find useful include:

- FV to return the future value of savings using the interest rate, number of regular payments and amount of each payment
- PMT to return the regular payments for a loan using the interest rate, number of regular payments and amount of the loan
- PV to return the present value of a loan using the interest rate, number of regular payments and amount of each payment. This is how much the loan is worth without the interest payments.

Conditional

Conditional functions to provide one of several results which you will find useful include:

- COUNTIF to count how many cells in a range meet a criterion
- COUNTIFS to count how many cells in a range meet several criteria
- IF uses a condition to produce one of two possible results (the condition can be true or false, e.g. A3>12 which will be true if a cell holds a number bigger than 12)
- SUMIF to add cells in a range meet a criterion
- SUMIFS to add cells in a range meet several criteria.

Logical
Logical functions to compare items producing true or false which you will find useful include: ● AND to return true if all of its arguments are true ● NOT to make true into false (or false into true) ● OR to return true if any of its arguments are true.

Table 11.2: The five different types of functions

Check your understanding

1 What are the similarities and differences between functions and formulas?
2 Give an example of a circular reference with how it could be prevented.
3 Show how a function of each type could be used.

3 Select and use tools and techniques to present and format spreadsheet information

Planning a spreadsheet can save time when you actually create it as there will be less need to rearrange parts of the spreadsheet. You can plan both the layout and the calculations. Remember that:

✓ A good layout will make the spreadsheet easy to understand and to use.
✓ Arranging cells so that similar items are close together with a space or line to separate them from others will help to make the spreadsheet easy to understand.
✓ Arranging the spreadsheet so that cells used for data entry are close together will help to make it easy to use.
✓ Planning the calculations can be useful as you will need to think carefully about the data these need and ensure the spreadsheet has everything necessary to produce the required results.
✓ Formatting the spreadsheet will make it easier to use and ensure it looks professional.

There are many tools and techniques that you can use to format spreadsheet cells, rows, columns and worksheets which are explained in this section.

Case study: Building a carpentry business (3)

Rich has decided to buy a more fuel-efficient van. He needs to take out a loan in order to pay for it and he would like some help with working out and comparing interest rates and monthly repayment amounts.

3.1 Present and format information

How you present information is very important, as it needs to be accessible and easy to read. Formatting tools and techniques will help achieve this.

Numbers and currency

Numbers can be formatted in many ways including currency, percentage and to control the number of decimal places.

Currency format is perfect for numbers in cells that represent money. The currency format puts the £ sign at the start of the number and sets the number of decimal places shown. Many spreadsheets have zero decimal places for currency-formatted large numbers, as the number of pence can make it harder to understand the amounts.

When currency format is used for numbers in cells that represent small amounts of money the number of decimal places is usually set to 2 so the pence value can be seen.

People expect money numbers to line up making them easy to read. For this reason you should avoid having different numbers of decimal places in the same column.

Percentages

Percentages are used in many different ways, such as calculating the commission sales people are due when they sell items. Spreadsheets are very useful when you need to work with percentages or convert numbers to percentages,

If you type 10% into a cell it will be treated as a percentage. This means you can multiply another cell by this to get the percentage. For example, if you create a formula to multiply the value in cell B4, which is in this example is 200, by a 10% value (which would appear in cell C1), you will see 20 as the result. The formula for this would look like **=B4 * C1**.

Entering a number into a cell as a percentage is easy. You can also format a number already in a cell as a percentage. To do this, you need to understand how percentages work – for example, that 50% represents a half and is 0.5 as a number. Here are some other numbers and their percentage equivalents:

- 10% = 0.1
- 25% = 0.25
- 100% = 1
- 500% = 5.

Number of decimal places

Columns of figures should have the same number of decimal places so that the numbers align. This will make them easy to understand. It is very difficult to make sense of numbers which have a mixture of decimal places, as small numbers with decimal places (e.g. 3.45) look very similar to larger numbers with no decimal places (e.g. 345).

Font and alignment

The font can be changed by selecting a cell(s) and clicking on the **Font** combo box. Other properties of the font can also be set, such as the point size and whether it is bold or italic.

Alignment is where in a cell you see the contents. A cell(s) can be aligned by selecting, then clicking on either the **Align Left**, **Center**, or **Align Right** buttons in the ribbon, to align to the left, centre or right. You can also align cells to top, middle or bottom.

Activity: Working out loan repayment options

Your parents have offered to lend Rich the money he needs to buy a new van. They have also offered to loan him the money to pay for the insurance. They would like the loan paid back with regular payments at an interest rate which is half way between the interest rate on a savings account and the interest rate on a standard bank loan.

1   Research savings and bank loan interest rates. Identify three different interest rates for a savings account and three different interest rates for a bank loan.

2   Produce a spreadsheet which shows the cost of Rich's loan using the information from Step 1. It should look at the different interest rates, payment periods and the different loan amounts.

   ● The spreadsheet needs to have cells where you can enter the loan amount and interest rates. You need to use these to calculate the interest rate for your parent's loan.

   ● There needs to be a table with 6, 12, 18, 24, 30, 36, 42 and 48 as column headings – these numbers represent the number of months it could take for replaying the loan.

   ● Under these headings there needs to be rows to show the monthly payments, total cost of the loan and amount of interest paid.

   ● Add further analysis to show how much more interest your parents will earn from their savings and how much Rich will save from not using a bank.

   ● Add one or more charts to illustrate the costs of the loan for the different repayment periods.

Date and time formats

Date and time formats show numbers as points in time. In this system the decimal part of a number is the time. For example, 0.25 displays as 6:00 am, as six o'clock in the morning is a quarter of the way through the day.

The whole part of a number formatted as a date treats it as the number of days after the start of the last century, so 1 shows as 01/01/1900 or the number shown as 01/01/2012 would have 40,909 behind it.

Wrap text

Cell alignment can be set to wrap text. This means that text in the cell will start a new line inside the cell if it does not fit the width of the cell.

3.2 Format rows and columns

Formatting rows and columns usually involves changing how high or wide they are.

Height and width

The row height is how tall a row is. The column width is how wide a column is.

> #### *How to adjust row height*
>
> In this example, we're going to adjust the height of row 6.
>
> 1. On the left-hand side of the worksheet, right click on the number 6 (which denotes row 6).
> 2. Right click the row button, then select **Row Height**.
> 3. In the dialog box, type in the height you require. Then click **OK**.
>
> Alternatively, you can place your cursor over the row number, click on the bottom line and then drag the line to the required size.

Setting the column width is very similar to the row height. You just click on the column letter you want to adjust and select **Column Width** from the drop-down menu.

Hide

A lot of professional spreadsheets hide columns or rows which are not wanted in the printouts or to be seen by the spreadsheet user. This is useful if the spreadsheet has cells with part calculations where a difficult and complex calculation has been carried out using several cells.

You can hide a column or row by right clicking on the column or row button then selecting **Hide**.

Freeze

Freezing the pane, row or column is essential for large spreadsheets when you want to move around lots of cells while keeping the names you have typed in for rows and columns in view.

To do this, position the cursor at the top left of the cells which you want to move around, then go to the **View** menu and select the **Freeze panes** options. You can select whether to freeze panes, the top row or the first column.

Freezing the pane keeps both the rows above the cursor and columns to the left on the screen as you move around the data cells. Freezing the row or column keeps the rows above the cursor or the columns to the left on the screen as you move around the data cells.

To stop freezing your spreadsheet, go to the **View** menu, and select the **Freeze panes** options again.

3.3 Format charts and graphs

Charts and graphs need to be chosen carefully and set up to give meaning to and explain the data in your spreadsheet.

Chart type

Creating a chart or graph is as simple as selecting the cells which have the data to be used in the chart then using the **Insert** toolbar to click on the chart type you want.

Chart type	Why use this chart?
Pie chart	To show how figures contribute to a total such as the mix of sugars, fats and proteins in a food product.
Bar chart	To show how items compare such as sales of different products.
Single line graph	To show how something changes over time such as temperature in a room.
Area chart	This is used for similar reasons to a single line graph.
Column chart	This is used for similar reasons to a bar chart.
X-Y scatter graph	To show data where numbers have a relationship to other numbers such as ice cream sales and temperature.
Stock chart	To show how items have changed over a period.
Radar chart	To show differently how items have sold over a period.
Doughnut chart	To compare two or more pie charts.
Surface chart	To show how three sets of numbers relate together.

Table 11.3: The range of different charts you can choose in Microsoft® Excel®

In the following section you will see how different charts can be used to display and compare information. The charts will show the different types of sound equipment hired in 2011 and 2012. Types of hire were divided into:

- dry hires – deliver and collect
- indoors – equipment delivered, set up and collected
- outdoors – marquees or similar.

Pie chart

Two pie charts have been used in the example. They have been shown side-by-side so that the types of hire for each year can be clearly seen and compared.

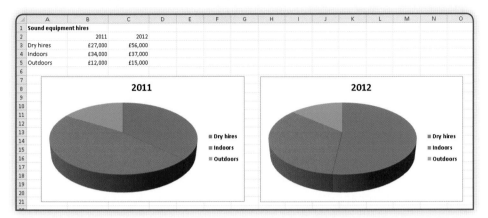

Figure 11.8: Example of how a pie chart can be used to compare information side-by-side

How to create a pie chart

To create a chart you will need to have already entered the data into your spreadsheet.

1. Highlight the cells which contain the data you want to see displayed as a pie chart.
2. Go to the **Insert** menu and select an option from the **Pie** collection.
3. Go to the **Layout** menu (in **Chart Tools**), and select **Chart title**. Select **Above chart** and type in your pie chart's title.
4. Right click the legend, then select **Font** to make the font larger and bold.

Bar chart

The bar charts in Figure 11.9 compare the incomes from types of hire in 2011 and 2012.

How to create a bar chart

To create a chart you will need to have already entered the data into your spreadsheet.

1. Highlight the cells which contain the data you want to see displayed as a bar chart.
2. Go to the **Insert** menu and select an option from the **Bar** collection.
3. You need to add a title to your bar chart. Go to the **Layout** menu (in **Chart Tools**), and select Chart title. Select **Above chart** and type in your bar chart's title.
4. You might need to rotate your title. Go to the **Layout** menu and select **Axis Titles**. Then select **Primary Vertical Axis Title** and then **Rotated Title** .

continued

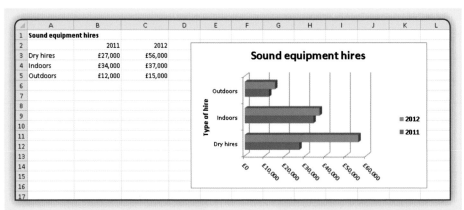

Figure 11.9: An example of how a bar chart can be used to compare information

5. Right click the legend, then select **Font** to make the font larger and bold.

6. You can also change the custom angle, which will make it easier to read amounts. Right click on the axis labels under the bar chart then choose **Format Axis**. Then select **Custom angle** to 45°. (See Figure 11.10.)

Figure 11.10: Format Axis dialog box can change the Custom angle to 45°

Single line graph

The single line graphs in Figure 11.11 show how the incomes from types of hire in 2012 varied during the months January to December.

How to create a single line graph

To create a chart you will need to have already entered the data into your spreadsheet.

1. Highlight the cells which contain the data you want to see displayed as a single line graph.
2. Go to the **Insert** menu, and select an option from the **Line** collection.

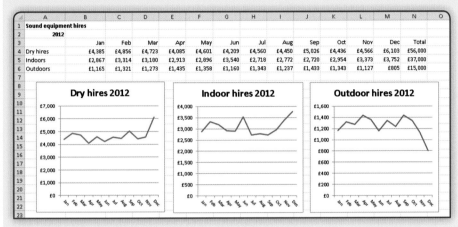

Figure 11.11: An example of how a single line graph can be used to compare information

Area chart

The area chart in Figure 11.12 compares how the incomes from types of hire in 2012 varied during the months January to December.

How to create an area chart

To create a chart you will need to have already entered the data into your spreadsheet.

1. Highlight the cells which contain the data you want to see displayed as an area chart.
2. Go to the **Insert** menu, and select an option from the **Area** collection.
3. To change the perspective values of your chart, right click on your chart and select **3-D Rotation.**

continued

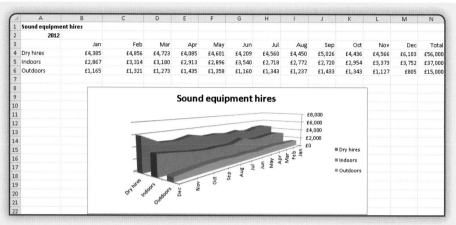

Figure 11.12: An example of how an area chart can be used to compare different types of information

Column chart

The column chart in Figure 11.13 compares the incomes from types of hire in 2011 and 2012.

How to create a column chart

To create a chart you will need to have already entered the data into your spreadsheet.

1. Highlight the cells which contain the data you want to see displayed as a column chart.

2. Go to the **Insert** menu, and select the column chart option from the **Column** collection.

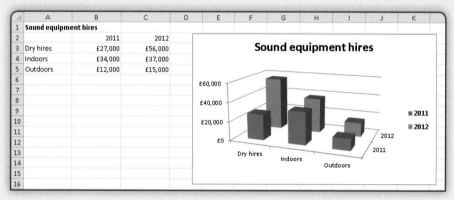

Figure 11.13: An example of how a column chart can be used to compare information

continued

3. To change the perspective values of your chart, right click on your chart and select **3-D Rotation.**

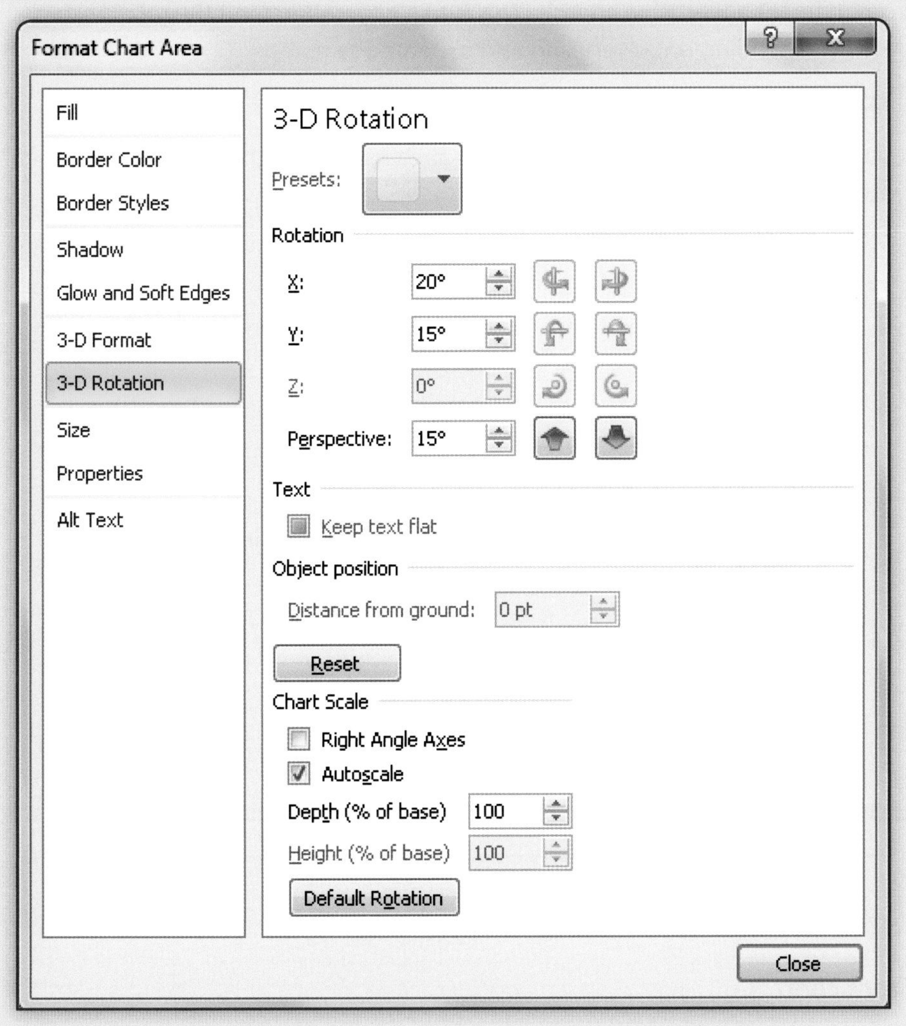

Figure 11.14: Using the Format Chart Area dialog box to control 3D rotation

X-Y scatter graph

The X-Y scatter graph in Figure 11.5 plots the sales figures that were recorded from different advertising spends. This is to try to understand the relationship between spending on advertising and expected sales.

> #### How to create an X-Y scatter graph
>
> To create a chart you will need to have already entered the data into your spreadsheet.
>
> 1. Highlight the cells which contain the data you want to see displayed as an X-Y scatter graph chart.
>
> 2. Go to the **Insert** menu, and select an option (e.g. **Scatter with only Markers**) from the **Scatter** collection.
>
> 3. Right click on the data in the scatter graph to add a linear **Trendline**.

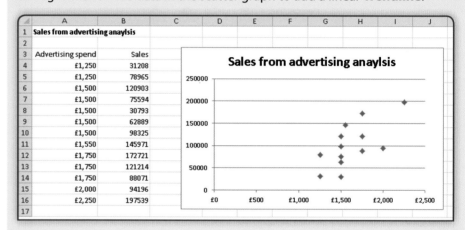

	A	B
1	Sales from advertising anaylsis	
2		
3	Advertising spend	Sales
4	£1,250	31208
5	£1,250	78965
6	£1,500	120903
7	£1,500	75594
8	£1,500	30793
9	£1,500	62889
10	£1,500	98325
11	£1,550	145971
12	£1,750	172721
13	£1,750	121214
14	£1,750	88071
15	£2,000	94196
16	£2,250	197539
17		

Figure 11.15: An example of how a X-Y scatter graph can be used to compare information

Stock chart

The stock chart in Figure 11.16 shows the range of values from high to low for each share issue with the current value shown.

(See page 259 for information on 'How to create a stock chart'.)

How to create a stock chart

To create a chart you will need to have already entered the data into your spreadsheet.

1. Highlight the cells which contain the data you want to see displayed as a stock chart.

2. Go to the **Insert** menu, and select an option from the **Other Charts** collection.

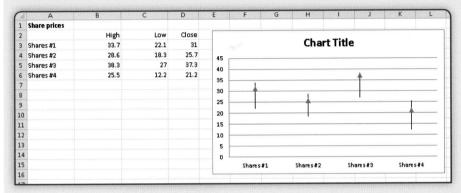

Figure 11.16: An example of how a stock chart can be used to compare information

Radar chart

The radar chart in Figure 11.17 compares how the incomes from types of hire in 2012 varied during the months January to December.

How to create a radar chart

To create a chart you will need to have already entered the data into your spreadsheet.

1. Highlight the cells which contain the data you want to see displayed as a radar chart.

2. Go to the **Insert** menu, and select **Radar chart** from the **Other Charts** collection.

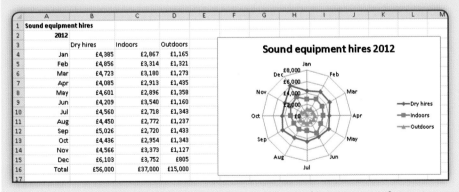

Figure 11.17: An example of how a radar chart can be used to compare information

Doughnut chart

The doughnut chart in Figure 11.18 shows the mix of types of hire in 2011 and 2012.

How to create a doughnut chart

To create a chart you will need to have already entered the data into your spreadsheet.

1. Highlight the cells which contain the data you want to see displayed as a doughnut chart.

2. Go to the **Insert** menu, and select **Doughnut chart** from the **Other Charts** collection.

3. Use the **Insert** toolbar to add the callout shapes for the years identifying rings in the doughnut. (See Figure 11.18.)

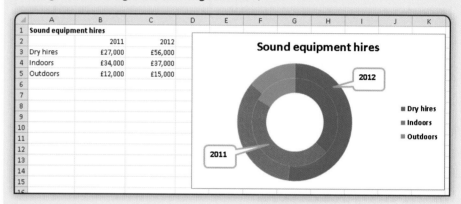

Figure 11.18: An example of how a doughnut chart can be used to compare information

Surface chart

The surface chart in Figure 11.19 plots numbers to show their relative sizes. These numbers are the row and column headings multiplied together.

How to create a surface chart

To create a chart you will need to have already entered the data into your spreadsheet.

1. Highlight the cells which contain the data you want to see displayed as a surface chart.

2. Go to the **Insert** menu, and select an option from the **Surface** collection.

3. To change the perspective values of your chart, right click on your chart and select **3-D Rotation.**

continued

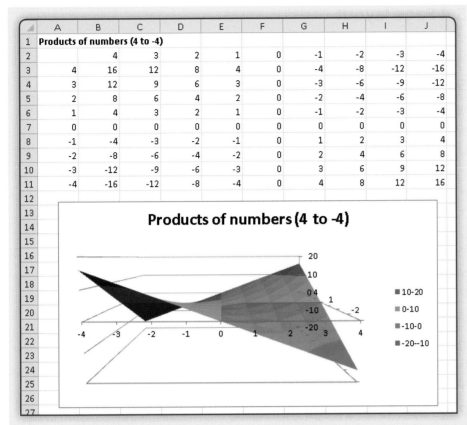

◢	A	B	C	D	E	F	G	H	I	J
1	Products of numbers (4 to -4)									
2		4	3	2	1	0	-1	-2	-3	-4
3	4	16	12	8	4	0	-4	-8	-12	-16
4	3	12	9	6	3	0	-3	-6	-9	-12
5	2	8	6	4	2	0	-2	-4	-6	-8
6	1	4	3	2	1	0	-1	-2	-3	-4
7	0	0	0	0	0	0	0	0	0	0
8	-1	-4	-3	-2	-1	0	1	2	3	4
9	-2	-8	-6	-4	-2	0	2	4	6	8
10	-3	-12	-9	-6	-3	0	3	6	9	12
11	-4	-16	-12	-8	-4	0	4	8	12	16

Figure 11.19: An example of how a surface chart can be used to compare information

Title, axis titles and legend

After you have inserted a new chart you should add in the following features:

- a title to give a name to the chart
- axis titles to name the data at the left and bottom of the chart
- a legend to identify what colours in the chart represent.

To change any of the above features, you need to click on the chart to select it. When selected, the **Charts** toolbar will open. Click on the **Layout** toolbar to insert a chart title, axis title or legend.

Move, resize and change chart type

To move or resize a chart you need to select the edge of the box around the chart. It is then very easy to drag the chart to another place using the mouse.

You can change the size of the chart when selected by using the mouse on one of the corners or the middle of a side. There is a visual indication you have found where to resize the chart when the mouse pointer changes to a double-ended arrow.

When the chart is selected, you can use the **Design** toolbar under the **Chart** tools to change the chart type.

3.4 Page layout

Excel® offers a number of tools to help with the page layout to ensure that the spreadsheet prints as required.

Size, orientation and margins

When you use the **File** toolbar to select **Print**, Excel® shows you a preview of what the spreadsheet will look like on paper. There are tools here to set:

- orientation for printing landscape or portrait
- paper size for printers that can use larger paper such as A3
- margins to control how much white space is left around the edge of the paper
- scaling to affect the size of the spreadsheet on paper, for example to fit to one page.

The **Page** tab of the **Page Setup** dialog box also includes some of the options seen in the **File Print** screen, as well as giving more control over the size of the print. For example, the **Fit to** options here could force the print into two pages.

Header and footer

The **Header/Footer** tab of the **Page Setup** dialog box offers a lot of control over headers or footers where you can set page numbers, date and time, as well as other information such as the file name.

Page breaks and page numbers

When you return from the **Print Preview** there will be dashed lines in your spreadsheet to show the edges of pages.

You can force page breaks in your spreadsheet by placing the cursor under and to the right of where you want the new page to start, then select the **Breaks** option from the **Page Layout** toolbar.

Date and time

You can add in the date and time to the footer. Go to the **Page Setup** dialog box and select the **Header/Footer** tab. Click the **Custom footer** option and then click the **Insert Time** and **Insert Date** options.

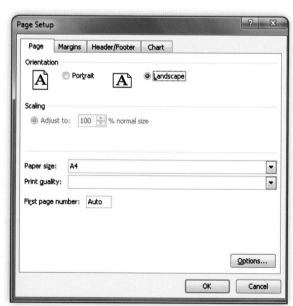

Figure 11.20: The Page Setup dialog box

3.5 Check spreadsheet information

You will need to check the information in your spreadsheet to ensure that it is correct and the calculations are accurate and free from errors.

Any errors you find must be corrected. You can do this by entering good data or calculations to replace the errors or you could edit the problem cells to correct them.

Accuracy of numbers, formulas and any text

Accuracy of data entry (i.e. adding the correct numbers to the spreadsheet) is very important and you need to check carefully that all the numbers are correct. You should always check back over your work to ensure that the data you have typed in on the spreadsheet matches the original information you were given.

Check that text is accurate (i.e. spelled correctly), capital letters have been used consistently and that cells have been appropriately labelled. Formulas and their results will also need to be checked. In certain instances, in order to successfully do this you will need to know the results of the calculations.

Suitability of charts and graphs

You will need to check the suitability of your charts and graphs. Consider how well they help to make the data in your spreadsheet understood. This may be difficult as they were your choice so you could ask someone else how well they think your charts explain the data.

Reveal formulas

You can reveal formulas by clicking on **Show Formulas** in the **Formulas** toolbar. This formula view can help you to identify errors such as when a calculation has been typed over with a number.

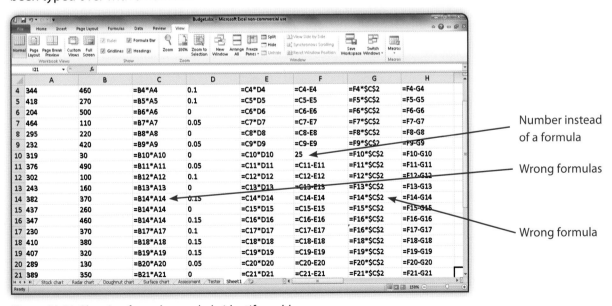

Figure 11.21: Showing formulas can help identify problems

Layout and formatting

Review the layout and formatting to consider whether it looks professional and makes the data in the spreadsheet easy to understand and edit. How clear do you think the overall spreadsheet is?

You will need to consider the **validity** and accuracy of your analysis. Ask yourself:

- Did the spreadsheet meet the requirements?
- Did the calculations produce their expected results?
- Was the spreadsheet fit for purpose?

You have to make sure your final spreadsheets clearly show and explain the data inside them. Try to look at the whole work and decide whether it communicates the meaning wanted in the requirements.

3.6 Problems with spreadsheets

To find errors you need to know the results that your calculations are expected to produce and to be able to check carefully that the numbers feeding into these calculations are correct, as well as the results shown.

You should also have some other numbers you can use as test data to back up the calculations work as required. These numbers may be provided, but you will probably decide yourself what the numbers are and also calculate the expected results from them being used by your calculations.

You can also explain how when you edit a calculation giving a bad result. Excel® uses colours to show the cells used by the formula or function (see section 1.2).

Using the Help function

You may need help with setting up your spreadsheet or to solve problems that may arise once you have set it up. Excel's® **Help** facility has information on spreadsheet functions and formatting features. To start Help press the **F1** key.

There is also a lot of help available on the Internet where you will find good explanations and examples of how to set up and use calculations and formatting in Excel®.

Sorting out errors in formulas, circular reference

You will, of course, sort out all the errors you find in your formulas and functions, including any circular references. These calculations must work correctly and you will need to test them thoroughly to ensure they do.

Check your understanding

1 Find an example of how each type of chart is used from the Internet.
2 Create a table showing examples of common errors in spreadsheets with how they could be avoided.
3 Find examples of good and bad formatted spreadsheets.

ASSESSMENT ACTIVITY

You work for a local building firm which specialises in building conservatories, replacing windows and repairing driveways.

The firm has a sales team consisting of three sales people and a sales director. Each member of the sales team earns a commission per sale: £200 for windows, £150 for driveways and £250 for conservatories. The sales director, Rana, has been looking at the sales figures for the last year in order to identify the most popular products and the best performing member(s) of the sales team.

Rana would like your help with producing a spreadsheet to help him analysis the data and to see how many sales each team member is making.

The sales have been divided down into quarterly periods throughout the year (spring, summer, autumn and winter). The spreadsheet should contain five pages – one for each quarterly period and a summary page.

The summary page needs to include the following data:

- Graphs or charts which show how the products have sold and how the sales team have performed. This information should be presented in separate charts.
- The sales team's rankings, in order of their performance.
- The sales team's commissions (per person).
- The products' rankings according to their sales figures (most profitable first).
- The commission paid per product.
- Further analysis of the figures (i.e. such as calculating averages).

Person	Item	Spring	Summer	Autumn	Winter
Andrea	Windows	5	7	6	5
	Driveways	2	0	1	2
	Conservatories	1	1	1	0
Gary	Windows	7	8	5	7
	Driveways	0	0	1	0
	Conservatories	1	2	2	1
Sagaal	Windows	6	8	10	7
	Driveways	3	1	2	1
	Conservatories	0	2	3	2
Terry	Windows	4	3	2	5
	Driveways	2	0	1	0
	Conservatories	4	3	3	2

Task 1

1 Plan out how you are going to produce the spreadsheet. Create a document to record this information and explain how the calculations will work and the numbers they will require.

2 Create your spreadsheet.

3 Add calculations to your spreadsheet which show:

- the total amount of products sold
- the total amount of commission
- the total amount sold per sales person.

Calculate the above for each quarterly period and add that information to your summary page.

4 Save your spreadsheet to a folder named 'Quarterly sales' and name the spreadsheet 'Sales 2012'.

Task 2

1 Produce sketches to plan how the spreadsheet will be structured and annotate these to show how the calculations on the summary page will work.

2 Add the calculations you planned to your summary page.

3 Implement your planning sketches to the summary page. Show how the sales team rank in order of their sales performance and identify the top sellers.

Task 3

1 Annotate your planning sketches to identify any formatting requirements.

2 Format your spreadsheet to ensure it looks professional.

3 Create charts or graphs to show and compare how the sales team have performed.

4 Create charts or graphs to show product sales over the period.

5 Use the Print Preview view to confirm the spreadsheet will print out correctly. Make any adjustments you think necessary to the page layout at this point.

6 Produce a checklist to ensure that the information from your spreadsheet meets the requirements.

7 Use your checklist to confirm everything is working correctly. Make any corrections which are needed.

8 Add a brief description of any corrections made to your checklist.

9 Produce a guide to finding errors in spreadsheet formulas with explanations of how each of the errors could occur.

10 Write a short report describing how you responded to the problems you had with producing your spreadsheet.

Website software

As a member of society in the 21st century, the Internet is likely to be a core part of your life – something which has always been there and which naturally blends with other aspects. It can be used to communicate research, play games, learn, shop and share experiences with others.

The Internet is made up of billions of web pages and in this unit you will learn how to make a website of your own. You will design and create a website of at least five web pages, with at least two different types of content on each page. You will add hyperlinks so that users can easily navigate around all your pages. You will add at least one feature to help users with special needs access your site. When you have checked and tested your website, you will upload it so that it can be viewed on the Internet or an intranet.

Learning outcomes

After completing this unit you should be able to achieve the following learning outcomes.

» **LO1**   Create structures and styles for websites

» **LO2**   Use website software tools to prepare content for websites

» **LO3**   Publish websites

1 Create structures and styles for websites

1.1 Content and layout

From a user's perspective, the two crucial elements of a website are content and layout. Content includes words, images, video and sound. Layout refers to the positioning of the content.

Web page content

Your web pages could include a range of content, such as:

- text – headings, main (body) text and captions for images
- images – photos, simple **graphics** and diagrams
- numbers – tables, charts and graphs
- moving images – animation and video clips
- sound – background music, video soundtracks and clips which play when clicked.

When creating a website, think about the software that the user will have on their computer. Most will be able to play common video file types, so if you wanted to include a video there would be a high chance that most of your users would be able to see and hear it. However, if you wanted to include a Flash® animation, remember that mobile devices generally do not support Flash® Player®. You could risk denying your users' access to that content.

> **Key term**
>
> **Graphics** – this is another term for images or pictures.

Case study: Nourish Restaurant (Part 1)

Nourish is a new restaurant opening near where you live. It is part of a chain of restaurants in towns and cities across the UK. The company that owns the restaurant chain has decided it needs a website to advertise its restaurants, including menus, special offers, customer reviews and the sources of its produce.

You have been asked to design the website. Before starting work, you need to think about its purpose and who it is aimed at (i.e. the audience). This will help you decide how it will look, including the:

- structure
- style
- content.

A restaurant website should be aimed at its customers. Its web pages could include high-quality photos of the restaurant and the food it serves; the food and drinks menus; its opening times; special offers; and the facility to book online. Customers will need to find it easy to navigate between pages.

In contrast, a school website would be aimed at its pupils and their parents. It would include information about the school, term dates, a newsletter and photos of school activities and trips. Its web pages would include useful links to other pages.

Web page layout

You also need to decide the layout of the web pages. For example, you could include a **side bar** or a **frame**. You need to choose a suitable background, such as one colour, a **gradient**, a pattern, a texture or a picture.

Consistency across all web pages on a site is an important aspect to consider when designing your layout. If a website is consistent, then users will come to recognise it and they will know they are still within your particular site when moving from page to page. The elements which could be the same in the layout are a **side bar** on the left of the page, the logo in the top left corner and text wrapped around all of the graphics. Using a consistent **house style** can also be useful.

Key terms

Side bar – an area at the side of a web page which usually contains navigation buttons or hyperlinks. Within the same website, this tends to be identical on every web page.
Frames – used for controlling the layout of a web page. Each frame is a separate page and can have a scroll bar, often containing navigation buttons.
Gradient – a colour range which fades gradually from one colour to another colour (i.e. black to grey to white).
Consistency – the same formatting and layout used across all pages.
House style – the same formatting across pages, including font, font size, colour, etc.

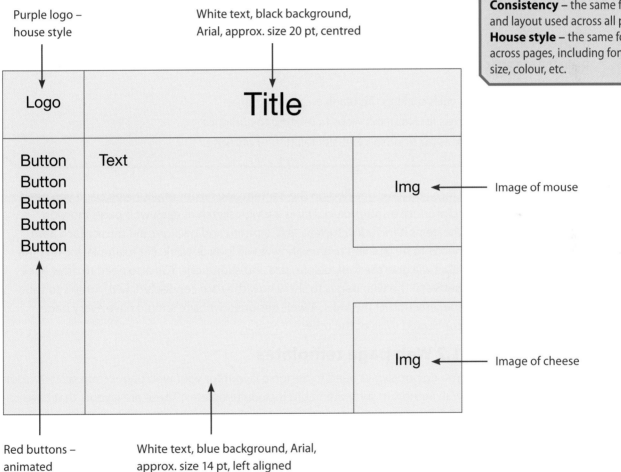

Purple logo – house style

White text, black background, Arial, approx. size 20 pt, centred

Logo

Title

Button
Button
Button
Button
Button

Text

Img — Image of mouse

Img — Image of cheese

Red buttons – animated

White text, blue background, Arial, approx. size 14 pt, left aligned

Figure 12.1: An example layout for a webpage

Look at the website of a well-known restaurant chain, such as Nando's, McDonald's or Frankie and Benny's.

1   Get a sheet of A4 plain paper and carry out the following steps:

    a In the top left corner, write who you think the audience of the website is and draw a circle around this.

    b In the top right corner, write what you think the purpose of the website is and draw a circle around this.

    c On the left side of the page, write a list of all the parts of the content on the main web page.

    d On the right side of the page, write a list of all the parts of the layout on the main web page.

2   Draw lines to connect the audience and purpose with the content and layout.

3   Do you think the audience and purpose affects the content and layout of a website? Why?

Consider the audience and purpose of Nourish's website. (*See the case study on page 268.*)

4   Get a new sheet of A4 plain paper and carry out the following steps.

    a In the top left corner, write who you think the audience is and draw a circle around this.

    b In the top right corner, write what you think the purpose of the website is and draw a circle around this.

    c Draw five lines from each circle to the blank area of the page.

    d Write five content ideas for Nourish's website relating to audience.

    e Write five content ideas for Nourish's website relating to purpose.

Once you have decided on the content and layout of your web page you need to produce a storyboard. This is a rough sketch of each web page showing the items it includes, such as text, a photo and background music. Each item needs to be labelled to show how it will look or work. For example, for text the label will give the font, colour, size and alignment. You also need to draw lines between the web pages to show how they are connected, with arrows to show the direction of the links. A well-designed website should have every page connected to all of the others.

1.2 Web page templates

You do not always need to design a layout for your web pages from scratch. Your web authoring software might include templates. These are layouts that have already been designed for you to use. For example, a template may have boxes where you type in your content. As you type, the template will automatically put the text into a pre-selected font and colour. You can also find templates on the Internet, although some sites will charge a fee for you to use them.

Your storyboard will help you to select the right template. When selecting a template, make sure that you think about the following things.

- Will your design work in the template you have chosen?
- Can you adapt the layout to suit your design?

- Can you add extra pages or delete ones that you do not want to use?
- How much technical knowledge will you need to use the template? Will you be able to create the web pages as you have designed them on your storyboard?
- Does the template come with tools to help you edit it (as sites such as WordPress™ and Blogger™ do)? If not, can you put it into a web page editor (such as Dreamweaver®) or edit it in a different way?
- Can you upload the template to the correct location so that it will be seen on the Internet?

Design layout

Design layout will vary but may include the following.

- **Text**: this can include letters, numbers and symbols. You need different styles of text in a web page, such as body text (the main text of the page), headings (the titles and subtitles) and captions (text which labels images).
- **Images**: web pages can include photographs or diagrams.
- **Numbers**: these can be represented on a web page as tables, charts or graphs.
- **Background**: a web page can be a single colour, a gradient, a pattern or even a texture. You can also choose to use an image as your background.
- **Structure**: this includes using frames which control the different sections of your web page or side bars which often contain navigation hyperlinks.
- **Moving images**: this can include animations or video clips.
- **Sound**: this can include background music, soundtracks to videos or animations, or sound clips which are linked to buttons.

Web page styles

Styles give web pages a consistent appearance. They help to give your website its own identity so that the user knows when they are on your site. Visitors will find your site easy to understand if your pages use the same style.

The styles you choose will depend on your website design. Consider:

- typeface – the size, colour and type of font and the alignment of headings, body text and captions
- lines – the type, thickness and colour of borders, tables and diagrams
- alignment – the positioning of the text, e.g. left, right or centred.

> **Did you know?**
>
> On average, you have eight seconds to grab someone's attention when they first visit your website. It is important that your website looks professional, appealing and easy to navigate. Templates will give your website this professional look. If you use the same template every time, then your web pages will look consistent in style and layout. This will appeal to users and make your website easy to get around.

Activity: Looking for consistency

1 Find three websites which have a consistent style across all of their web pages.
2 Describe five ways in which each website is consistent.
3 State what you have learned from this and how you will use this knowledge to improve the website for Nourish.

1.3 Website navigation features

Visitors to your website should enjoy using it and want to return. You can use a range of web page features to make your site user friendly, such as:

- navigation
- sound
- multimedia.

Web page features

Navigation

Users need to be able to easily find their way round your website. There are different tools that you can use to help them navigate. See Table 12.1 for a list of navigation tools.

Action button	When clicked, this performs an action. This could be a **hyperlink** which, when clicked, takes the user to another web page. This could also be a **Print**, **Submit** or **Search** button.
Menu	This is also known as a **navigation** or **nav bar**. It is usually at the left side of a web page, but can also be at the right or at the top. It contains a set of links which can access other parts of the website. A good design will put the menu in the same place on every web page with the links in the same order, and the page you are on highlighted, to show where you are on the site.
Hyperlink	By clicking on a **hyperlink** the user is taken to another page in the website, or an external website. A text hyperlink is a word or set of words which have been turned into a hyperlink. They often appear blue and underlined and when clicked on take you to the destination. Images can also be turned into hyperlinks. A button hyperlink is a special animation which has been made to be a hyperlink.
Hot spot	This is an area which has been made into a hyperlink. It could be an area on an image or a section of the text. When you click on any part of the **hot spot** you will be taken to another web page on the website.
Pop-up	This is a window which 'pops up' on the user's screen. It could be a separate mini-window which perhaps contains further information or, more frequently, it contains advertisements trying to catch the user's attention so they will click on them.

Table 12.1: Website navigation tools

Activity: Analyse website features

1 Find at least two different websites with:
- action buttons
- menus
- hyperlinks
- hot spots.
2 Analyse the features. Explain briefly:
- what is good about each feature
- what is bad about each feature
- how each of the features affects a user's experience.

Sound

Sound on a website can include background music for a page, a soundtrack to a video clip, or sound clips which can be played when a button is clicked.

Multimedia

Multimedia is where different elements have been combined; for example, sound and visuals in the form of an animation, or a video clip with a soundtrack.

1.4 Effect of copyright law and permissions

You do not need to produce all of the content for your website. You can use content created by other people, but you need to be aware of copyright laws when finding information for your web pages. These cover:

- downloads of music from the Internet
- use of other people's images
- use of other people's video clips or animations.

It is against the law to use someone's work without getting permission from the copyright holder.

Acknowledgement of sources and avoiding plagiarism

When you use someone else's work you must always acknowledge the source. This includes stating:

- who created the content
- where you got it (e.g. title and ISBN of a book)
- the date you got it.

Plagiarism means using someone else's work and pretending it is your own. This is taken very seriously and can lead to poor marks or even expulsion from college courses. You could also be sued by the owner of the work. Even accidental plagiarism could have serious consequences.

Did you know?

Copyright is a law which protects people's work and stops others from copying it. In the UK this law is part of a bigger law called the Copyright Designs and Patents Act 1988. As soon as someone has created something which is physical (e.g. a book, a painting, a written piece of music, a saved image or a web page) it is protected under that law. If anyone tried to copy it or pretend it was their own, the real author could take them to court and sue them.

1.5 Access issues

Some users may have difficulty accessing your website. This may be because:

- they have special needs, such as a visual or hearing impairment
- they are using a computer with a low specification or have a slow Internet connection.

When designing your site you need to make sure that all users can access the features on every page. Table 12.2 explain the different ways that users might experience difficulties accessing your website.

Font and font size	Is the text in a suitable font and font size? Select a font that all users will find easy to read. You could include a button on every web page to make the text size larger for people with a visual impairment.
Font colour and background colours	Is the font colour visible against the background? A light-coloured font on a light background will be difficult to read, as will black text on a dark background.
Screen readers	Can your web pages be read by a **screen reader**?
Captions	Do captions explain clearly what the images are? This is important for users who may have difficulty seeing the images.
Hyperlinks	Are the hyperlinks easy to use? Make sure that they are easy to click on.

Table 12.2: The different ways users might experience difficulties accessing your website

Download speeds

There are several browsers which your users might be using, including Internet Explorer®, Google™ Chrome™, Safari and Firefox. Each browser is similar, but interprets web pages differently. Browsers can have an effect on the speed on which a web page is loaded as some can read the code faster than others.

The speed of a web page will also depend on the Internet connection being used. For example, a 50 MB connection will be much faster than a 4 MB connection. In addition, a user on their mobile phone on a wireless connection will be slower than a user on a cabled connection.

Some users may not be able to access your website because they are using different technology. For example, if your site uses a lot of animation made in Flash® or large, high-quality graphics, then users with lower Internet speeds may find the site too slow and not visit it.

1.6 File types

When creating your website you are likely to use several different file types.
Table 12.3 shows some which you might come across.

Full name	Extension	Description
Web pages		
Hypertext mark-up language	.htm, .html	HTML is the basic language in which web pages are written. Web pages made in Dreamweaver® usually use these extensions.
Text		
Rich text format	.rtf	A format used to allow Microsoft® Word® documents to be opened in other word-processing software.
Microsoft® Word® document	.doc	A document made in Microsoft® Word®.
Portable document format (PDF)	.pdf	A document file which can be opened in all systems and is also locked, meaning it cannot be edited. Adobe® Acrobat® is free software which can be used to read PDF documents.
Images		
Graphics interchange format	.gif	Usually small files, which are good for websites. Can also have a transparent background, but often can be lower quality. Can be produced from Adobe® Photoshop® and similar graphics software. Can also be used to save small animations.
Joint photographic experts' group	.jpg, .jpeg	Usually a larger file than GIF but often higher quality. Good for photographs. Can be produced from Photoshop® and similar graphics software.
Adobe® Photoshop Drawing®	.psd	An image created in Photoshop® which can only be opened in Photoshop®. This file type needs to be saved as a different file type before being used on a web page.
Tagged image file format	.tiff	It can store both bitmap and vector images.
Charts and graphs		
Microsoft® Excel®	.xls	A spreadsheet made in Microsoft® Excel®.
Sound		
Microsoft® WAVE®	.wav	A sound file suitable for playing on Windows® systems and Microsoft® software, such as Windows® Media Player®. Often a large file as it is uncompressed.
MPEG-2 Audio Layer III	.mp3	A sound file suitable for playing on all systems. Often a very small file as it is compressed and is lower quality.

Table 12.3: File types used in making web pages

1.7 Store and retrieve files effectively

When creating a website, you are working with a lot of files. For each web page you do not just need to save the page itself, but also each image, video clip and other files separately. It is important that you know how to manage these files carefully and accurately.

Create and name

Your web pages need to have sensible names, especially as the file names will usually appear in the address bar of the user's browser. You should also make sure that your homepage is called 'index', as your web server will be looking for this file to become the homepage when you upload it.

When you save files for your website, make sure you use sensible file names. This is very important for images and other content which you bring into the web page, as you will need to locate them when you want to insert them. If you do not use appropriate file names when you save, it may be difficult to find your content when you are ready to use it.

Save and Save As

There are usually two options for saving your files: **Save** and **Save As**. Use Save As the first time you save a file as it will always give you a chance to enter a file name and find the correct save location. After that you should always use Save because it will save to the same file name and this will make saving faster. You only need to use Save As again after this point if you want to change the file name.

Folders

You are advised to create a new folder and save all of your website files into it, including your web pages, images, sound files, videos, etc. This makes uploading the website onto a web server easier, once you reach that point.

Find

The **Find** tool allows you to type in text and it will search for where it is used in your web page. This can be useful if you are looking for where you have entered specific text.

Version control

As you develop your website, you can save different versions of each page. This can let you experiment with layouts and formatting. You can go back to an earlier version if needed. You can create different versions of each page by saving it with the same file name but with v1, v2, v3, etc. on the end, and then FINAL on the end of your completed web page. This should make the files easier to find and you can decide which version of a page you want to use.

Import and export data

Importing data could be where you insert an image into your web page, or add a video clip or similar multimedia element. Although it will appear in the web page, it is saved separately and you must make sure once it has been included in the web page, that the file is not removed, renamed or deleted, as these actions will remove it from the web page.

Check your understanding

1 Name five types of content you could include in your web pages.
2 What is a storyboard and why is it important?
3 Name three things you need to consider when choosing or creating a template.
4 State one way you could improve:
   a text
   b video
   c an image before adding it to a web page.
5 How does copyright law affect the use of other people's images in your website?
6 What are access issues?
7 What are the differences between .gif, .jpg and .png?
8 Name three things you need to consider about storing files for your website.

2 Use website software tools to prepare content for websites

When preparing content for your web pages you need to make sure it is right for your site. Always keep in mind the purpose of your website and the audience it is aimed at.

Case study: Nourish Restaurant (Part 2)

The owners of Nourish are pleased with your designs for the restaurant's website. They have asked you to prepare the content for the site.

Before you can prepare content for the site, you need to start thinking about:

- Layouts for different pages. The website will be displaying different types of information (e.g. menus, special offers, customer reviews) so you'll need to look at how different types of information can be combined to present the best user experience.
- Client requirements. What is Nourish's vision for the website? How does it want the content presented?
- Content. What does the content consist of? What level of formatting and editing does it require? What software tools do you require to develop it?

2.1 Combine information

A web page gives you a great opportunity to combine different types of information, including text, images, numbers and multimedia elements like video and sound.

Combine images with text

Text can be combined with images; for example, you could add captions to your images to explain what they show, as in magazines and newspapers.

Presentation with audio and/or video

When using pre-recorded audio or video clips, you may not need to use the whole clip. You can edit clips before adding them to your web pages. A shorter clip with important information will encourage users to watch or listen. They may lose interest if the clip is too long.

Numbers with charts and graphs

Numbers can be presented in charts and graphs on web pages. These can be used to present complicated data visually and make it easy to understand for users. These could include bar charts and pie charts.

Text alignment

Text on a web page, just like a word-processed document, can be aligned left, right and centre. This refers to where the text is placed on the page.

- Centre is good for titles and headings.
- Left is usual for body text.
- Right can be used for other types of text, such as subtitles.

Text wrap

Text can be wrapped around images, which means that the letters will flow around the shape of the image. It can give the impression that the image has been placed into the text and the words have been forced out of the way.

Behind, in front and grouping

The order of elements can be changed to bring parts to the front or to send them to the back. This allows you to move parts to be over the top or behind others. Also, different graphic elements can be grouped which means they are joined together and can be affected together, such as resized and moved.

2.2 Editing and formatting techniques

When creating your web pages, you should make sure that you are using the tools available to match your design and produce a high-quality product.

See Table 12.4 for further explanation on the tools you can use to help you achieve this.

Select	Select means choosing an element to alter. This could be an image where you use the cursor to select it, or text which you can highlight.
Copy and paste	**Copy** and **Paste** can create another of whatever has been selected, whereas **Cut** and **Paste** will move something from one place to another.
Find and replace	**Find and Replace** allows you to look for a word and replace it with another word – it can be used to automatically replace all particular words in a document. Hold down the **Ctrl** key and then hold down the **F** key on the keyboard. This will pull up the **Find and Replace** box.
Undo and redo	**Undo** will remove the last action you undertook. **Redo** will redo an action which has been undone, or will repeat the last action that was taken.
Resize	**Resize** will make an image larger or smaller – to constrain proportions (keep it in proportion) you can hold the **Shift** key to make sure it does not stretch.
Crop	Using the **Crop** function will remove unwanted parts of an image.

Table 12.4: Tools available to help improve the editing process

2.3 Development techniques

There are many ways in which you can develop your web pages, and use software tools to improve your site and make a better final product.

When using content from other sources, such as text or images from the Internet, you may need to change the file type so that it is suitable for a web page. If you are converting a document to be shown as a web page, your file type should be .html. Therefore, you need to change it from a .docx file.

How to convert a document to html

1. Open the document in word-processing software such as Microsoft® Word®.
2. Click **File**, then **Save As**.
3. From the drop-down menu select the right folder location to save the file in.
4. Give the file a meaningful file name.
5. In the drop-down box beneath the file name, choose **Web Page (*.htm, *.html)**.
6. Click **Save**.

Alternatively, you may wish to use a word-processed document on your web page. You will need to turn it into a **.rtf file**. In Step 5 of the 'How to convert a document to html' (page 185), select **Rich Text Format (*.rtf)** instead.

You may also need to convert an image (for example, from a .jpg), which can be a large file to a .gif which is smaller and allows you to have a transparent background.

How to convert an image into .gif

1. Open the image in a graphics package such as Adobe® Photoshop®.
2. Click **File**. Then choose **Save As**.
3. From the drop-down menu, select the right folder location to save the file in.
4. Give the file a meaningful file name.
5. In the drop-down box beneath the file name, choose **CompuServe GIF (*.gif)**.
6. Click **Save**.
7. Another window will then pop up. Check that the settings match your requirements for the image (e.g. it supports transparency if you want a transparent background).
8. Click **OK**.
9. Another window will pop up. Click **OK**.

There may be other file types you wish to convert, such as .pdf into a .doc so you can edit it, or a .wma to a .mp3. You can also extract the soundtrack of a video by converting it from a movie file type (such as .avi) to an audio file type (such as .mp3). You can use software to do these conversions if you wish, or websites such as **www.convertfiles.com** or **www.zamzar.com**.

2.4 Evaluating requirements and outcomes

Your web pages must meet your users' needs and should look professional. You will need to check:

- text
- layout
- images.

Text

Whether you have written the text yourself or taken it from another source, think about the wording. Does the text make sense? Is it interesting to read? If not, try rewording the text to improve it.

It is important to proof-read the text carefully so that you spot any spelling or grammar mistakes. A spell checker program will help you to find wrongly spelt words and correct them. Programs such as Dreamweaver® do not have a spell checker function. Instead, you could copy your text into a Microsoft® Word®

document and use **Spell Check**. Word® also has a grammar checker which checks your punctuation, grammar and sentence structure.

Also look at the way the text appears on the page.

- Is the text easily readable? If not, you may need to choose a different type face or size.
- Are lots of words split across lines? Too many hyphens can make text harder to read.

Layout

There are several layout features you can include in your web pages.

- **Page layout** is the overall design of the page and placing of different elements. Make sure your elements are easy to read, images are well placed and hyperlinks are easy to use.
- **Margins** are the spaces around the edge of a web page, between the edge of the screen and your content. You should consider how much margin you will have – not too much to lose space for your web page elements but not going right to the edge.
- **Line breaks** and **page breaks**.
- **Tables** are grids made up of cells, rows and columns which can hold data. They can be really useful on a web page to display data clearly and to make data easier to understand for your users.
- **Frames** are a system of layout for web pages, where each part of the page is actually a separate page that is saved by itself.

Images

When using images in a web page, you need to consider their alignment and orientation. Alignment is where they are positioned on the page, e.g. left, right or centred. Orientation is which way around they are; for example, **portrait** (up and down) or **landscape** (across ways).

Also consider the colour mode and how many colours are used in the image, which will have an effect on the quality of the image. The file type which is used for images can also have an effect on the number of colours used. For example, a .gif has less colours available than a .jpg.

Filters can create a quick, distinctive effect on an image. For example, they might turn a picture black and white or put the photographic image into a style which mimics a hand-drawn image. Most graphics software has quick and easy ways to add a filter to the image.

It is a good idea to check that the file formats you have used for your images are suitable. Smaller file sizes will load faster on the Internet. Resaving a .jpg image as a .gif will make the file size smaller, but check that you do not lose too much quality by doing this.

When using images, you need to make sure that they are not pixelated. **Pixelation** happens when a bitmap image is stretched too far. If an image pixelates when you enlarge it to the size you want, you can either use the image at a smaller size or find a different image. If it is an image you have created, re-open the original and think about the file type you have used. Perhaps using a .jpg image would be more suitable than a .gif.

When you put an image that has a large file size onto a web page it loads at the original size, even if you make the image smaller in the web design software. This means that your page will take longer to show. It is always best to resize your images to the size you want *before* you put them into your web pages. This is known as optimising the image. You could also reduce the size of the image by cropping out any areas which are not needed.

You should also consider the resolution of an image, which is the number of pixels per square inch (or square centimetre).

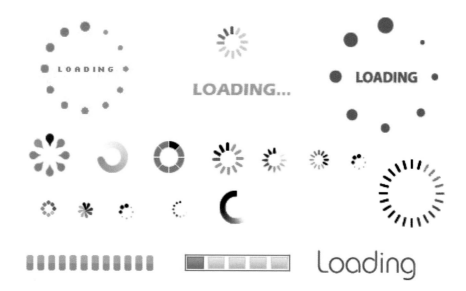

Figure 12.2: If a web page is taking a long time to load you will probably see a similar icon to those shown here

Check your understanding

1 Describe five types of hyperlink and how they might be used.
2 Explain why you might need to change the file format of three different files.
3 What is hyphenation and how might it affect text on a web page?

3 Publish websites

Case study: Nourish Restaurant (Part 3)

The owners of Nourish like their new website. Before you can upload it to the Internet, you need to test it and deal with any problems.

The things you need to think about include:

- Testing methods. You need to ensure that: all the content is on the site; pages load; hyperlinks work; navigation is user friendly; website works in different browsers; and that the site is fir for purpose and meets the client's requirements.

- Issues. If any issues are found during the testing stage then you need to know how to resolve these issues and ensure that they are fixed within the final version.

- Publishing/uploading. You need to ensure that once all the content is uploading that all the files have been accounted for and that they are displaying correctly.

3.1 Testing methods

Before your website goes online, you need to test that all elements are working. Things you need to consider include:

- that pages load correctly
- that images load on the pages – and that they are the correct images
- that hyperlinks work when clicked and that they take you to the right page
- that the website is user friendly and your navigation works
- that users with special needs or lower specification technology can access the website.

There are three main testing methods.

1. View your web pages in several Internet browsers, such as Internet Explorer®, Firefox, Safari and Google™ Chrome™, to see what they will actually look like on the Internet. To do this in Dreamweaver®, press **F12** at the top of your keyboard. This will allow you to check that:

   - the text is readable
   - the images are correctly sized and not pixelated
   - the layout of the content is correct.

2. Check that you can navigate fully and easily around the pages in your site.

3. Check that external links work, such as a hyperlink to another website.

You could use a test plan to make sure that you test every feature in your site. Table 12.5 shows an extract from a test plan.

Test number	What I'm testing	Web page	How I'm testing it	Expected result	Actual result	Success or failure	Date problem corrected
1	A hyperlink from the homepage to the Contact us page	Index.html	Left click once on the Home button	Index.html opens	Index.html open	Success	

Table 12.5: Example of a test plan

When testing your site you might find it helpful to answer the questions in Table 12.6. If possible, also ask some users from your intended audience to test your website. They can give you feedback about their experience and you can make any changes before it goes online.

Purpose	● Does it meet your purpose? ● Is it suitable for your audience? ● Will it attract the audience, and why?
Content	● Does it give the information needed? ● Is it clear? ● Is it easy to find and ordered well? ● Is it interesting? ● Is the language suitable? Does it avoid slang or jargon? ● Has the text been spell checked and proof-read? Have any spelling and grammar mistakes been corrected?
Layout and style	● Is the layout clear? ● Is the font easy to read? ● Do the colours of the font and background work well together? Is the text clearly visible? ● Does the style give the web pages a consistent appearance?
User friendly	● Is the navigation clear? ● Do the hyperlinks work correctly? ● Would a first-time user be able to get around the site easily? ● Is the site designed so that it is suitable for both a new visitor to the site and one who visits regularly? ● Can the site be viewed equally well in different software browsers?
Access	● Is it suitable for all users, including those with a disability? ● Can people with lower specification computers and/or slow Internet connections use the site?

Table 12.6: Questions to consider when testing your website

3.2 Identifying issues: problems with websites

Once you have tested your website you will need to fix any problems you find. These are the sorts of problems you may come across.

- Content is missing.
- Content is not suitable for the template, e.g. it does not fit or there are parts which are not suitably positioned.
- Text is missing or is not readable.
- Images are oriented or sized wrongly.
- Navigation does not work.
- Multimedia features may not work correctly. For example:
  - sound levels may be too low or too loud
  - sound and images are not **synchronised**
  - images may be blurred because the resolution is wrong.

3.3 Upload and publish website

Uploading is the system of putting web pages and their associated files (images, sound files, etc.) onto a web server or equivalent. Uploading is a term which comes from putting the files 'up' for others to see – the opposite of downloading, which is taking files from a server to your own computer. Websites must be uploaded and published so that they become available on the Internet (or network where they are being published).

Publishing is the process of allowing others to see your website. You may have uploaded your web pages onto a web server, but you need to publish them to make sure they can be seen by others.

Use file exchange programme to upload and publish

You can upload your web pages to the Internet using **File transfer protocol (FTP)**. This can usually be done straight to a **web server** through web design software or you can use specialist software such as CuteFTP™.

HTTP is another protocol which is used for viewing web pages. You may have noticed these letters at the front of some website addresses. It is this protocol that looks at a web address and knows that it needs to find the web page and display it on the screen.

You will also need to upload any files associated with the website, including images, videos and buttons. If these files are not uploaded, when the website is viewed online there will be gaps where this content is meant to appear.

> **Did you know?**
>
> When you find a problem you will need to find a solution to fix it, or if you are unable to fix it you will need to find a way around the problem. For example, make a blurred image smaller so that the blurring is less obvious, or replace it with another image.

> **Key terms**
>
> **Synchronise** – in multimedia, sound should be lined up well with the images which appear on screen so they are synchronised.
>
> **File transfer protocol (FTP)** – FTP is a system of uploading pages to a web server (or similar system) and is a standard method of working.
>
> **Web server** – a computer, usually with a large hard drive, special operating system and good Internet connection, onto which web pages are loaded so that others can see them over the Internet.

> **Remember**
>
> Every website you design and put on the Internet shows your professionalism, as well as the business or topic that the site is about. If you upload a poor-quality website, you are likely to get less work as a web designer in the future. Employers will look at your work and see its quality before hiring you. The same also applies to any public social networking or similar content which you put onto the Internet. Employers will search online to check a candidate before hiring them.

Check your understanding

1 What are the three main testing methods?
2 Why is it important to always upload high-quality websites?
3 What is FTP and how is it used?

ASSESSMENT ACTIVITY

Task 1 – Create structures and styles for websites

Create a design portfolio for Nourish's new website. The purpose is to present the portfolio (of several documents) to the owners and get their approval before creating the website. The website should contain at least five web pages, including the homepage.

The portfolio should include:

- a storyboard for each page in the website
- a description of the content for each page (which must include at least two types of content on each page)
- an overview of the purpose of the website and the target audience
- a template which you have created for the website
- prepared content ready to be put into the website, including organising it, combining it and using different software (you do not need to create all of the content yourself)
- a range of styles you have selected to use on the website to keep the appearance consistent and easy to understand
- a list of sources used with dates, identifying any copyright constraints which apply
- a description of access issues for your website
- a list of content created, with the file types used and the reasons for using them
- a demonstration of good file management, showing folders and sensible file names.

Task 2 – Use website software tools to prepare content for websites

Create the website you have designed.

Make sure you use:

- a variety of editing and development techniques
- clear text and images on your pages with good layout
- a range of features to help users navigate around the site and access the information
- suitable file formats.

Task 3 – Publish websites

1 When you have completed the website, check the web pages against your design. Use IT tools to ensure that text, layout and images meet your purpose and the needs of the audience. Make corrections as necessary.

2 Use testing methods to check that everything on your website works as planned and can be viewed correctly in a browser.

3 Fix any problems that you came across during testing. Describe how you dealt with them.

4 Upload your website using a suitable program so it can be viewed on the Internet or an intranet.

Word-processing software

This unit will provide you with the knowledge and skills that you need to edit, combine, structure, format and present information using a word processor.

This unit will introduce you to a range of documents that are featured in different types of organisations. Using a variety of templates, tables and forms, you will then be expected to take responsibility for producing your own documents that will meet a particular purpose or function.

Learning outcomes

After completing this unit you should be able to achieve the following learning outcomes.

» **LO1** Enter and combine text and other information accurately within word-processing documents

» **LO2** Create and modify layout and structures for word-processing documents

» **LO3** Use word-processing software tools to format and present documents effectively to meet requirements

1 Enter and combine text and other information accurately within word-processing documents

Most word-processed documents are made up of more than just text. Even simple letters can include small logos, while reports often use a wide variety of charts and images to support the text.

1.1 Types of information

Documents can be made up of different types of information, including:

- text
- numbers and graphics, such as tables and charts
- photographs and other images
- simple graphic images, such as lines and borders.

The type of information you need in a document will depend on the purpose of the document and who will be reading it. It is important to know who the audience is (i.e. who the information is aimed at), and what its purpose is (i.e. to persuade, to inform, to inspire, to entertain). This level of detail will help you identify what type(s) of information are required. Consider the two examples below and think about how the information needs to be presented to the relevant audiences:.

- A poster advertising a swimming course for beginners will look very different from a poster advertising the opening of a local shop for children's clothing. The layout, choice of images and fonts will be different. The information on the swimming poster is likely to be concise and factual, the text will be shown in a large font and one or two images used designed to catch the attention of passers-by (see Figure 13.1).
- A guide produced for a local authority hearing service needs to be appropriate for the widest range of potential readers. It is likely that the users of the clinic will include the elderly, who may need easily readable large-sized fonts and a straightforward layout style. Graphic images will be useful for example photos of hearing aids rather than text descriptions. Other graphic objects that might be needed could include location maps.

Hyperlinks

Documents can also contain other types of information, like **hyperlinks**. Hyperlinks allow the user to 'jump' out of the document to another location, such as a file, picture, web page or program. If the hyperlink links to a web page, the user needs to be working on a computer connected to the Internet. You can also use a hyperlink to 'jump' to other parts of the documents or to external reference documents or web pages.

See *Unit 6 section 1.1* (*page 64*) for more information on how to insert a hyperlink.

Charts and objects

In certain situations, charts can be more effective than text as a way of showing or communicating an idea. This can also be the case for spreadsheets, graphics and presentations. See *Unit 10 Presentation software* and *Unit 11 Spreadsheet software* for more information on how charts and objects are used within spreadsheets and presentations.

Case study: Millhouse Swimming Centre

Millhouse Swimming Centre has been struggling to get people signed up for swimming lessons. To try and boost registration numbers, the centre has decided to offer swimming sessions aimed at different age groups.

Your manager has asked you to help out with this task.

1   Using the information featured in Figure 13.1, come up with a design for three new posters aimed at:
    a   primary school pupils
    b   working adults
    c   over 60s.
    You can make changes to the image, the 'Come and get fit' strap line, fonts, and the layout.
    Produce hand-drawn designs and some notes explaining the differences between the posters.

Beginners Swimming
4-week course
Starts Wednesday 12 September

All Welcome
'Come and get fit'

£25.00 Full
£15.00 Under 12s
£10.00 Over 60s

Millhouse Swimming Centre
enquiries@millhouseswimming.com
01806 457341

Figure 13.1: An example poster

1.2 Techniques and input methods

There are different ways to input text into a system.

- For text that already exists as a clear printed copy, you could use an electronic method such as **optical character recognition**.
- You can usually input text from another software application into Microsoft® Word® using an importing function. If the applications are in the same suite of software, such as Microsoft® Excel® and Microsoft® Word®, you can **Copy** and **Paste**. (*See page 297* for more information on copy and paste.)
- For new information, you are likely to use a keyboard to input the text. Keyboards are the normal input device for computers, laptops, mobile phones and other portable devices.

Key term

Optical character recognition (OCR) – a means of digitising text using a compatible scanner. It can be useful if you have a clear printed copy of the text you wish to input or adapt. The scanning process is often available within a graphics scanner or photocopier. Many OCR systems cannot recognise complex layouts, such as combinations of text boxes, columns and images. Like voice recognition, the results of OCR scanning can need time-consuming checks and edits to get them right.

Other input methods

Other input methods include:

- voice recognition
- touch screen
- stylus.

Voice recognition

Voice recognition is an alternative to typing on a keyboard. You talk to the computer and the software converts your words to text, which then appears on the computer screen. Usually, the software needs 'training' to recognise your voice. Text inputted in this way needs careful proof-reading.

Once set up correctly though, voice recognition can be a fast way to input text. It can also help people with disabilities, particularly those who find it difficult or painful to type.

Figure 13.2: How words can be miscommunicated

Touch screen

Touch screen technology is where an electronic device, such as a mobile phone, tablet computer or computer game, recognises the touch of a finger and responds to this. A lot of smartphones use this technology.

Stylus

A stylus is a small pointing and drawing device, similar in look and size to a small pencil. It can be used to make selections from menus and also input handwritten text into some computers.

When it is vital for a document to be accurate, such as in the production of medicine information leaflets, it is important to choose the right input device.

Keyboard skills

Figure 13.3 shows a typical keyboard layout. However, you may find some slight differences in the keyboard you use. It is always important that the final text is checked very carefully for mistakes (proof-read). Although there are proofing tools within the software (described later in *section 3.3 on page 330*), you must also read the text carefully, correcting errors as they are identified.

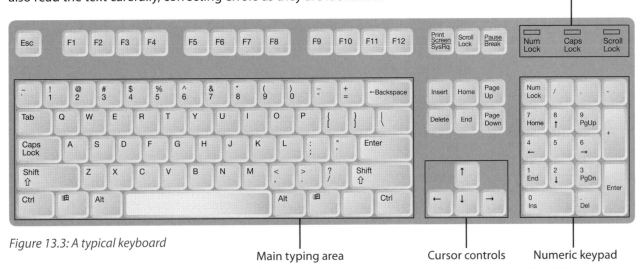

Indicator lights

Main typing area

Cursor controls

Numeric keypad

Figure 13.3: A typical keyboard

The most commonly used keys are the character keys A to Z. They are arranged on the keyboard in the same order as old-fashioned typewriters. The top line of letters begins with QWERTY and this is known as the **QWERTY keyboard**.

Table 13.1 describes some of the other keys that you may use regularly.

<table>
<tr><td colspan="2">Key term</td></tr>
<tr><td colspan="2">Clipboard – a temporary place where text and images are stored when you either cut or copy things. Anything in the clipboard can be pasted in the same or another document.</td></tr>
</table>

Shift key	Shift ⇧	When you press and hold the **Shift** key, any alphabet keys you press at the same time will type as capital letters (upper case). Holding down the **Shift** key will allow you to type the top character on keys where two symbols are shown, such as the @ symbol, the £ symbol or the & symbol.
Caps Lock key	Caps Lock	When you press the **Caps Lock** key once, all of the alphabet keys you type will be in capitals. Press the key again to return to lower case letters.
Print Screen key	Print Screen SysRq	When you press the **Print Screen** key, an image of your current screen is taken and placed on the **clipboard**.
Delete key	Delete	When you press the **Delete** key, the character to the right of the cursor is deleted.
Backspace key	←Backspace	When you press the **Backspace** key the character to the left of the cursor is deleted.
Ctrl key	Ctrl	The **Ctrl** or **Control** key is always used together with another key to provide shortcuts. For example, when it is pressed with the letter 'P', it takes the user to the **Print** dialog box.

Table 13.1: Keyboard keys that are regularly used

Some operations are also available as **keyboard shortcuts**. In some circumstances and with practice, using a shortcut can increase efficiency as it avoids the need to switch from the keyboard to the mouse and then back again.

For more information on using keyboard shortcuts to format text, *see section 3.1 on page 324.*

1.3 Selecting and using templates

A template is like a 'fill in the blanks' document where the user is given a document with most of the fixed titles, structures and fonts already entered.

Templates can be:

- simple word-processed documents that can be reused
- special files that are created using word-processing software – the templates contain placeholders which prompt the user to type in their own information.

Existing templates

Microsoft® Word® provides a number of templates. Some of them will have been automatically downloaded when you installed Word®, while others are available from the Microsoft® website.

When you select a new document, the different template types will be displayed (see Figure 13.4). The **Available Templates** displayed at the top of the window are already installed on your computer.

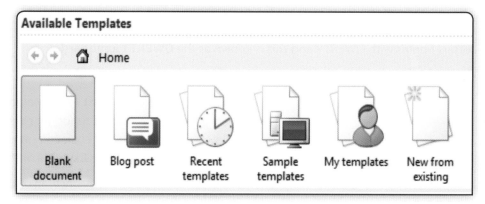

Figure 13.4: Available templates

The **Sample Templates** folder will be the same for everyone with the same version of Word®. As new templates are created, modified or downloaded, they are stored in each user's **My Templates** folder. Two commonly used templates are the **Blank document** and **Blog post**.

Activity: Choosing the right template

Microsoft® Word® 2010 is populated with a number of different template types. Have a look at the templates and identify templates you could use for the following:

- party invitation
- company report
- certificate
- checklist
- letter
- newsletter
- flyers
- planners.

Using the Internet, find other examples of template types.

How to use an existing template

1. Select the **File** menu and click **New**.

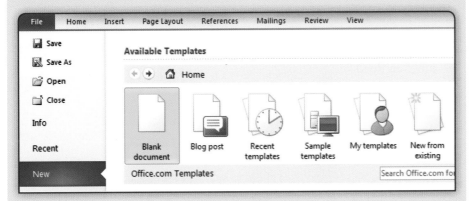

Figure 13.5: Available Templates in Microsoft Word®

2. In **Available Templates**, select **Sample templates**.

3. In the **Available Templates** window that appears, choose **Equity Letter**.

4. Below the **Equity Letter** that appears on the right side of the screen, click **Create**. A new document is created based on the **Equity Letter** template. Figure 13.5 shows the top part of the template.

- The information shown in square brackets are placeholders – they act as a prompt for what to type.
- **<Computer name>** will show on your computer as your name or your company's name.

continued

5. Click **[Pick the date]** and in the box that appears, click the down arrow and choose the date from the calendar that is displayed.

6. Click on the other placeholders and replace them with the text shown in Figure 13.6.

7. In the **File** menu, click on the **Align text right** icon to align the sender details to the right, as is usual in the UK (as shown in Figure 13.6).

21/11/2011

Peter Jones
Jones' Fabrications Ltd
Unit 7 Hartington Industrial Estate
Peterborough
PE4 5TY

Jane Peter Motors
Junction Road
LONDON
FT5 6HY

Re: Your Enquiry last week

Dear Jane,

Many thanks for your enquiry. We will be able to produce the mouldings that you need by the beginning of March. Please let me know if this date is agreeable and we will produce a detailed costing.

Regards,

Peter Jones

Manager
Jones' Fabrications Ltd

Figure 13.6: A completed template

8. Save the document using an appropriate file name..

Create new templates for common documents

Part of your job may involve you having to send out similar documents such as letters, reports, and so on. To save time you can create your own template and store it in your computer's **Templates** folder, or in a network drive. The template can be loaded when required and used to quickly produce documents in the same style.

The available styles are shown in the **Styles** section of the **Home** menu. To see all of the styles available, click the down arrow on the right-hand side (see Figure 13.7). All newly installed systems will show the same set of styles. However, as new ones are created or existing ones modified, the sets will change.

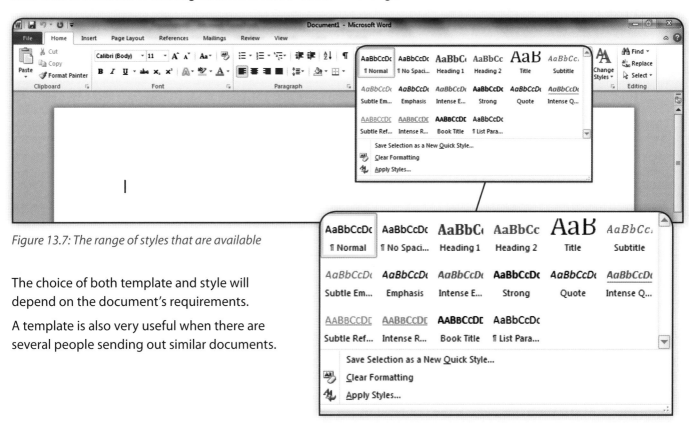

Figure 13.7: The range of styles that are available

The choice of both template and style will depend on the document's requirements.

A template is also very useful when there are several people sending out similar documents.

Activity: Create a new jobs letter template

You work in an educational institution and you need to create a jobs letter template which students can use to help produce job application letters.

1 Create a new blank document.

2 Add the text as shown below. Adapt the letter according to your own circumstances or details. However, be wary of putting in too much personal detail unless you are confident that the document will be kept secure.

3 The text shown in **RED** will act as placeholders to indicate which bits of the document are to be overwritten with the information relevant to each particular application.

4 When you are comfortable with the content, fonts and layout of the letter, save the document as a template in your **Templates** folder.

145 Park Avenue
St Albans
AL2 7HG
Email: Jo.newbury32375@aol.com
Phone: 01705 8789986

Date: (INSERT DATE)
(Name of contact)
(Company Name)
(Company Address)
(PostCode)

Dear (INSERT FORMAL NAME e.g. Mr or Mrs …),

I am writing in response to the advert that I saw in (enter newspaper, website, etc.). Please find attached my curriculum vitae which details my qualifications, experience and interests. I also enclose a completed application form.

At the moment I am in the last term of a BTEC First Diploma in I&CT, and will be available if needed to start work in three weeks' time.

Yours faithfully,

(remember to sign it)

Jo Newbury

Figure 13.8: Creating a new template

1.4 Editing tools and techniques

To use the editing tools successfully, you need to be able to highlight text. There are two ways to do this.

1. To highlight a single word, double click it – you can tell it is highlighted because the background colour changes.

2. To highlight larger amounts of text, click at the start of the section, then hold and drag the cursor over the words. At the end of the section you wish to highlight, unclick and the background colour of the selected text changes.

To select other objects such as graphic images, clicking on the object will highlight it ready for any editing operation.

Copy, Cut and Paste

The **Cut**, **Copy** and **Paste** functions allow you to recreate text or images in a quick and efficient manner.

How to copy and paste text from one place in a document to another

1. Highlight the text and either click **Copy** in the **Home** menu or press **Ctrl+C**. The Copy and Paste icons are shown in Figure 13.9.

2. Move the cursor to where you want the text to be copied to and then either choose **Paste** or press **Ctrl+V**. The text is copied to the new position.

Figure 13.9: Cut, Copy and Paste icons

Moving text to another part of a document is similar to copying and pasting. In this case you cut, or delete, the text and then paste it where you want it to appear.

How to cut and paste text from one place in a document to another

1. Highlight the text and either click **Cut** in the **Home** menu (see Figure 13.9) or press **Ctrl+X**.

2. Move the cursor or insertion point to where you want the text to be placed and then either select **Paste** or press **Ctrl+V**. The text is moved to its new position.

You can also use these techniques to copy material or move it to another document.

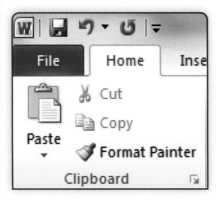

Figure 13.10: Undo and Redo icons

Figure 13.11: 'Find' and 'Replace' icons

Undo and Redo

Undo allows you to go back a step and undo an action that you have carried out. For example, if you deleted a piece of text in error, you can undo the delete by clicking the Undo icon in the top left-hand corner of the screen. **Redo** repeats the last action you did. You can find the Redo icon in the top left-hand corner of the screen.

Drag and drop

Another way to move text is to 'drag and drop'. Highlight the text to be moved and then click and hold the mouse button and 'drag' it to the new location. Unclicking 'drops' the text into its new place in the document.

Find and Replace

The **Find** and **Replace** functions are very useful.

- **Find** allows you to search for a word or a piece of text in a document.
- **Replace** enables you to find a word or piece of text and then replace it with another word or piece of text. For example, in a business letter changing a customer name that has been spelt incorrectly would need to be found every time it appears and replaced. Using the Replace function is easier than looking through the letter and changing the name individually each time it appears.

How to use the Find function

1. Place the cursor at the start of the document. Click the **Find** icon on the right-hand side of the **Home** menu (see Figure 13.11).
2. In the **Find and Replace** dialog box that appears, type the word(s) you are searching for in the **Find what** box.
3. Click **Find Next**. The word is automatically highlighted the first time it appears in the document.
4. The **Find and Replace** dialog box remains open. Click **Find Next** again, and if the word appears again in the document it will be highlighted.
5. Repeat until every word is found. Click **Close** to close the message box.
6. Click the **Close** icon at the top of the **Find and Replace** dialog box to close it.

How to use the Replace function

1. Click the **Replace** icon on the right-hand side of the **Home** menu (see Figure 13.11).
2. In the **Find and Replace** dialog box that appears, type the word(s) you want to replace in the **Find what** box. Type the word(s) that you want to replace them with in the **Replace with** box.

continued

3. Click **Replace** and the word(s) will automatically be replaced with the new word(s). If the word(s) that you want to replace appear several times in the document click **Replace All** to automatically replace every instance with the new word(s).

4. When all the word(s) have been replaced, a pop-up box appears with the message **Word has finished searching the document**. Click **Close** to close the message box.

5. Click the **Close** icon at the top of the **Find and Replace** dialog box to close it.

Insert

To insert new text in your document, move the cursor to where you want the text to appear and type in text. Normally, the keyboard is in **Insert** mode (see the cursor controls in *Figure 13.3 on page 291*). This means that as you type new text, the existing text will be pushed to the right.

To replace existing text with new text, highlight the text you want to replace and type in the new text.

To insert a new paragraph, press the **Enter** key. To add an extra blank line, press **Enter** twice.

When you reach the end of a line, Word® automatically wraps the text to the next line.

Delete

You can delete characters to the right of the cursor by pressing the **Delete** key. You can delete characters to the left of the cursor by pressing the **Backspace** key.

To delete several lines or paragraphs of text, highlight the text to be deleted and press the **Delete** key.

Size, crop and position

There are a number of editing tools available which make editing images easier.

When an image is selected, **handles** appear around the edge of the image and these can be used to change the size of the image. The image can be moved using a hold and drag technique when the cursor is inside an image. **Cropping** an image means to select a portion of it. For example, you take a photo of a group of people but later decide that you only need one face. You can crop the photo to show just a single face. The **Crop** icon can be found in the **Picture Tools** menu, which is automatically displayed when an image is selected.

The process of cropping is described in *Unit 9 Imaging software* (*page 165*) and *Unit 10 Presentation software* (*page 218*).

1.5 Combine and merge information

Word-processed documents tend to be mostly text. Sometimes, though, you need to include other types of information to support the text. For example, an instruction booklet could include diagrams to help the reader understand what needs to be done. A sales report could use charts and tables to put across information in a visual way.

Deciding when to combine information in a word-processed document will be based on:

- the requirements of the new document
- its audience
- the format or application package in which the information, or data, is stored.

If the information to be used is already available in a different document or application package, it may be easy to bring it in from that source. This is an efficient way of working as it is quicker to take information directly without having to retype or recreate it, and will also result in fewer errors. A simple example is copying a photo from your Documents folder to use in a family newsletter. See Table 13.2 for examples of more complex situations where you could combine or merge information from other software or documents.

Adding a spreadsheet	• An end-of-year company report may be mainly text. It could also usefully include part of a spreadsheet from Microsoft® Excel® to illustrate the state of the company finances.
Adding graphs	• A document that summarises the results of a market survey could include some graphs that show the trends in the data collected.
Mail merge	• A local sports club could merge a database of all of its members with a standard letter at the end of the year asking them to renew their subscriptions. This is called a mail merge (for more information, see the *Mail merge documents and labels* section on *page 213*).
Combining documents	• A garden centre company with a number of different branches needs to make sure that there is a common source of information about prices – prices increase every so often but also fall during special promotions. One way that this can be achieved is to create a master price list and then link the information in this list to all other documents, so that when prices change they are automatically shown in every related document.

Table 13.2: Examples of situations where you could combine or merge information from other software or documents

Insert, size and position

Microsoft® Word® provides a number of basic graphic shapes that can be inserted individually, or combined together and inserted into a document. Some examples of graphic shapes are shown in Figure 13.12.

Figure 13.12: Example shapes

How to insert a graphic shape in a Word® document

1. Select the **Insert** menu and click the **Shapes** icon.

2. In the drop-down menu that appears, choose a shape of your choice.

3. Place the cursor where you want the shape to be in your document. Then click and drag the shape until it is the required size.

4. Click in a space away from the shape to complete the process.

The size and proportions of a shape can easily be changed using the **handles** that appear when the shape is selected. There are a number of handle types, including size handles and rotation handles (see Figure 13.13). For example, putting the cursor over a corner handle, and then clicking and dragging the handle will make the shape larger or smaller.

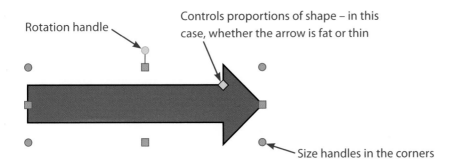

Figure 13.13: Handles used to manipulate shapes

The position of a shape can easily be changed. To move a shape, click on the shape and then hold and drag it to a new position.

Wrapping text

When you insert an object or an image (such as a shape, graph or photo) into a document, you need to decide whether to **wrap** the text around the image. For example, do you want the text to keep tight to the edge of the image? Or do you want the image to appear in the middle of the text with space around it? Figure 13.14 shows the different wrapping options. The **Behind text** option may only be suitable for graphics or shapes that are almost transparent so that the text is still visible.

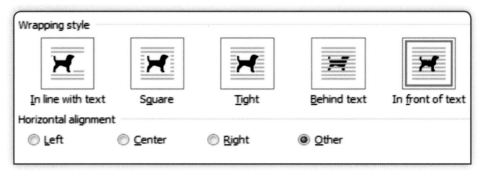

Figure 13.14: Wrapping options

Order and group

Individual shapes can be combined into more complex images and then 'grouped' so that they can be manipulated as one new shape.

After the individual images have been inserted and arranged, hold down the **Ctrl** key and then click on each of the images in turn. When all have been selected, group them using the **Group** option (see Figure 13.15).

Figure 13.15: The Group option

If you look at Figure 13.16, you will see that this was created using the three basic shapes shown in Figure 13.12. The wrapping of the shape was set to square to allow it to be placed at the side of the text.

Figure 13.16: A grouped object

Activity: Creating a company logo

Your manager at Millhouse Swimming Centre was impressed with your poster designs and has asked you to create a simple company logo. It will be used in a variety of material, including headed notepaper. Your manager has asked you to come up with three ideas – but she would like to see either a stylised pool or diving board incorporated in the design.

1 Open a new Word® document. Using a series of simple shapes, create three potential new logos.

2 When you have completed the logos, group the individual objects. Then **Copy** and **Paste** the new grouped object a few times. Experiment by changing the size of each. Make at least one of the logos small enough to be used for headed notepaper.

3 **Save** and **Print** the document. Decide which of the three logos is the most appropriate.

Hyperlinks

Hyperlinks allow the user to 'jump' out of their current location (i.e. a document) to another location (i.e. a file, a web page or program). See *Unit 6 Using email, page 70*, more details.

Link information in a document to another source

When the information already exists in another form, the best way of combining the information is by creating a direct link from the new document to the source. Any changes to the source data will appear automatically in the new document.

In the 'How to link documents' step-by-step guide, you will create a spreadsheet document and link this to a word-processed memo document.

See section *Building spreadsheets* in *Unit 11 Spreadsheet software*, page 234, for more information on creating spreadsheets.

How to link documents

1. Open your spreadsheet program, then open a new worksheet.

2. Create a simple table and populate it with the information shown below.

Sales category	Revenue
Shrubs	£17,858.54
Vegetable plants	£1,441.20
Flowering plants	£10,751.52
Café	£25,090.90
Garden tools	£7,557.39
Garden chemicals	£3,672.83
Seeds	£4,095.58
Garden furniture	£4,764.75
Total	**£75,232.71**

Table 13.3: Sales categories and revenue

continued

3. Save the workbook and give it a meaningful file name.

4. Open a new Word® document. Create a memo with the following text.

To: All employees
Date: 12 December
Subject: Sales 2011–12

We are pleased to report that the total sales figures for this year have increased 3% on this time last year.

This is very positive in the light of the current economic climate and the directors have again agreed that a bonus of £200 will be paid to all employees in their January salary.

Happy New Year!

The Directors

Figure 13.17: Word® document memo

5. Save the memo with a meaningful file name.

6. Open your worksheet, then highlight and copy the final total figure.

7. Switch to the Word® document and highlight the required characters.

8. In the **Home** menu, click the arrow below the **Paste** icon and choose **Paste Special**. (See Figure 13.18.)

9. From the options, choose to paste the information as **Unformatted Text** and make sure that the **Paste link** button is selected.

10. Select **OK** to paste the data from the total cell over the required characters.

11. Save both files again.

12. Increase the value of one of the figures in the spreadsheet as if there were some late sales made.

13. Check the memo document – the total sales figure should have changed to reflect the new total figure in the worksheet.

continued

The 'Paste link' box needs to be selected

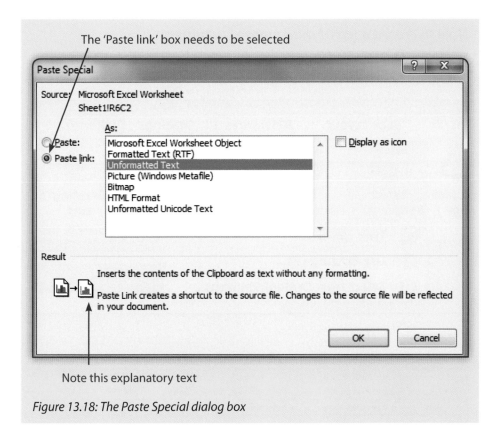

Note this explanatory text

Figure 13.18: The Paste Special dialog box

Activity: Linking documents

1 Using the spreadsheet that you created for the 'How to link documents' guide, create a graph of the data.
2 Link the graph to your sales memo. (If you need help with this then refer back to the 'How to link documents' guide.)
3 Make changes to the values in the spreadsheet and check that the graph changes similarly and automatically.

Mail merge documents and labels

Companies often send letters and targeted advertising materials to many customers. Instead of writing the letters or producing the labels individually, they can use the **Mail merge** feature.

A list of customer names and addresses is needed to feed the mail merge. This can either be created within the word-processing software or using other software such as a spreadsheet or a database. In the 'How to create a list of mail merge customers' guide on page 306, the list is created using Word®.

How to create a list of mail merge customers

1. Choose **Mailings** and then choose the **Select Recipients** option.
2. Choose **Type New List**. (See Figure 13.19.)

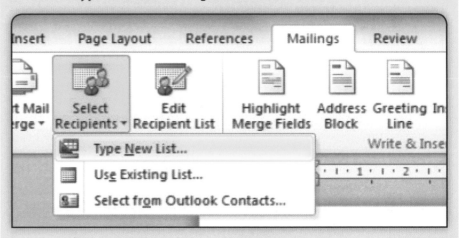

Figure 13.19: The Type New List option

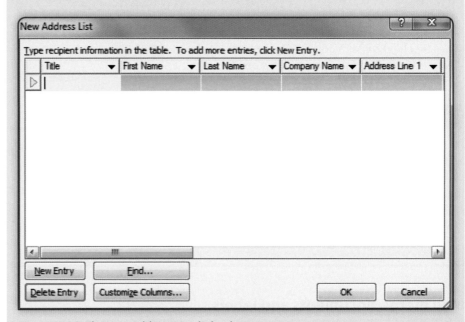

Figure 13.20: The New Address List dialog box

3. A blank **Address List** with some standard columns (fields) will be displayed (see Figure 13.20). You will need to customise the fields to suit your needs.
4. Within the **Customize Columns** option, use the **Add** button to add in new fields and the **Delete** button to delete uncesessary fields.

continued

5. The **Customize Address List** shows the result of the customisation. (See Figure 13.21.)

6. When you have completed the customisation, click the **OK** button.

Figure 13.21: Result of customising address list fields

You are now in a position to add records.

7. Add some sample customer details (see Figure 13.22). You can always edit the records and add new ones using the **Edit Recipient List** option.

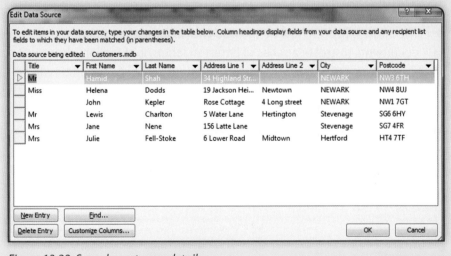

Figure 13.22: Sample customer details

continued

8. Once the address list has been created, select **OK**. You will be asked to save this file. Provide a meaningful name and choose the location to store it in. The normal location for a stand-alone machine is 'My Data Sources' within the 'My Documents' folder.

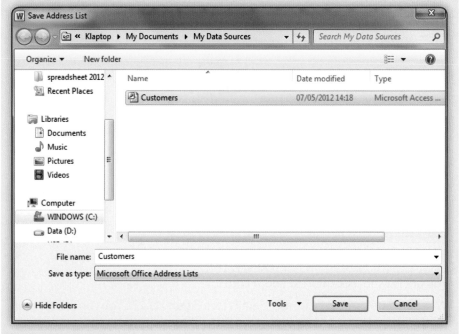

Figure 13.23: Saving the address list

9. The address list can now be merged with a number of different documents to create a series of letters or labels. In this example we will show how a letter that tells customers about some special offers can be created. You can either send letters to every customer in the list, or just a limited number of them.

10. Select **Edit Recipient List** from the menu (see Figure 13.24).

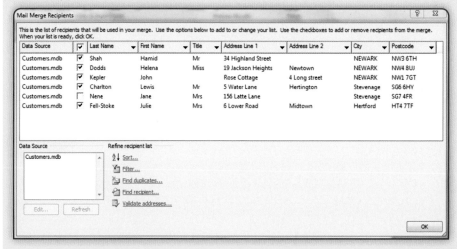

Figure 13.24: The Edit Recipient List option

continued

11. Check boxes are displayed at the side of each record. In Figure 13.24, Jane Nene has been deselected because you are not going to send her a letter. Click **OK** and you will be returned to the main Word® window.

12. You have now created the address list and chosen which people you intend to send letters to. Now you need to create the letter itself.

13. If necessary, start a new blank document.

14. Lay out the fixed text and any images you intend to use, and then use the **Insert Merge Field** option to put the fields into the appropriate places. Figure 13.25 shows the fields that have already been inserted.

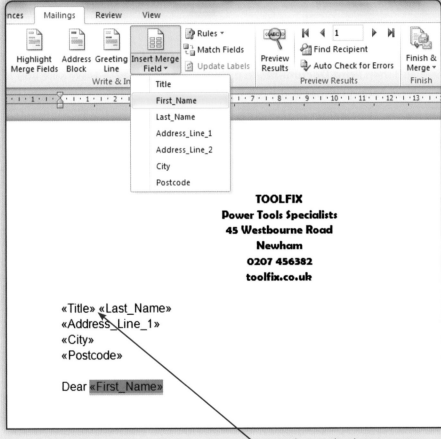

Figure 13.25: The Insert Merge Field option

Note the need to leave a space between the merge fields

15. Once you have completed the document, save it under an appropriate file name.

16. The mail merge is now complete. However, it is usual to review the letters before sending them to the printer. Click on the **Preview Results** icon (see Figure 13.26) and check through the letters using the arrows.

continued

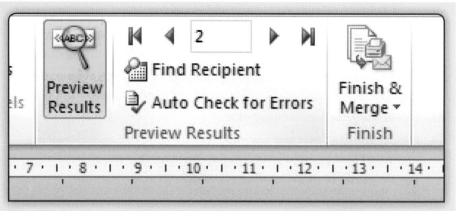

Figure 13.26: The Preview Results icon

17. If the letters are correct then you can select the **Finish & Merge** icon and then **Print Documents** to produce the mail merge. Make sure you have enough paper in the printer!

Activity: Using mail merge to produce labels

The Centre's management team has decided that as an incentive, all registered members will be given their own clothes locker.

You have been asked to produce labels that can be stuck onto each locker. Each label should contain the member's name, membership number and the Centre's logo.

1 Create a list containing the relevant information for 15 members.
2 Use the **mail merge** facility to produce a set of labels. If possible, use real labels but if these are not available, print them on ordinary paper.

1.6 Store and retrieve files effectively

If you have stored (saved) and opened files in other Microsoft® packages such as Excel®, you will find the process very similar to Word®.

Name

It is good practice to use a logical rule for naming files, one that will help manage the different versions that you might create. One simple solution is to add the text version at the end of the file name, such as ver3 for version 3 (see the section on version control on the next page). Alternatively, you can add the date to the end of the file name.

Save As

The first time you save a file you will need to use the **Save As** option in the **File** menu. This option allows you to:

- give the file an appropriate name
- choose the location where you want to save it.

Normally the file is saved in your own **Documents** folder, but check with your tutor or supervisor to find out what location you are expected to use, and any other local guidelines.

Find

If needed, files can be found using the **Search** facility. Check with your tutor or supervisor if you need help finding your files.

Share

Microsoft® Word® 2010 supports users **sharing** a file. This allows them to work on it, possibly at the same time, over a network. This feature only works when the computers are running Sharepoint software.

Version control

In many situations, you will be creating a number of versions of the same file. It is usual to keep track of the different versions using the name of the file.

Often, you will need to make additions or amendments to a file. If you need to keep a record of these changes, it is easiest to use different versions of the same file name. For example, if you create a file called 'Work experience report' and then update it, the new version could be called 'Work experience report v2'. The v2 refers to version 2.

Import/export

Word® does not have any specific **Import** or **Export** menu choices. However, it is possible to import information from other types of files and also export a Word® document to a number of different file types.

In a similar way, when using **Save As**, it is possible to choose a variety of different file types (file formats) that can then be read by other types of software. Three commonly used examples are PDF, web page and plain text. The web page is particular useful as it allows a Word® document to be converted (exported) to a form that can be used on the Internet.

File size

It is useful to have an awareness of the amount of disk space that a given file occupies. The file size is measured in kilobytes (KB) or megabytes (MB). Typical text-only files can be fairly small – one page of text may be only 20 or 30 kilobytes. File sizes can, however, increase dramatically if graphic images are included. File size is not usually a problem unless the file is being attached to an email, and in some situations it is necessary to zip files so that they occupy less space.

Folders

Folders are excellent ways to organise your files. It is a good idea to create a folder for each project you work on, and then you can save all of that project's information in the folder. This will keep all relevant information together, in the same place.

Activity: Creating an information leaflet

You have been asked to create an information leaflet. You have been given the basic information that you need to include (see below). The leaflet needs to be A4 size, landscape format and in a two-column layout. This will allow the leaflet to be folded into A5 size. You will need to produce two pages that when placed back to back will fill both sides of the A5 leaflet. The leaflet is designed to be used by adults, including older adults.

The text can be re-ordered as needed and the choice of layout, fonts, etc is left up to you – if any suitable images are available these can also be added. The overall style of the leaflet should be consistent with the poster developed earlier.

Your tutor may make a document with this 'raw' text already entered available to you. Otherwise, the text will need to be entered.

Millhouse Swimming Centre
High Street
Millhouse
Cambridge
CK8 7PH
Contact enquiries@Millhouseswimming.com
Phone 01806 457341

Millhouse is your local swimming pool and sports centre where you can enjoy swimming and other fitness activities using quality facilities. Membership is free. However, users must complete an application form and obtain a leisure card to gain access. Bring your completed application form along to reception and we will issue you with a card. Join today and get fit with us!

Opening times
Weekdays: 7.30am to 8.00pm
Saturdays: 9.00am to 6.00pm
Sundays: 9.00 am to 1.00pm.

Millhouse has a wide range of facilities, including:
fitness studio
swimming pool
thermal spa
café
gym
aerobics studio.

You can also book our sports hall for birthday parties or other events.

Email us for more details and costs.

1   Describe the reasons why organisations and individuals use templates.

2   Describe the possible drawbacks of using voice or optical character recognition input devices.

3   Explain a possible problem if someone chooses to use the automatic Find and Replace function to replace the word 'end' with the word 'finish'.

4   You are asked to produce a document that shows the calories that are in different three-course menus. What type of information would you include – unformatted text, text with tabs, a table or a bar chart?

2 Create and modify layout and structures for word-processing documents

2.1 Document requirements for structure and style

The structure of a document normally refers to the way in which the whole document is organised. Formal documents, especially longer ones, are typically organised into paragraphs and chapters. Layout refers to how the information is set out on the page, including aspects such as the number of columns used. The style of a document includes the fonts, colours and other formatting that it uses to display the information.

Document layout and house style

Many text documents require structure (e.g. paragraph sections, headings, bullet points, etc.) in order to make them more accessible and easier to read.

Organisations often use their own layouts for documents in the form of templates. They may also have their own 'house style' which uses the organisation's colours, fonts and logos. This gives the organisation its image.

The layout and style used will often depend on the purpose of the document. Here are some examples.

- Reference documents, such as dictionaries and information manuals, must be carefully ordered to allow users to access different parts of the document quickly and easily. In these cases, tools such as indexes and contents pages are useful.
- Novels require little structure apart from chapters. This is because most readers will read the text from the beginning to the end. The text needs only to be clear and readable. Page numbers are essential given that readers will not typically finish the novel in one go and will need to remember their place.
- Company reports are often read by a wide audience, including those outside of the organisation. They must be carefully structured because typically users will want to access various parts easily. Reports will use the organisation's house style, including colours, fonts and logos, to ensure that the corporate image is maintained.

2.2 Tables and forms

Forms

A form is a structured document where you fill in information in certain places. You are likely to have filled in forms previously (e.g. to join a course, register an email address, join a library, etc.). Nowadays, many forms are online and you complete them by placing the cursor in the correct text box before you type in the relevant information.

Form fields can be used to control information that is being entered into a document. A variety of controls are available, including drop-down boxes, check boxes and text boxes. Figure 13.27 shows how forms can be used to collect information from a student. Check boxes and drop-down boxes are both excellent ways of ensuring accurate data entry.

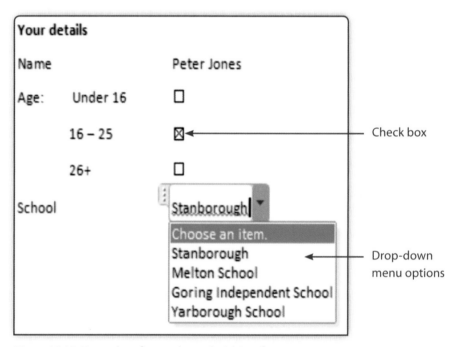

Figure 13.27: Examples of controls used within a form

The facility to insert form fields is in a **Developer tab** but is not available in the default Word® 2010 ribbon installation. It is possible to add the Developer tab through **Customize** within the **File Options**.

Tables

Tables are a good way of organising or presenting information in a document. They display information that is naturally divided into different but related sections (see Table 13.4).

Seed list		
Name	**Price**	**Estimated number of seeds in packet**
sweetcorn	£2.25	100
runner beans	£2.99	50
sprouts	£2.45	500
broccoli	£1.85	100
onions	£2.25	200
beetroot	£1.55	200
cabbages	£3.30	200
carrots	£1.30	200
lettuces	£2.00	700
parsnips	£2.55	100

Table 13.4: A table showing a seed list with prices table

Insert and delete cells, rows and columns

Once you have created a table, you may need to add or delete a row or column depending on the information you are entering. You may also need to add or delete information in an existing table which will involve adding or deleting a cell, row or column.

How to create a table and enter information

1. Select the **Insert** tab and choose **Table**.

2. In the **Insert Table** drop-down box that appears, slide over the boxes to select the number of rows and columns in your table (you can create a table up to a maximum of 10 columns and 8 rows using this method). Click to create the table in your document.

3. To enter information into the table, click in each cell and type in the information. Press the **Tab** key to move the cursor to the next cell.

> ### *How to insert or delete a row or column in a table*
>
> 1. To insert a column, right click in the column next to where you want the column to appear.
> 2. In the drop-down menu that appears, choose **Insert** and click **Insert Columns to the Left** to insert a column to the left of the column you are in, or **Insert Columns to the Right** to insert a column to the right of the column you are in.
> 3. To insert a row, right click in the row above or below where you want the row to appear.
> 4. In the drop-down menu that appears, select **Insert** and click **Insert Rows Above** or **Insert Rows Below** to insert a row above or below the row you are in.
> 5. To delete a row or a column, click in the row or column you want to delete and then right click.
> 6. In the drop-down menu that appears, select **Delete Cells**.
> 7. In the **Delete Cells** dialog box that appears, select either **Delete entire row** or **Delete entire column** and click **OK** to delete.

Adjust row height and column width

Normally, the row height automatically adjusts to suit the size of the text used. However, it can be changed in a variety of ways. The easiest way is to right click when the cursor is inside a table and then select the **Properties** option. This provides a window with a number of choices, including how you can set the row height to a specific number.

The column width can also be changed within the Properties window.

Merge and split cells

In some circumstances, it is useful to merge a number of cells within a table. An example is shown in Table 13.5, where you might want a 'Sales' heading over two columns.

	Sales	Sales
Section	Month 1	Month 2
Trees	£3,303.33	£2,365.99
Shrubs	£1,256.79	£1,293.41
Vegetable plants	£125.53	£166.09
Flowering plants – perennials	£704.11	£1,296.61
Flowering plants – annuals	£387.74	£324.22
Bulbs	£125.90	£105.74
Total	**£5,903.41**	**£5,552.06**

Table 13.5: Sales table 1

Sales		
Section	Month 1	Month 2
Trees	£3,303.33	£2,365.99
Shrubs	£1,256.79	£1,293.41
Vegetable plants	£125.53	£166.09
Flowering plants - perennials	£704.11	£1,296.61
Flowering plants - annuals	£387.74	£324.22
Bulbs	£125.90	£105.74
Total	**£5,903.41**	**£5,552.06**

Table 13.6: Sales table 1 showing merged cells

How to merge cells

1. Highlight the cells you wish to merge.
2. Right click and then select the **Merge Cells** option from the display list.

How to split cells

1. Highlight the cell you wish to split.
2. Right click and then select the **Split Cells** option from the display list.

You can choose to split cells into two or more cells, and also either split them to add new rows or to add more columns.

Merged and split cells can present problems though, if the table is going to be sorted later.

Convert text to table

If you already have some text that you wish to convert into a table, it is possible to do so directly without having to create the blank table and then copy and paste the information into each cell separately.

The text must have separators that will be used to divide up the material into the different cells. The separators can be commas or tabs. The example text below uses commas and refers to the number of absent learners from a school over a week.

**Mon, Tues, Wed, Thurs, Fri
15,7,12,8,31**

The command to convert text to table can be found within the **Insert Table** menu option. After highlighting all of the text and selecting **Convert Text to Table**, Word® displays a window (see Figure 13.28).

> **Did you know?**
>
> The properties of a table refer to a number of details, such as the column width, the row height, the borders and shading used, cell alignment and the cell margins. These details can be changed in a variety of ways but right clicking when the cursor is inside a table and selecting Table Properties from the list gives you access to all of the properties. Other objects, such as pictures or graphic shapes, also have properties. However, the nature of them will vary according to the type of object.

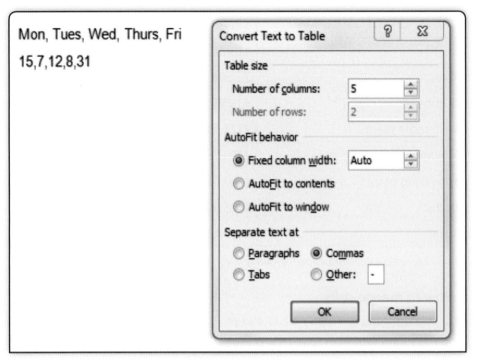

Figure 13.28: The Convert Text to Table window

Word® has automatically recognised that there are two rows and five columns. The commas that were placed between the numbers have successfully been recognised as separators. Table 13.7 shows how the information is then displayed.

Mon	Tues	Wed	Thurs	Fri
15	7	12	8	31

Table 13.7: How information is displayed when you use the command to convert text to a table

Horizontal and vertical text alignment

Information in table cells can be aligned to the left, centre or right within the cell, as with normal text. Unlike ordinary text, information in cells can also be aligned to the top of the cell, the middle of the cell, or the bottom.

How to align cells

1. Highlight the relevant cells.
2. Right click, then choose the **Cell Alignment** option and choose your preferred option from the list.

Borders and shading

Borders define the edges of various objects, including tables. Borders and shading can increase the visual impact of a table. After placing the cursor inside an existing table, the **Table Tools** menu will be displayed. Use the options within the **Design** menu to select your effect. See Figure 13.29 for an example of the pre-set table styles which can be used.

Figure 13.29: Pre-set table styles

Sort

It is possible for information in a table to be sorted on one or more columns.

The **Sort** options can be found within the **Layout** tab of the **Table Tools** menu. The Table Tools menu is automatically displayed when the cursor is inside a table.

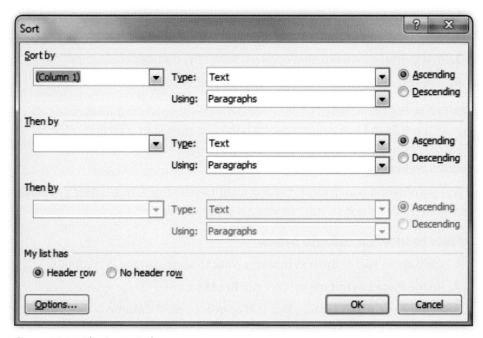

Figure 13.30: The Sort window

You can sort data in a variety of ways and by one or more columns. In the example screenshot (Figure 13.30), the choice has been made to sort the information in ascending order by Column 1.

2.3 Columns

Columns are commonly used in newspapers and textbooks because you can fit more text on a page than in one column. Shorter lines are also easier to read.

Add and delete columns

In Word®, when you type into the document the text automatically runs across the entire width of the page (excluding page margins). This means that the text is displaying in a single column. You can change this so that text displays in two or more columns. You can change the entire document, or you can select sections of the document to change. If you are producing text on a standard A4-size page, it is best practice not to select more than two columns of text; otherwise it would be very hard to read it.

To convert the whole document to column format, select **More Columns** in the **Columns** drop-down menu. The **Apply to** option at the bottom of the window allows you to apply the change to the whole document or just from that point forward.

> #### How to convert existing one-column text into two or more columns
> 1. Highlight the text that you want to convert into columns.
> 2. Select the **Page Layout** menu and click the **Columns** icon.
> 3. In the drop-down box that appears, select the number of columns.
> 4. The text automatically changes the number of columns.

The text in the columns will snake around the page, similar to a newspaper layout. It will fill the first column on the page and then start a second column. If you have more text than can fit on a single page, it will scroll over to the first column on the next page, and so on.

If you are entering text in a column and want to start a new one before you have completely filled the first, you can insert a column break.

> #### How to insert a column break
> 1. Click at the end of the text that you want to appear in the first column.
> 2. In the **Page Layout** menu, click the **Breaks** icon.
> 3. In the **Page Breaks** dialog box that appears, select **Column** break.

Modify column width

All aspects of columns can be changed, including:

- the width of the column – columns can be of equal width or unequal width
- the width of spacing between columns.

How to modify the column width

1. Place the cursor in the column section in your document.

2. Select the **Page Layout** menu and click the **Columns** icon.

3. In the drop-down box that appears, choose **More Columns**.

4. In the **Columns** dialog box that appears, change the width and spacing of your columns.

5. Click **OK** to change the width of your columns.

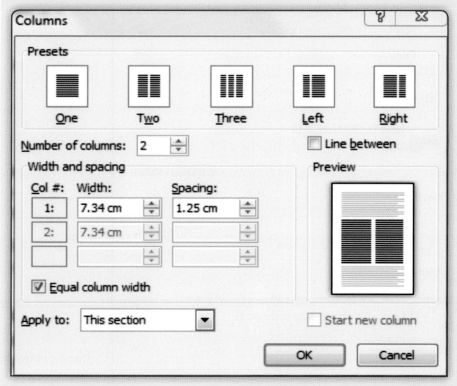

Figure 13.31: How to change the width and spacing of columns

2.4 Styles

Heading styles

In some formal documents, such as reports, the information is divided into chapters or sections. To help the reader find their way around the document, it is important that the different levels of headings all use the same style, so that the structure of the document is clear. For example, look at the headings in this book and you will find that all of the unit titles, main headings, subheadings, and so on have their own style. This helps the reader to see how all of the material interrelates.

You can format the style of each heading separately, but a quicker way is to use the available styles provided by Word® as part of the **Home** menu. Use the same style for all similar headings.

2.5 Page layouts

The **Page Layout Page Setup** menu provides a number of options that control such aspects as paper size, orientation and margins. All of the options shown here, as well as others, can also be seen when you select the **Print** option in the **File** menu. In Word® 2010, a preview of the printed image is displayed, and various page layout choices are presented on the left.

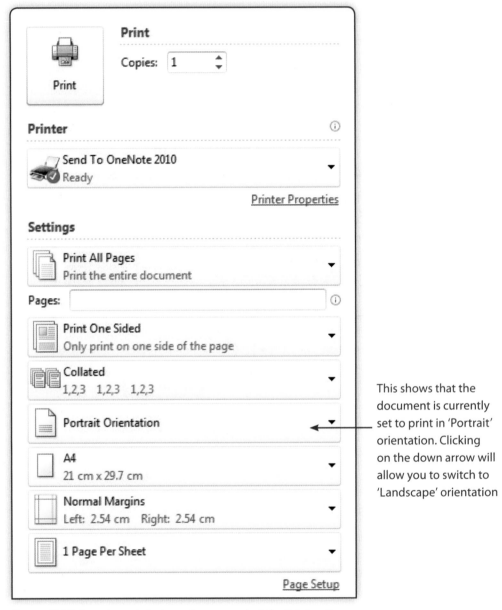

This shows that the document is currently set to print in 'Portrait' orientation. Clicking on the down arrow will allow you to switch to 'Landscape' orientation

Figure 13.32: Page layout choices when you select the Print option in the File menu

The default paper size used in most printers is A4, although a number of other sizes are available. A3 can be used where you want larger printed output, perhaps for posters. It is important to match your choice of paper size within the software with the actual paper in the printer. Books and magazines have a wide range of different sizes.

In a similar way, the normal orientation is portrait – this means that the height is greater than the width. This can be changed to landscape easily and often does not involve changing the paper in the printer.

Margins

Margins refer to the space between the text and the side and top of the page. The gap between the text and the side/top of the page can be changed, making it wider or smaller. Click the **Page Layout** tab and select **Margins** to see the different margin settings available. You can also click **Custom Margins** to set your own depth and width.

Header and footer

The **header** is the space at the top of the page. It usually contains a document title, logos, etc. The **footer** is the space at the bottom of the page and it usually contains the page number.

Click **Insert** and then select either the **Header** or **Footer** tab to see the available options. It is good practice for a document to have page numbers and a title.

Check your understanding

1 Describe what application package might be more appropriate for the seeds sales table if you were going to include a number of equations and totals.
2 Why is it sensible to use heading styles in a long document rather than formatting each title separately?
3 Note three advantages of using standard layouts or templates for similar documents.

3 Use word-processing software tools to format and present documents effectively to meet requirements

You need to decide the best way to format and present a document so that its meaning is clear to readers. For example, individual characters or words can be formatted to show how the words would be emphasised if the text was being read out loud rather than read from the printed page. To give the document its structure, the text can be divided into paragraphs with headings or chapters.

3.1 Techniques to format characters

Word® provides a number of formatting techniques, to help you:

- communicate the meaning of the text within a document
- emphasise particular words or sections.

You can format words or characters by selecting the appropriate icon from the **Home** menu, or using a keyboard shortcut such as **Ctrl+B** to make the text bold. Some of the keyboard shortcuts used to format characters are shown in Table 13.8.

Open the Font dialog box to change the formatting of characters	**Ctrl+D**
Change the case of letters	**Shift+F3**
Change all letters to capitals	**Ctrl+Shift+A**
Make text bold	**Ctrl+B**
Underline text	**Ctrl+U**
Double underline text	**Ctrl+Shift+D**
Italicise text	**Ctrl+I**
Change letters to small capitals	**Ctrl+Shift+K**
Change text to subscript	**Ctrl+Equal Sign**
Change text to superscript	**Ctrl+Shift+Plus Sign**

Table 13.8: Common keyboard shortcuts used to format characters

Size and font style

There are a wide variety of different fonts (or typefaces) that can be used to format text. Examples include:

- **STENCIL FONT**
- Arial Font
- **IMPACT Font**
- Comic Sans Font

Choosing the right font can improve the look of a document, although it is important not to switch fonts too often. Many organisations ask for particular fonts to be used for their external communications to give a consistent image.

There are two main families of fonts: the SERIF (note the decorative curls at the ends) and the SANS SERIF. It is generally accepted that large volumes of text are easier to read if they are formatted in a serif font.

How to change the typeface or font size

1. Highlight the text you want to change.
2. Within the **Home** menu, go to the **Font** section. From the drop-down boxes choose the typeface and font size you'd like to use.

Colour, bold, underline and italic

It is a good idea to highlight any words that you would emphasise if you were speaking them out loud. You could also highlight words that are significant in other ways. Ways of emphasising words include:

- changing the colour of the word
- making the word bold
- italicising the word
- underlining the word.

The font section allows you to change the font of the highlighted text. Click on the down arrow to see the font options

This tool allows you to change the size of the text

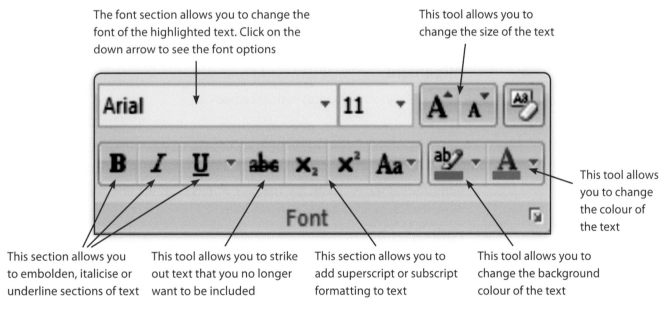

This tool allows you to change the colour of the text

This section allows you to embolden, italicise or underline sections of text

This tool allows you to strike out text that you no longer want to be included

This section allows you to add superscript or subscript formatting to text

This tool allows you to change the background colour of the text

Figure 13.33: Formatting icons

Superscript and subscript

In the same way that characters and words are emboldened or underlined, they can also be formatted as ^{superscript} or $_{\text{subscript}}$.

These options are available in the Font section near **Bold**, **Italic** and **Underline** (see Figure 13.33).

Special characters and symbols

Word® has special symbol fonts that can be used as long as you know what character represents which symbol. For example, the letters a, b, c, d, e, f, g, h, i, j with the Wingdings font applied to them become:

♋ ♌ ♍ ♎ ♏ ♐ ♑ ♒ ♓ ♋

Many common symbols can be inserted directly into the text from the **Symbols** section of the **Insert** menu by clicking the **Symbol** icon and selecting a symbol such as:

© ™ ≥ ≤ ☺

The **Symbols** section also allows you to insert a range of equations. Click on the **Equation** icon and select an equation, such as the one shown in Figure 13.34.

$$(x + a)^{n+1} = \sum_{k=0}^{n} \binom{n}{k} x^k a^{n-k}$$

Figure 13.34: Example of an equation inserted from the Symbols section

3.2 Format paragraphs

Paragraphs in a document should be formatted so that the text is clear and understandable to the reader. There are a range of formatting techniques which you can use and these are covered below.

Alignment

Text is usually left aligned, as in this textbook, or

it may be right aligned, as here,

or centred, as in this example.

You may wish your document to look more formal, in which case you could justify both sides of the text with the margins. In this case, the text will automatically space itself across the page, as shown here.

Line spacing

Most word-processed documents automatically appear in single line spacing and this generally suits most purposes. Sometimes though you may want to increase the size of the line spacing; for example, to 1.5 lines or double line spacing.

> ### How to change line spacing
> 1. Highlight the section you wish to change.
> 2. Go to the **Home** tab, and within the **Paragraph** section select the **Line spacing** icon (which has an arrow pointing upwards and an arrow pointing downwards).
> 3. Choose the appropriate option from the drop-down menu.

Tabs and indents

Tabs and indents are used to achieve similar effects but are quite different in the way they operate.

You will see a series of tab stops on the ruler (see Figure 13.35) but you can create your own for particular situations. When the left tab icon is displayed, click on the ruler where you want the tabs to be. In the example screenshot, tabs have already been set at 2 cm and 5 cm.

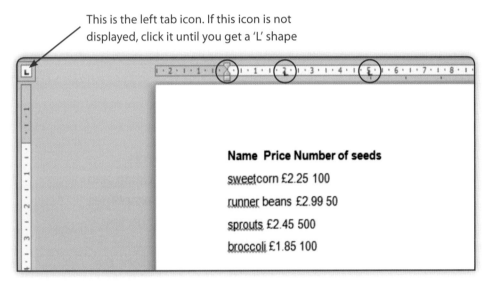

Figure 13.35: Tab stops on the ruler

Figure 13.36 shows the situation when the third tab is set at 7 cm and each of the lines of text are tabbed forward using the keyboard tab key. This technique is appropriate for simple columns of information when you do not need to create an actual table.

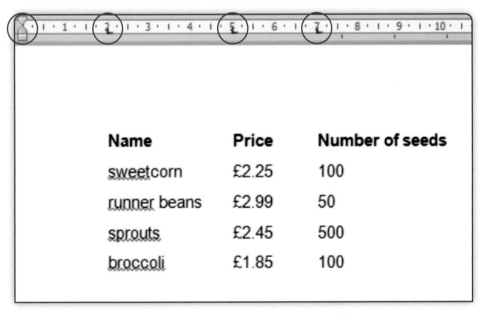

Figure 13.36: How text is tabbed forward using the keyboard tab key

Indents are similar in that they impact how information is 'pushed in' from the left-hand margin, but the are useful when working with paragraphs rather than tabular information. Figure 13.37 shows the indent icons on the ruler. In each case the indent is moved by clicking, holding and dragging to the required location. The example text has been set with a first line 'pushed in' (indented) to the 4 cm mark, the left indent set at 2.75 cm and the right indent at 11 cm. This feature can be used to bring attention to a small amount of text within a document.

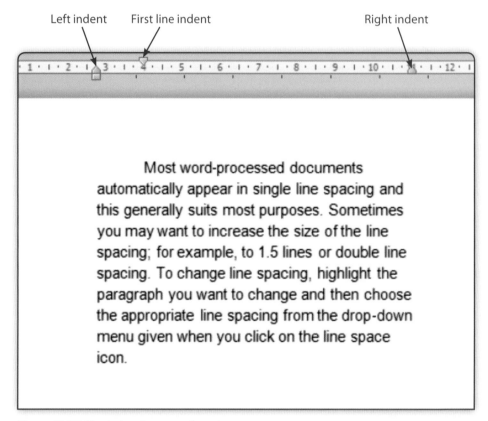

Figure 13.37: The indent icons on the ruler

Borders and shading

When individual characters, words and paragraphs are entered, they are normally given a white background without any borders – as in this paragraph. It is possible, however, to highlight them using borders and shading . The border options are available in the **Paragraph** section of the **Home** menu, although they can be applied to individual characters and words as well. Shading options are provided in the **Font** section of the **Home** menu. You need to select and highlight the character, word or paragraph first and then apply the border or shading.

Bullets and numbering

You may decide to use bullets or a numbered list when you have a list of items that you want to show separately from the main text.

- Bullets/lists help to show clearly where each item starts, and you will see many examples in this textbook.
- The bullet/list style you choose may also **indent** the text, which adds to the presentation.

How to add bullet points

1. Highlight the text you want to mark with bullet points.
2. Go to the **Home** menu and click on the **Bullets** icon within the **Paragraph** section.
3. The **Bullet Library** will display and you can choose what type of bullet point you'd like.

To add a numbered list, choose the **Numbering** icon in Step 2 (rather than the Bullets icon).

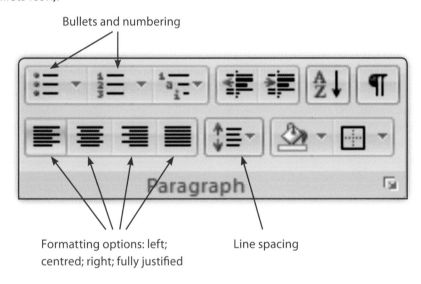

Bullets and numbering

Formatting options: left; centred; right; fully justified

Line spacing

Figure 13.38: Paragraph icons

Activity: Formatting choices in different types of documents

Look at a number of different types of documents, such as reports, magazines and advertisements. Your tutor may provide a set for you, or you could look in the library.

For each one, identify the formatting that is being used and comment on whether you think that the formatting choices are appropriate.

3.3 Check word-processed documents

Documents need to be carefully checked to make sure that:

- the layout looks correct
- there are no spelling or grammatical errors.

For business documents these checks are essential, as it is unprofessional for incorrect and poorly presented information to be sent to a customer or supplier.

Spell check and grammar check

Word® is supplied with a dictionary and a spell check and grammar facility which will check the spelling and grammar in a document. Misspelt words will appear with a red wavy line under them, while a green wavy line means that the text may have a grammatical error.

To check the highlighted word or phrase, right click on it. A drop-down menu will appear and you will either be given an alternative word or told what the problem is.

You should also check your own work very carefully. Watch out for words that are spelled correctly but may not make sense in the context in which they appear, such as 'there' and 'their'.

Make sure that your language setting is correct (i.e. that it is set to English UK rather than English US, as this could account for some of the spelling errors). You can change your language settings by selecting the **Language** tab in the **Options** menu.

Activity: The perils of relying on the automated spell checker

1   Look at the text below.

> Prince Charles is the currant air to the throne.

2   Open up a new document and enter this text.
3   Although none of the words will be identified as misspelled, some of them are definitely wrong.
4   Read the text and check the words carefully. Note down the words that you think are wrong.
5   Explain why the spell checker did not spot them as spelling mistakes.
6   Find some other examples of this type of error. Use them to produce a simple poster that can be used to advise learners on the perils of relying on the automatic spell checker.

Breaks

When text reaches the end of a line, it wraps over to the next line automatically. A new paragraph can be started by pressing the return or enter key.

You can insert a line break by pressing **Shift** and **Enter**. A new line is then started, with single line spacing separating the two lines.

A page break forces the beginning of a new page.

How to insert a page break

1. Select **Breaks** from the **Page Layout** menu.

2. Select **Page** (see Figure 13.39).

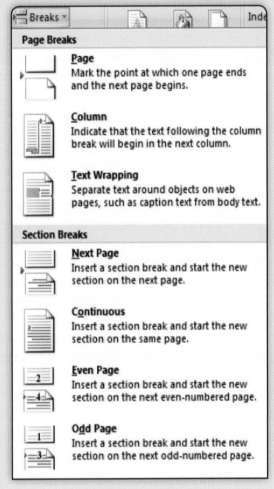

Figure 13.39: The Page Breaks window

If you wish to see what breaks and other hidden formatting symbols appear in a document, select the **Show/Hide** icon on the toolbar.

Print preview

You can preview documents prior to printing them. Choose the **Print** option in the **File** menu, and on the right-hand side of the screen the document will appear in preview mode. You can magnify the image and scroll through the pages to make sure that it will print correctly.

3.4 Quality problems with documents

A number of potential quality problems can affect documents, which you need to check for when you proof-read and review the document. They include the following.

- Errors in the content: these are difficult to spot just by reviewing and proof-reading the document. You need to refer back to the source of the information to make sure that you have entered everything correctly. The importance of this will change from one document to another. For instance, final assignments, police interview records and formal company reports are examples of where accuracy is vital.
- If the document includes calculations, you need to check these using a different method, for example a calculator or spreadsheet. A rough estimate is always useful, but you may also need to check for accuracy.
- Previewing the document is a useful way to check the overall style, structure and layout of the text before printing. Many users work in **Print Layout** so that they are viewing the document as if it were printed copy, but it is also a good idea to check margins, headers and footers, and so on using an actual printout.
- Inserted images, if not carefully formatted, can often change their position because of later changes to the whole document. Getting the properties and wrapping characteristics correct can be complicated, and their size, position and orientation needs to be checked to ensure that they are displayed correctly.
- If styles are used consistently there should be few issues, but sometimes paragraphs or characters may have been formatted directly instead of using the set of styles, and later changes to these styles will not be applied to all parts of the document.

How you deal with quality issues will depend on what the problem is. For example, orphans can usually be sorted out by inserting a new page break before every title or main heading. Care needs to be taken not to waste space.

Sometimes quality problems will result from mistakes made in the production of the document. For example, you may have set one section to be landscape orientation but a follow-up section break was not inserted, resulting in the rest of the document appearing in landscape orientation too. Once you spot these errors, they are not difficult to sort out.

Other quality issues are more complex and may result from decisions made about the style and structure of the document, or the quality of the images chosen. In these cases, it is important to think about the purpose of the document and its intended audience and, if necessary, to make changes to the design. In some cases changes will be easy. For example, if the styles have been used consistently it should be possible to make wholesale changes to the look of the document by changing the styles at source.

ASSESSMENT ACTIVITY

You have been asked by a local band to help them with their publicity.

Task 1 – Enter and combine text and other information accurately within word-processing documents

Create a structured document containing information about the group itself. It should include an overview of the members of the band, for example their backgrounds, photographs, musical histories, instruments played or role in the band. (You can either make up information about the band or use information about a real band.)

The document should be structured with appropriate styles applied to the headings, and include:

- page numbers
- at least two different fonts
- at least one image
- a number of different text formats
- hyperlinks to appropriate related websites.

Task 2 – Create and modify layout and structures for word-processing documents

Create a second document that covers the following topics.

- How did the band get together?
- What type of music do they play?
- Who are their musical influences?
- What are their best/worst gig memories and stories?
- What would they like to be doing in the future?

The document should be in the form of an article for a music magazine and be in portrait column format with at least one page showing a large image in landscape orientation.

Task 3 – Use word-processing software tools to format and present documents effectively to meet requirements

Create two further documents and two templates related to the marketing of a concert by the band in your local area. The first document will be a poster and the second a small card.

The poster and card can use some of the same material and styles. The poster can be A4 or A3 size. The card will be about the size of a typical company business card and designed to be left in clubs, bus stations, and so on, or handed out to individuals.

Given that other events are being planned, create templates for these two documents to save time when creating further materials. For the purposes of the assessment, the poster should include a number of graphic shapes, suitably chosen, positioned, sized and grouped.

Note

You will be asked to meet with your tutor at the end of the assessment to talk through the formatting and layout choices you have made. Your tutor may also need to check that you are familiar with some of the techniques not demonstrated by the documents created for this project.

For all documents it is important that you have checked carefully that there are no obvious spelling or grammar problems (i.e. fix any problems you find). Remember to choose meaningful file names for your documents and store the documents and templates in the most appropriate place.

Glossary

A

Archive – a storage area which is not immediately accessible but can be accessed if needed. If your house has a loft or a garage you can use it like an archive. You put things in a loft or garage which you do not want to throw away but need to use only occasionally.

Aspect ratio – refers to the ratio of the width to the height of an image or display monitor. If you change the aspect ratio of an image, for example by making it wider without changing the height by the same amount, it will look stretched.

Attach – an attachment is a file which is included in an email, such as a word processed document or a spreadsheet. You 'attach' this file to an email if you want to send it on to someone else.

Attachments – these are files (e.g. a photograph or a word-processed document) which are linked to emails and sent along with them to the recipient.

Axis (plural is axes) – these are the lines running along the edge of the chart which are labelled to give meaning to the chart contents. Charts and graphs usually have two axes.

B

Bandwidth – network bandwidth capacity is how much data can travel through a connection at any time.

Bcc – with Bcc the person you send the email to does not see the email addresses of the people you Bcc it it (whereas with Cc they do see the names)

Bitmap image – made up of dots know as pixels. Millions of different colour pixels make a lifelike image.

Blog – An online journal where people post diary entries.

C

Cache – memory in a web browser. This is when pages are kept on your computer so they do not need to be downloaded again from the Internet. This can make revisiting a web page a lot quicker.

Cc – a copy of the email is sent to addresses you add to the Cc box. The email is not directly to them but they might need to know what's happening.

Circular reference – if you use the cell holding a function as one of the cells used by the function you create a circular function, so-called because the spreadsheet goes round in circles trying to work it out, giving up with an error message.

Clip art – a single piece of ready-made art, often appearing as a bitmap or a combination of drawn shapes.

Clipboard – a temporary place where text and images are stored when you either cut or copy things. Anything in the clipboard can be pasted in the same or another document.

Colour balance – sometimes called white balance of an image; is the intensity of the pixels in the image of each of the three primary colours (red, green and blue) that make up the image.

Composite primary key – when two or more fields are used as the primary key.

Consistency – the same formatting and layout used across all pages.

Contrast – the difference in brightness between the dark and light areas of an image.

Copyright – this is a law which protects the creator of original works (music, art, photographs, etc.) from people copying and using their work without permission .For example, you cannot use someone else's photograph on an advertising leaflet or blog without getting their permission to do so.

D

Domains – within the Internet a domain is a geographical area (more properly called a country code top level domain). For example, an email address ending in .uk comes from an address in the UK; while an email ending in .cn originates from the People's Republic of China.

Data feed – a data feed is when a website sends fresh or changed information to your browser.

Data validation rule – used in a table to reject data entries that are obviously wrong

Default sequence – is how a table automatically sorts a new record into place

Desktop publishing – or DTP, is the use of application software (e.g. Microsoft® Publisher®) to create complex printed documents which combine text, graphics and other features. Examples of documents that might be produced using DTP software include magazines, brochures and newsletters.

E

Emoticons – graphics to visually show emotions such as smiley or sad faces.

Encrypt – change data into a code so it can only be read by authorised users. The encrypted data will need to be decrypted by the receiving system so it can be understood.

F

File transfer protocol (FTP) – FTP is a system of uploading pages to a web server (or similar system) and is a standard method of working.

Firewall – this is software which helps protect a computer network by monitoring incoming and outgoing network traffic. It decides what information should be allowed through and what information should be blocked or flagged up as being potentially threatening.

Flagging – is a method of highlighting important email, perhaps ones you need to reply to or do something about. Outlook® puts a red coloured flag next to emails you flag as a reminder.

Frames – are used for controlling the layout of a web page. Each frame is a separate page and can have a scroll bar, often containing navigation buttons.

G

GIGO – Garbage In Garbage Out. This term is used to show how important it is to input good data into an IT system as bad data will always produce bad results.

Gradient – a colour range which fades gradually from one colour to another colour (i.e. black to grey to white).

Graphics – a general term used to describe pictures, photos, clip art, SmartArt, charts, diagrams and individual shapes such as arrows or boxes. In Microsoft® PowerPoint®, graphics may also be referred to as illustrations.

Graphics tablet – also known as a digitising tablet. This is an input device which allows you to draw images just as you would using a pen and paper. You can also trace over an existing piece of artwork by taping it to the top of the tablet.

H

Hard drive – refers to the disc drive located inside you desktop or laptop computer. This disc is used to store the computer's operating system, applications programs like Microsoft® Office® 2010 and all your folders.

Header – text that prints at the top of every page. It is often used to give the title of the worksheet and maybe the author.

High resolution – this refers to the number of pixels in the image. The higher the resolution of an image the bigger the file it occupies. Depending on the type of image a low resolution image might have a size of 0.1MB, while a high resolution image might be 3MB or more.

House style – the same formatting across pages including font, font size, colour, etc.

HTML format – when an email or a web page uses HTML (Hyper Text Mark-up Language) to improve the appearance.

Hyperlink – a hyperlink is a graphic or piece of text which, when clicked on, takes the user to another slide or website. Text hyperlinks are usually underlined.

Hyper Text Markup Language (HTML) – behind every web page, used by browsers to understand how to display the page. HTML is plain text with commands on how to lay out the page and where the images are stored on the web server hosting the page.

I

Identifier – is a field (or fields) different for each record, such as a reference number

Import – the process of moving files from one location to another location.

Indent – this is when text or a graphic is set in from the edge of a page or another section of text.

InPrivate browsing – can be turned on using the Tools menu. The browser will now not remember any sites you visit in the History or anywhere else.

Input mask – a set of rules which governs the type and length of information a user is allowed to enter in a particular field.

Integrated services digital network (ISDN) – a service introduced in the late 1980s by BT for businesses providing a good connection to the Internet and voice calls.

Intensity – in this context intensity refers to the brightness of the individual coloured pixels. By varying the brightness of the red, green and blue pixels a range of different colours can be reproduced.

Internet service provider (ISP) – a company that provides users with Internet services. Most people make a regular payment to their ISP to keep the Internet connection working.

IP address – most devices on a network have an IP address which needs to be different for each of them. An IP address consists of four numbers separated by full stops. Each of these numbers needs to be in the 0–255 range.

ISDN – Integrated services digital network: a service introduced in the late 1980s by BT for businesses providing a good connection to the Internet and voice calls.

K

Keyboard shortcuts – when specific key combinations are used to trigger an action or to activate a menu command or toolbar button. For example, if you highlight a section of text and then you hold down the Ctrl key and then C key, you will copy that piece of text. If you then hold down the Ctrl key and then the V key, you will be able to paste the copied piece of text.

Kilo bits per second (kbps) – a measure of data transfer speed over a communication which is approximately a thousand bits every second.

L

Layers - layers allow different parts of an image to be separated and edited individually.

Local system –where you use an email client program like Microsoft® Outlook® running on your computer. Your emails are stored locally on your computer.

M

MAC address – every network communication device such as a network card or a router has a Media Access Control (MAC) address in the electronic circuits which is unique to that device. No two devices have the same MAC address. This is used in security systems to help authenticate connected devices.

Macro –an automated set of commands which achieves some tasks in an application program.

Mail merge – when information stored on a database (e.g. people's names, company names and addresses) is dropped into a letter template. This process means that the same letter can be sent to hundreds of people and that the system inserts everyone's name and address, rather than each name and address having to be added to the letter manually.

Malware – is short for malicious software and is a general term applied to types of hostile or intrusive code or software. This type of software is often used by hackers to disrupt network operations or gain unauthorised access to computer systems or sensitive information.

Medium – in this context the medium is how the image will be presented. Paper, a computer monitor and a HD projector are all examples of mediums through which the image might be viewed.

Mega bits per second (mbps) – a measure of data transfer speed, which is approximately a million bits every second. Several broadband providers currently advertise up to 20 mbps, although very few actually achieve this.

Megabytes and kilobytes – file sizes are generally measured in kilobytes or megabytes. All files are made up a binary data, known as bits (1s and 0s) and these are grouped together in sets of 8 known as a byte (8 bits = 1 byte). 1024 bytes makes a kilobyte (KB), and 1024 kilobytes makes a megabyte (MB).

Memory stick – a robust, portable storage device used to store and transfer files from one computer to another. You will usually connect a memory stick to your computer via a USB port.

Modem – a device for transmitting and receiving data. The word, modem, is made from MODulator and DEModulator. These were used in old dial-up modems to turn data into sound that could be sent through an ordinary voice telephone system (modulate) and also to receive the sound made by another modem to translate back into data (demodulate).

N

Netiquette –general guidelines for using email which can help prevent misunderstandings.

Network – a group of connected computers. A network may simply link two computers within a home, or it may connect thousands of computers worldwide.

Not null/null – Null is when an empty field with no data in a table is said to have a null value.

O

Optimising features – helpful tools that allow you to improve (optimise) your computer's performance.

Optical character recognition (OCR) – this is a means of digitising text using a compatible scanner. It can be useful if you have a clear printed copy of the text you wish to input or adapt. The scanning process is often available within a graphics scanner or photocopier. Many OCR systems cannot recognise complex layouts such as combinations of text boxes, columns and images. Like voice recognition, the results of OCR scanning can need time consuming checks and edits to get it right.

P

Packet – when data is transmitted, it is broken down into thousands of small pieces of data, called packets. Each packet is sent independently to the receiving system. When the packets arrive they are put back together so that the data appears complete once again.

Phishing – this is a technique used to obtain individuals' personal details. Phishing emails are designed to look like official emails (e.g. from your bank) and will ask you to click a link and provide personal information (e.g. your name, address and online banking login passwords). If you enter you details on the fake page then your details will become available to the people behind the phising email, who could use them to steal money from your account.

PIN– short for personal identification number. If you have a debit or credit card, then you will have a PIN for that card. It is a secret number only you know which you enter at a bank machine in order to take money out of your account.

Pixelation – this describes when a picture has been stretched too far and the image becomes blocky.

Placeholder – this is a box with dotted borders in a slide layout that show where content can be placed.

Plagiarism – passing other people's work off as your own.

Planning – the process of breaking down a large project or task into several smaller tasks, or sub-tasks, and identifying what you need to do in order to complete each sub-task.

Podcast – a podcast is a recording which can be downloaded then heard on a media player.

Primary key – a table can have one or more fields set as the primary key. The primary key has two purposes: the table automatically sorts on the primary key to put the data into order; it keeps each record unique because the primary key cannot have the same data in different records.

Project milestones – are dates when significant events are planned to occur within a project. For example, you might include a milestone in your schedule such as 'Project proposal agreed by customer'.

Protocol – a set of rules used by computers to control how they communicate. There are many protocols including the wireless application protocol.

R

Record – a record is all the fields in a row in a table where information is kept about one person or item.

Replicate – to copy or reproduce something.

Resolution – this is the number of pixels per inch or centimetre in an image. The higher the resolution, the better the quality of the image.

Ribbon – this is the name of the tabbed menu bar at the top of the Outlook® window. All Microsoft® Office® 2010 products use a ribbon menu bar.

Router – a device that sends and receives data between systems through the Internet.

S

Scale – scaling an image means increasing or decreasing its size.

Schedule – is a list of tasks and the dates you plan to start and complete them.

Screen reader – a screen reader is used by blind users. It speaks the words on the screen and, if the correct code has been used, will read out a caption explaining what each image contains.

Search operators – are used to help find records, e.g. text filter to find records which begin with S

Search engine – a website where you can enter something you want to find on the Internet. The search engine then shows you a list of websites that contain the information you want.

Sequences – are different orders that data can be arranged in such as A-Z

Sharing – is when more than one user can access the same file and work on it at the same time as another user.

Side bar – an area at the side of a web page which usually contains navigation buttons or hyperlinks. Within the same website, this tends to be identical on every web page.

SmartArt – this is a series of specialist graphics available with Microsoft® software, that allow you to create a variety of effective diagrams, e.g. cycles, processes, organisational structures and many more. They can be adapted for particular purposes.

Software licensing – unless the software you are using is classified as 'freeware' or open source then you will need to purchase a licence to use it. Using unlicensed software breaks copyright law.

SSID – service set identifier. Every WiFi system has a SSID which is the name of the network. The SSID is the name you see when searching for a connection in the available networks.

Synchronise – in multimedia, sound should be lined up well with the images which appear on screen so they are synchronised.

T

Template – a template is a standard slide layout. Once chosen for a new slide, however, placeholders can be adapted and new ones added.

Text language – abbreviated language used in text messages such as 'btw' (by the way).

Trojan horse – or Trojan, is a malicious file or program which is used to steal information or harm the host computer or network. Often Trojans look like legitimate or harmless files. The term derives from Greek mythology. The Trojans were planning to attack the city of Troy so they gave the people of Troy a gift of a giant wooden horse. Trojan soldiers were hidden inside the horse: during the night the soldiers slipped out, opened the gates and the Trojan forces entered the city and destroyed Troy.

U

USB memory stick – a device used to store files which plugs into the USB port on a computer.

V

Validation text – shows when a validation rule is broken. This needs to clearly explain what the rule will allow so the user can get their data entry accepted.

Validity – valid results are useful and helpful, meeting the purpose for which they are intended.

Vector image – made up of objects such as circles and rectangles. Used for diagrams, cartoons and non-life-like images.

W

WAP – an acronym that has several possible meanings including wireless application protocol and wireless access point.

Wireless access point – a device that can receive and transmit WiFi. A wireless router is a WAP, although WAP usually refers to a device used by organisations to enable their employees to connect laptops to the LAN.

Webmail – where you access your email using an Internet browser. All your emails are stored on the email service provider servers (e.g. Gmail, Hotmail).

Web server – a computer, usually with a large hard drive, special operating system and good Internet connection, onto which web pages are loaded so that others can see them over the Internet.

Website hosting – the website host provides storage and Internet connections for a website.

Working offline – this is when your computer is not connected to the Internet.

Z

Zip files – a zip file contains one or more files that have been compressed to reduce their file size. Zip files usually use the .zip extension and can be unzipped using many freely available utility programs.

Index